Queen Victoria's Early Letters

Queen Victoria's Early Letters

Edited by

JOHN RAYMOND

The Macmillan Company

NEW YORK

Library of Congress Catalog Card Number: 63–15934

FIRST PUBLISHED 1907
REVISED EDITION © JOHN RAYMOND 1963

FIRST PUBLISHED IN THE UNITED STATES OF AMERICA
BY THE MACMILLAN COMPANY, 1963

Made and printed in Great Britain
by William Clowes and Sons, Limited, London and Beccles

Contents

LIST OF ILLUSTRATIONS   vii

ACKNOWLEDGMENT   ix

INTRODUCTION   1

The Letters

1821-1835	7
1836	12
1837	14
1838	27
1839	30
1840	40
1841	45
1842	75
1843	83
1844	94
1845	103
1846	118
1847	129
1848	133

Contents

1849	154
1850	161
1851	179
1852	188
1853	195
1854	195
1855	206
1856	216
1857	221
1858	226
1859	237
1860	258
1861	273
INDEX	295

List of Illustrations

facing page

Queen Victoria's First Council, 20th June 1837   22
From a print after the painting by Sir David Wilkie

King Leopold   23
From an early photograph

Baron Stockmar   23
From a portrait by F. Winterhalter

Queen Victoria in 1838   38
From a lithograph by Edwin Dalton after Sir William Ross

Prince Albert in 1840   38
From a sketch by Sir George Hayter for his painting 'The Royal Marriage'

Queen Victoria and Prince Albert, c. 1840   39
From a sketch by John Doyle

'Susannah and the Elders': the young Queen riding with Lord Melbourne and Lord John Russell, 1837   39
From a sketch by John Doyle

The Duke of Wellington and Sir Robert Peel   118
From the painting by F. Winterhalter

Lord Palmerston   119
From an engraving after an early photograph

Lord John Russell 119
  From an engraving by D. J. Pound after a photograph by Mayall

Buckingham Palace: the Princess Royal sitting for a portrait by Winterhalter 134
  From an engraving by William Radclyffe after Sir John Gilbert

The State Visit of the Emperor Napoleon III: Queen Victoria and Prince Albert with the Emperor and Empress at Covent Garden, 19th April 1855 135
  From a lithograph by G. H. Thomas after Louis Haghe

Acknowledgment

The illustrations facing pages 23 (bottom), 38 (bottom), 118 and 135 are reproduced by Gracious Permission of Her Majesty the Queen.

The Publishers also wish to thank the following for permission to reproduce illustrations appearing in this book:

The Trustees of the British Museum for the illustrations facing pages 38 (top) and 39 (both); the Mansell Collection for page 22; and the *Radio Times* Hulton Picture Library for pages 23 (top) and 119 (both).

The first page of a letter from Queen Victoria to the Earl of Liverpool, written in 1842, is reproduced on the cover of this book by permission of the Trustees of the British Museum (Add. Ms. 38190, f. 146).

Introduction

MY DEAREST VICTORIA,—I have to thank you for your dear kind letter of the 12th. Madame de Sévigné says, with great truth, that a letter to be a good letter ought to be as if one heard the person speak; your dear letters are always so, and you would therefore be praised by Madame de Sévigné, and that very deservedly.

The comparison was not of the happiest, yet there was a hidden truth in Uncle Leopold's words. Queen Victoria was no verbal artist, as her journals and diaries show. Yet, in her letters, we can hear her authentic voice—rebuking, consoling, confirming, cajoling, upbraiding —in accents unlike those of any British sovereign (Queen Elizabeth I not excepted).

Born in 1819, a Queen in her nineteenth year, Victoria's was the longest and greatest reign in British history. Long after her death she remained a revered but remote and mysterious figure—an imperial matriarch, Kipling's black-garbed Widow at Windsor, owning half of creation:

> 'Ave you 'eard o' the Widow at Windsor
> With a hairy gold crown on 'er 'head?
> She 'as ships on the foam—she 'as millions at 'ome
> An' she pays us poor beggars in red.
> (Ow, poor beggars in red)
> There's 'er nick on the cavalry 'orses,
> There's 'er mark on the medical stores—
> An' 'er troopers you'll find with a fair wind be'ind
> That takes us to various wars.
> (Poor beggars!—barbarious wars!)

The Queen first emerged from the thickly veiled mists of sovereignty when the first series of her letters was published in 1907. The task of editing was entrusted to two important juniors of the Edwardian Establishment, A. C. Benson, a melancholic don and former Eton schoolmaster, the son of an Archbishop of Canterbury, and Reginald Baliol Brett, second Lord Esher (1852–1930), the most eminent courtier of his generation and one of the Queen's intimate friends. John Morley, a Liberal Cabinet Minister and the official biographer of Gladstone, read and criticized the manuscript in draft, and the book was published, in three handsome volumes, by John Murray.

In their preface, the editors called attention to the method by which they had selected their material. 'It became clear that the only satisfactory plan was to publish specimens of such documents as would serve to bring out the development of the Queen's character and disposition, and to give typical instances of her methods in dealing with political and social matters—to produce, in fact, a book for British citizens and British subjects, rather than a book for students of political history. That the inner working of the unwritten constitution of the country; that some of the unrealized checks and balances; that the delicate equipoise of the component parts of the executive machinery should stand revealed was inevitable. We had thought it best, throughout to abstain from unnecessary comment and illustration.' The same method has been pursued in the present selection from the original series.

Most of Queen Victoria's story, as related in these letters and memoranda, covering her life up to the time of Prince Albert's death in 1861, speaks for itself and requires little in the way of comment from an editor. There are, however, certain important facts about the young Princess's upbringing and early connections which are not brought out by her correspondence and do deserve mention, if the reader is to follow the background and hidden nuances of the period. And first, perhaps, a word about her parentage.

Nine of George III's fifteen children were sons, two of whom died young. Princess Charlotte, George IV's daughter was, until her death in 1817, his only legitimate grandchild and, therefore, the direct heir to the British Throne. George III's second son, the Duke of York, was childless. On Princess Charlotte's death, the old King's third and fourth sons, the Duke of Clarence (later William IV) and the Duke of Kent together with a younger son, the Duke of Cambridge, all immediately married. The Duke of Kent's daughter was born two years later in 1819. Her mother, Princess Victoria of Saxe-Coburg, was the widow of Prince Charles of Leiningen. Her brother Leopold, later King of the Belgians, had been the unfortunate Princess Charlotte's husband.

In gratitude to the Czar, who had supplied the debt-ridden Duke with the funds needed to prosecute his marriage, the child was christened Victoria Alexandrina (the Regent, who detested Alexander I, refused to allow his own name to be added). Neither name was popular in British nurseries and, in 1831, it was proposed in Parliament that she should be named Elizabeth; others, including an uncle, William IV, whose own two daughters had both died in infancy, suggested she should take the name of her Aunt Charlotte. On the Duke of Kent's death the Duchess and her small daughter were placed under the care of their Uncle Leopold. George IV was kind but distant towards her, his brother William was genuinely fond of her. He wished her to assume a position at Court, make herself known to her future subjects, and generally prepare herself for the important fate that lay before her.

A powerful obstacle stood in the path of the King's good intentions. This was none other than Victoria's mother, whose dislike and distrust of William IV was cordially returned by the Monarch himself. From the first she jealously guarded the young Princess from any contact with the Court, even with society at large. The King disliked Victoria's Uncle Leopold on private and political grounds, and during the last years of his reign did everything he could to thwart Leopold's ever-growing influence over their young niece. The Coburgs were always of a managing disposition, and Leopold had early cast his lot with the Whigs, whom King William tolerated but did not affect. The quarrel between the King and Duchess inevitably centred round the person of Victoria. As the late Sir Charles Webster wrote in his famous essay on the 1837 Accession, 'the Duchess assumed complete control over her daughter and William was denied by her the usual rights of both uncle and sovereign. He always resented it. And the quarrel was developing into a public scandal when he died.'

The Duchess was a weak and foolish woman, much in the hands of her Comptroller, Sir John Conroy. This sinister person, whose name is absent from the *Dictionary of National Biography*, and occurs only once in these letters, played a great part in the circumstances of the Princess's childhood. An extract from Greville, for July 1833, throws a good deal of light on the relations between Claremont and the Palace.

> At Court yesterday, and Council for a foolish business. The King has been (not unnaturally) disgusted at the Duchess of Kent's progresses with her daughter through the kingdom, and amongst the rest with her sailings at the Isle of Wight, and the continual popping in the shape of salutes to Her Royal Highness. He did not choose that this latter practice should go on, and he signified his pleasure to Sir James Graham and Lord Hill, for salutes are matter of general order, both to army and navy. They (and Lord Grey) thought it better to make no order on the subject, and they opened a negotiation with the Duchess of Kent, to induce her of her own accord to waive the salutes, and when she went to the Isle of Wight to send word that as she was sailing about for her amusement she had rather they did not salute her whenever she appeared. The negotiation failed, for the Duchess insisted upon her right to be saluted, and would not give it up. Kemp told me he had heard that Conroy (who is a ridiculous fellow, a compound of 'Great Hussy' and the Chamberlain of the Princess of Navarre) had said 'that as Her Royal Highness's confidential adviser, he could not recommend her to give way on this point.' As she declined to accede to the proposals, nothing remained but to alter the regulations, and accordingly yesterday, by an Order in Council, the King changed them, and from this time the Royal Standard is only to be saluted when the King or the Queen are on board.

The Duchess's attitude to Conroy was so equivocal, Webster relates, that only one conclusion could be drawn from it. 'There is much evidence,' he goes on, that Conroy 'had the design of exploiting for his own purposes the position that Victoria must one day hold. . . . For long he seemed to have a great game to play, and Victoria was kept so far as possible from influences that would rival that of her mother, and thus his own.'

Avoiding the leaders of the two great parties, Conroy wooed the Radicals, particularly Lord Durham, whom he consulted about the future Queen's education, which later his lordship claimed to have influenced. Though their association was denounced by *The Times*, 'Victoria herself seems for a time to have been genuinely impressed with their radical point of view.' (Hence the references to 'our friend Mr Hume' and to O'Connell's speeches.)

Meanwhile, the young Princess's education proceeded. It was of a highly conventional kind, not at all specifically designed for a future sovereign—languages (German and French), music, watercolours and the general run of ladylike accomplishments. She was certainly no match for her handsome cousin, Prince Albert of Saxe-Coburg, whom Uncle Leopold had long ago picked out as her prospective bridegroom. King William, whose dislike of Leopold and his sister had extended itself over the years to cover all members of the Coburg family, hated the idea of this intended match and did everything to prevent it. In April 1836 he proposed to stop the Coburg Princes, Albert and Ernest, from visiting England, lest one or the other of them should aspire to the Princess's hand. His own candidate, a son of the Prince of Orange, was not favoured by Lord Melbourne and the British Cabinet. This, briefly, is the background to the Princess's early letters to her uncle and Leopold's wily but affectionate replies. The King of the Belgians has received a rough handling from posterity, notably by Lytton Strachey in his masterly but foreshortened study of Victoria (*Queen Victoria*, 1921), though Miss Joanna Richardson's recent biography has gone some way to make amends. As these letters show, he was not the frigid and ceremonial stick that Strachey makes him. He and his friend, Stockmar, were the two great formative influences of Victoria's public character. Her succeeding counsellors—Melbourne, Peel and above all, the Prince Consort himself, built on their solid Coburg foundations.

A final word about the method of selection. The aim of the present volume is to reveal Queen Victoria's essential character at the cost of the multifarious episodes and transactions, however colourful or momentous, that took place during the earlier half of her reign. Thus we have had to by-pass Lord Palmerston's Near Eastern policy and the vagaries of Mehemet Ali; the Opium War with China; the long and complicated question of the Spanish Marriage; the State of Afghanistan, and the condition of the Sikhs; the famous Bedchamber crisis, and the involved Ministerial Crisis of 1851 (the latter, as revealed in the Consort's own memoranda, is itself a superb theme for the political historian); we have been forced to expunge the long diplomatic preamble to the Crimean War, and to abridge the Queen's long and un-pacific relations with Lord Palmerston.

The result of this attempt should, if anything, be to heighten the portrayal and the Queen's personality. 'We see,' wrote her original editors, 'her character expand and deepen, schooled by mightly experience into patience and sagacity and wisdom, and yet never losing a particle of the strength, the decision, and the devotion with which she had been originally endowed. Up to the year 1861 the Queen's career was one of unexampled prosperity. She was happy in her temperament, in her health, in her education, in her wedded life, in her children. She saw a great Empire grow through troubled times in liberty and power and greatness; yet this prosperity brought with it no shadow of complacency, because the Queen felt with an increasing depth the anxieties and responsibilities inseparable from her great position. Her happiness, instead of making her self-absorbed, only quickened her beneficence and her womanly desire that her subjects should be enabled to enjoy a similar happiness based upon the same simple virtues. Nothing comes out more strongly in these documents than the laborious patience with which the Queen kept herself informed of the minutest details of political and social movements both in her own and other countries.'

With these sedate and appropriate sentiments the present editor is delighted to concur.

JOHN RAYMOND

1821–1835

[The first letter ever received by Queen Victoria appears to be the following little note, written by the Duchess of Clarence, afterwards Queen Adelaide, in May 1821, when the Princess entered upon her third year.]

MY DEAR LITTLE HEART,—I hope you are well and don't forget Aunt Adelaide, who loves you so fondly.

Loulou and Wilhelm desire their love to you, and Uncle William also.

God bless and preserve you is the constant prayer of your most truly affectionate Aunt,   ADELAIDE

The Duchess of Clarence to the Princess Victoria

24th May 1822

Uncle William and Aunt Adelaide send their love to *dear little Victoria* with their best wishes on her birthday, and hope that she will now become a *very good Girl*, being now *three years old*. Uncle William and Aunt Adelaide also beg little Victoria to give dear Mamma and to dear Sissi a kiss in their name, and to Aunt Augusta, Aunt Mary and Aunt Sophia too, and also to the *big Doll*. Uncle William and Aunt Adelaide are very sorry to be absent on that day and not to see their *dear, dear* little Victoria, as they are sure she will be very good and obedient to dear Mamma on that day, and on many, many others. They also hope that dear little Victoria will not forget them and know them again when Uncle and Aunt return.

To dear little Xandrina Victoria.

Kensington Palace, 25th November 1828

MY DEAREST UNCLE,—I wish you many happy returns of your birthday; I very often think of you, and I hope to see you soon again, for I am very fond of you. I see my Aunt Sophia often, who looks very well, and is very well. I use every day your pretty soup-basin. Is it very warm in Italy? It is so mild here, that I go out every day. Mama is tolerable well and am quite well. Your affectionate Niece,   VICTORIA

P.S.—I am very angry with you, Uncle, for you have never written to me once since you went, and that is a long while.

Prince Leopold* to the Princess Victoria

Paris, 20th April 1829

MY DEAREST LOVE,—Though in a few days I hope to have the happiness of seeing you, still I wish to recall myself even before that time to your recollection, and to tell you how delighted I shall be to embrace my dearest little child. I have travelled far over the world and shall be able to give you some curious information about various matters.

Stockmar, who was very ill, and whom I despaired of seeing here, did arrive before yesterday, and you may guess what pleasure it gave me. Now I will conclude; *au revoir*, and let me find you grown, blooming, and kind to your old and faithful Uncle,   LEOPOLD

The King of the Belgians to the Princess Victoria

Brussels, 22nd May 1832

MY DEAREST LOVE,—Let me offer you my *sincerest* and *best* wishes on the return of the anniversary of your birthday. May heaven protect and prosper you, and shower all its best blessings on you.

Time flies: it is now thirteen years that you came into the world of trouble; I therefore can hardly venture to call you any longer a little Princess.

This will make you feel, my dear Love, that you must give your attention more and more to graver matters. By the dispensation of Providence you are destined to fill a most eminent station; to fill it *well* must now become your study. A good heart and a trusty and honourable character are amongst the most indispensable qualifications for that position.

* Afterwards King of the Belgians.

You will always find in your Uncle that faithful friend which he has proved to you from your earliest infancy, and whenever you feel yourself in want of support or advice, call on him with perfect confidence.

If circumstances permitted my leaving Ostend early tomorrow morning, I should be able to place myself my birthday present into your fair hair; as this happiness has not fallen to my lot, your excellent mother has promised to act as my representative.

You will probably have little time to spare. I therefore conclude with the assurance of the sincere attachment and affection with which I shall ever be, my dearest Love, your faithful and devoted Friend and Uncle,   LEOPOLD R.

The Princess Victoria to the King of the Belgians

Tunbridge Wells, 22nd October 1834

MY DEAREST UNCLE,—You cannot conceive how happy you have made me, by your very kind letter, which, instead of tiring, delights me beyond everything. I must likewise say how very grateful I feel for the kind and excellent advice you gave me in it.

For the autographs I beg to return my best thanks. They are most valuable and interesting, and will be great additions to my collections. As I have not got Sully's Memoirs, I shall be delighted if you will be so good as to give them to me. Reading history is one of my greatest delights, and perhaps, dear Uncle, you might like to know which books in that line I am now reading. In my lessons with the Dean of Chester, I am reading Russell's *Modern Europe*, which is very interesting, and Clarendon's *History of the Rebellion*. It is drily written, but is full of instruction. I like reading different authors, of different opinions, by which means I learn not to lean on one particular side. Besides my lessons, I read Jones' account of the wars in Spain, Portugal and the South of France, from the year 1808 till 1814. It is well done, I think, and amuses me very much. In French, I am now in *La Rivalité de la France et de l'Espagne*, par Gaillard, which is very interesting. I have also begun Rollin. I am very fond of making tables of the Kings and Queens, as I go on, and I have lately finished one of the English Sovereigns and their consorts, as, of course, the history of my own country is one of my first duties. I should be fearful of tiring you with so long an account of myself, were I not sure you take so great an interest in my welfare.

Pray give my most affectionate love to *dearest* Aunt Louisa, and please say to the Queen of the French and the two Princesses how grateful I am for their kind remembrance of me.

Believe me always, my dearest Uncle, your very affectionate, very dutiful, and most attached Niece,   VICTORIA

The King of the Belgians to the Princess Victoria

Laeken, 2nd December 1834

MY DEAREST LOVE,—You have written a very clever, sharp little letter the other day, which gave me great pleasure. Sure enough, when I show you what a Queen ought not to be, I also ought to tell you what she should be, and this task I will very conscientiously take upon myself on the very first occasion which may offer itself for a confidential communication. Now I must conclude, to go to town. I must, however, say that I have given orders to send you Sully's Memoirs. As they have not been written exclusively for young ladies, it will be well to have Lehzen to read it with you, and to judge what ought to be left for some future time. And now God bless you! Ever, my beloved child, your attached Friend and Uncle,   LEOPOLD R.

The King of the Belgians to the Princess Victoria

Camp of Beverloo
(in the North of the Province of Limburg),
3rd August 1835

MY DEAR LOVE,—By your Mother's letter of the 31st ult°·, I learned of the serious and important action in your young life* which has passed recently, and I cannot let it pass without saying some words on the subject. I am perhaps rather strongly situated for a preaching— somewhat in the style of those of camp preachers who held forth to many thousand people on some heath in Scotland. I am also on an immense heath, surrounded by 16,000 men, mostly young and gay,

* The Princess was confirmed at the Chapel Royal, on 30th July 1835.

cooking, singing, working, and not very like the stern old Covenanters; however, I shall try. First of all, let me congratulate you that it passed happily and well off. Secondly, let me entreat you to look with a serious and reflective mind on the day which is past. Many are the religions, many the shades of those religions, but it must be confessed the principles of the Christian religion are the most perfect and the most beautiful that can be imagined. . . . There is one virtue which is particularly Christian; this is the knowledge of our own heart in *real humility*. *Hypocrisy* is a besetting sin of all times, but *particularly of the present*, and many are the wolves in sheep's clothes. I am sorry to say, with all my affection for old England, the very *state of its Society and politics* renders many in that country *essentially humbugs and deceivers*; the *appearance* of the thing is generally *more* considered than the *reality*; provided matters go off well, and opinion may be gained, *the real good is matter of the most perfect indifference*. Defend yourself, my dear love, against this system; let your dear character always be true and loyal; this does not *exclude prudence*—worldly concerns are now unfortunately so organised that you *must be cautious* or you may injure yourself and others—but it does not prevent the being sterling and true. Nothing in persons gives greater reliance, greater weight, than when they are known to be true. From your earliest childhood I was anxious to see in you this important virtue *saved* and *developed*, and *Lehzen* will still be able to recollect that. If it is God's pleasure that you should once fill the arduous situation to which you seem destined, you will find the importance of what I now say to you. And when others may tremble to have at last their real character found out, and to meet all the contempt which they may deserve, your mind and heart will be still and happy, because it will know that it acts honestly, that truth and goodness are the motives of its actions. I press you now against my heart; may God bless you as I wish and hope it, and may you always feel some affection for your sincerely devoted camp preacher and Uncle,   LEOPOLD R.

1836

The Princess Hohenlohe to the Princess Victoria

Stuttgart, 16th April 1836

... You will like our two Coburg cousins also, I think; they are more manly than I think the two others are, after the description. I am very fond of them both. Ernest is my favourite, although Albert is much handsomer, and cleverer too, but Ernest is so honest and good-natured. I shall be very curious to hear your opinion upon them. ...

The King of the Belgians to the Princess Victoria

13th May 1836

MY DEAREST CHILD,—I got this time a very small letter from your good little Ladyship, and I shall repay it probably in larger coin, as my letter going through a messenger of my own will become longer, as it will be more confidential than through the usual mode of conveyance.

I am really *astonished* at the conduct of your old Uncle the King; this invitation of the Prince of Orange and his sons, this forcing him upon others, is very extraordinary.* It is so, because persons in political stations and champions of great political passions cannot put aside their known character as you would lay your hat upon a table.

Not later than yesterday I got a half official communication from England, insinuating that it would be *highly* desirable that the visit of *your* relatives *should not take place this year—qu'en dites-vous?* The

---

* King Leopold had for some time cherished a hope of uniting the Princess Victoria in marriage with her cousin, Prince Albert of Coburg. He therefore arranged that the Prince, with his elder brother, Prince Ernest, should pay a visit to the Duchess of Kent at Kensington Palace. King William naturally opposed a scheme which he knew met with the approval of his sister-in-law. He accordingly invited the Prince of Orange and his two sons at the same time, and favoured the candidature of the younger son, Prince Alexander. The King (it is believed) went so far as to say that no other marriage should ever take place, and that the Duke of Saxe-Coburg and his son should never put foot in the country: they should not be allowed to land, and must go back whence they came.

12

relations of the Queen and the King, therefore, to the God-knows-what degree, are to come in shoals and rule the land, when *your relations* are to be *forbidden* the country, and that when, as you know, the whole of your relations have ever been very dutiful and kind to the King. Really and truly I never heard or saw anything like it, and I hope it will a *little rouse your spirit*; now that slavery is even abolished in the British Colonies, I do not comprehend *why your lot alone should be to be kept, a white little slavey in England*, for the pleasure of the Court, who never bought you, as I am not aware of their having gone to any expense on that head, or the King's even having *spent a sixpence for your existence*. I expect that my visits in England will also be prohibited by an Order in Council. Oh consistency and political or *other honesty*, where must one look for you!

I have not the least doubt that the King, in his passion for the Oranges, will be *excessively rude to your relations*; this, however, will not signify much; they are *your guests* and not *his*, and will therefore *not* mind it. . . .

The Princess Victoria to the King of the Belgians

7th June 1836

MY DEAREST UNCLE,—. . . I must thank you, my beloved Uncle, for the prospect of *great* happiness you have contributed to give me, in the person of dear Albert. Allow me, then, my dearest Uncle, to tell you how delighted I am with him, and how much I like him in every way. He possesses every quality that could be desired to render me perfectly happy. He is so sensible, so kind, and so good, and so amiable too. He has, besides, the most pleasing and delightful exterior and appearance you can possibly see.

I have only now to beg you, my dearest Uncle, to take care of the health of one, now *so dear* to me, and to take him under *your special* protection. I hope and trust that all will go on prosperously and well on this subject of so much importance to me. . . .   VICTORIA

1837

The Princess Victoria to the King of the Belgians

Claremont, 30th January 1837

MY DEAREST UNCLE,—... Our friend, Mr Hume, made a most violent speech at a dinner given to him and old George Byng at Drury Lane last week. He called Sir R. Peel and some other Tories 'the cloven foot,' which I think rather strong. I think that *great* violence and striving such a pity, on both sides, don't you, dear Uncle? They irritate one another so uselessly by calling one another fools, blockheads, liars, and so forth for no purpose. I think violence so bad in everything. They should imitate you, and be calm, for you have had, God knows! enough cause for irritation from your *worthy* Dutch neighbours and others. You will, I fear, laugh at my *politics*, but I like telling *you* my feelings, for you alone can put me right on such subjects.

The King of the Belgians to the Princess Victoria

Laeken, 11th April 1837

... As I believe the visit at Windsor is fixed for the 15th, I hope this letter will arrive in time. Perhaps the King will speak to you about the necessity of forming you an establishment.... Your position, having a Mother with whom you very naturally remain, would render a *complete* independent establishment perhaps matter of *real* inconvenience; still something like that which Charlotte had will become desirable. My idea, if it meets with your approbation, would be this: the Duchess of Northumberland would remain your first Lady, Baroness Lehzen would fill a similar position to that of Mrs Campbell, who had been Charlotte's governess in her younger days, and the Dean would step into the position which good Dr Short held. An Equerry, I do not think —as you will not go without your Mother—you would require. On the other hand, it may become matter of examination if you will perhaps like to have some young ladies attendants in the style of Lady Catherine

Jenkinson; should this be your wish, it would become necessary to make very good choices, else perhaps you would derive more trouble than comfort from the arrangement; *cela va sans dire,* that the choice could only be made by yourself, and that nobody should be given you *against* your wishes. Should the King speak to you on the subject, I would at once express this my wish if you should approve some such arrangement, and beg him to let *you choose.* Resist mildly but *positively* any nomination of a Gentleman other than the Dean; it is highly probable that any other would be put about you as a spy, and turn out at all events a great bore, which is better avoided. . . .

I received a messenger from Coburg. I enclose the letters and also a packet with fans. Ever, my beloved child, your faithfully attached Uncle and Friend,   LEOPOLD R.

The Princess Victoria to the King of the Belgians

2nd May 1837

. . . You may depend upon it that I shall profit by your excellent advice respecting Politics. Pray, dear Uncle, have you read Lord Palmerston's speech concerning the Spanish affairs, which he delivered the night of the division on Sir Henry Hardinge's motion? It is much admired. The Irish Tithes question came on last night in the House of Commons, and I am very anxious for the morning papers, to see what has been done. Lord Melbourne looks remarkably well, Lord Palmerston not very well, and as for poor little Lord John Russell, he is only a shadow of himself. It must be dreadfully fagging work for them; they sit so very late too, for when the Spanish question came on, the division only took place at four o'clock in the morning, and I saw them at the Drawing-Room the same day afterwards. . . .

The King of the Belgians to the Princess Victoria

Laeken, 25th May 1837

MY DEAREST CHILD,—You have had some battles and difficulties of which I am completely in the dark. The thing I am most curious to learn is what the King proposed to you concerning your establishment. . . . I shall reserve my opinion till I am better informed, but by what I heard I did not approve of it, because I thought it ill-timed. Stockmar will be able to do much. Two things seem necessary; not to be fettered by any establishment other than what will be *comfortable to you*, and then to avoid any breach with your mother. I have fully instructed Stockmar, and I must say he left me in such good disposition that I think he will be able to be of great use to you. The great thing is to act without precipitation and with caution. The King seems better again. I am very curious to know what he proposed; you will have it in your power to modify his proposition, as it is difficult your *approbation* should be dispensed with; it would be a great fault in your situation to *submit* to this. . . . They seemed to think the King dying, which does not appear to be the case. Be steady, my good child, and *not* put out by *anything*; as long as I live *you will not want a faithful friend and supporter*. . . .

Here your somewhat curious little soul has at least the outlines of things. . . .

26th—I received yesterday the whole of the papers concerning the King's propositions. I approve your letter to the King, as it is amiable and generous, and this in your position will always tell favourably. I think that if *he* is well advised he will chiefly consult *your wishes*. This is the footing on which you must place matters. It is not worth while to be told that one is in some sort of age when the consequence is that you are not consulted in what concerns you most personally. Avoid in future to say much about your great *youth* and *inexperience*. Who made the letter? Was it yourself, or came it from your Mother? You have now the Baron at your elbow, and even your Mother was most anxious for his arrival. *Speak sometimes with him*; it is necessary to accustom you to the thing.

About the King's health. I am doubtful what to think. We have foreseen the case and treated it formerly. The great thing would be to make no change, to keep Ministers and everything as it is, and to gain time; in this way *no one is hurt and no amour-propre blessé*. For this reason I lean to your keeping, to begin with, Sir Herbert Taylor for your *official* secretary, though I am not quite *decided* on the subject. He knows the manner in which the *daily business* is carried on; this is important. I believe him, and have found him to be an honest man, that would do for State matters; it would not be required that he should be your *confidential* adviser. Now I conclude, and send you this letter through Stockmar. My best regards to Lehzen. Ever your faithful Uncle and Friend,   LEOPOLD R.

The Princess Victoria to the King of the Belgians

26th May 1837

... The demonstrations of affection and kindness from all sides towards me on my birthday, were most gratifying. The park and streets were crowded all day as though something very extraordinary had happened. Yesterday I received twenty-two Addresses from various places, all very pretty and loyal; one in particular was very well written which was presented by Mr. Attwood from the Political Union at Birmingham. ...

The King of the Belgians to the Princess Victoria

Tuileries, 7th June 1837

... For the present the best plan is to continue to act as you have done hitherto; to avoid quarrels, but also to stick *firmly to your resolution when once taken*. The violence which is sometimes shown is so well known to you, you know also so well that you have nothing to fear from these people, that *you must keep up your usual cool spirit*, whatever may be tried in the House to *teaze you out of it*. I mean to wait some more detailed accounts of what is going on in England before I give my opinion on what ought to be done in the case that the King's disease should take a more fatal turn.

As I told you before, however, when we treated this subject verbally and in writing, I believe it to be your interest to act very mildly, *to begin by taking everything as the King leaves it*. By this system you avoid disappointing those whose hopes may remain unchanged, as your own choices, as it were, are not yet made. Parties, which at present are so nearly balanced, remain *in statu quo*, and you gain time.

I must conclude now this letter. My winding up is, keep your mind *cool* and *easy*; be *not alarmed* at the prospect of becoming perhaps sooner than you expected Queen; aid will not be wanting, and the great thing is that you should have some honest people about you who have your welfare *really at heart*. Stockmar will be in this respect all we can wish, and we must hope that *useful* occupation will prevent his health from suffering. Now once more God bless you. Ever, my dear child, your faithful Uncle and Friend,   LEOPOLD R.

The King of the Belgians to the Princess Victoria

Laeken, 17th June 1837

MY BELOVED CHILD,—... I shall to-day enter on the subject of what is to be done when the King ceases to live. The moment you get official communication of it, you will entrust Lord Melbourne with the office of retaining the present Administration as your Ministers. You will do this in that honest and kind way which is quite your own, and say some kind things on the subject. The fact is that the present Ministers are those who will serve you personally with the greatest *sincerity* and, I trust, attachment. For them, as well as for the Liberals at large, you are the *only* Sovereign that offers them *des chances d'existence et de durée*. With the exception of the Duke of Sussex, there is no *one* in the family that offers them anything like what they can reasonably hope from you, and your immediate successor, with the mustaches,* is enough to frighten them into the most violent attachment for you.

...The irksome position in which you have lived will have the merit to have given you the habit of *discretion* and *prudence*, as in your position you never can have *too much* of either. Great measures of State I hope you will be able to avoid at first. I have already—if you would read it over, and perhaps let Stockmar see it—written to you some months ago on the subject of the necessity of maintaining the influence of conservative principles, and of protecting the Church. You will do well to keep both objects in view. You will do wisely by showing yourself attached to the English Protestant Church as it exists in the State; you are particularly where you are, because you are a Protestant. I know you are averse to persecution, and you are right; miss, however, *no opportunity* to show your sincere feeling for the existing Church; it is *right* and *meet* that you should do so. I must repeat that you will do well as long as it will be possible to hurt no

* The Duke of Cumberland.

one's hopes or prospects. That this will not always, or very long, be possible is the consequence of the state of parties; still, one may be frank and honest, and still kind to all. Concerning foreign policy I shall write on some future occasion. In the meantime I trust you will protect the two Queens in the Peninsula, who are miserably ill off. I am sure, with your good sense you will not find it difficult to judge questions yourself. I cannot too much recommend this, as it will then become a habit, and even an amusement to you. Cultivate always a genuine feeling of right and wrong, and be very true and honourable in your dealings; this gives great strength. I have taken into consideration the advantage or disadvantage of my coming over to you *immediately*. The result of my *examen* is that I think it better to visit you later. If, however, you wanted me at any time, I should come in a moment. People might fancy I came to enslave you, while I glory in the contrary; and, thirdly, that they might be jealous, or *affect* it at least, of my coming, as if I thought of ruling the realm for *purposes of my own....*

The Princess Victoria to the King of the Belgians

19th June 1837

MY DEARLY BELOVED UNCLE,—... The King's state, I may fairly say, is *hopeless*; he may *perhaps* linger a few days, but he cannot recover *ultimately*. Yesterday the physicians declared he could not live till the morning, but to-day he is a little better; the great fear is his *excessive* weakness and no *pulse* at all. Poor old man! I feel sorry for him; he was always personally kind to me, and I should be ungrateful and devoid of feeling if I did not remember this.

I look forward to the event which it seems is likely to occur soon, with calmness and quietness; I am not alarmed at it, and yet I do not suppose myself quite equal to all; I trust, however, that with *good-will, honesty*, and *courage* I shall not, at all events, *fail....*

I need not add much more, dearest Uncle, but that I trust that the all-powerful Being who has so long watched over my destinies will guide and support me, in whatever situation and station it may please Him to place me! ...

Viscount Melbourne to Queen Victoria

South Street, 20th June 1837

Viscount Melbourne presents his humble duty to your Majesty, and being aware that your Majesty has already received the melancholy intelligence of the death of his late Majesty, will do himself the honour of waiting upon your Majesty a little before nine this morning. Viscount Melbourne has requested the Marquis of Lansdowne to name eleven as the hour for the meeting of the Council at Kensington Palace.

Queen Victoria to the King of the Belgians

20th June 1837 (half-past eight a.m.)

DEAREST, MOST BELOVED UNCLE,—Two words only, to tell you that my poor Uncle, the King, expired this morning at twelve minutes past two. The melancholy news were brought to me by Lord Conyngham and the Archbishop of Canterbury at six. I expect Lord Melbourne almost immediately, and hold a Council at eleven. Ever, my beloved Uncle, your devoted and attached Niece,   VICTORIA R.

Extract from the Queen's Journal

Tuesday, 20th June 1837

I was awoke at 6 o'clock by Mamma, who told me that the Archbishop of Canterbury and Lord Conyngham were here, and wished to see me. I got out of bed and went into my sitting-room (only in my dressing-gown) and *alone*, and saw them. Lord Conyngham (the Lord Chamberlain) then acquainted me that my poor Uncle, the King, was no more, and had expired at 12 minutes past 2 this morning, and consequently that I am *Queen*. Lord Conyngham knelt down and kissed my hand, at the same time delivering to me the official announcement of the poor King's demise. The Archbishop then told me that the Queen was desirous that he should come and tell me the details of the last moments of my good Uncle; he said that he had directed his mind to religion, and had died in a perfectly happy, quiet state of mind, and was quite prepared for his death. He added that the King's sufferings at the last were not very great but that there was a good deal of uneasiness. Lord Conyngham, whom I charged to express my feelings of condolence and sorrow to the poor Queen, returned directly to Windsor. I then went to my room and dressed.

Since it has pleased Providence to place me in this station, I shall do my utmost to fulfil my duty towards my country; I am very young and perhaps in many, though not in all things, inexperienced, but I am sure that very few have more real good-will and more real desire to do what is fit and right than I have.

Breakfasted, during which time good, faithful Stockmar came and talked to me. Wrote a letter to dear Uncle Leopold and a few words to dear good Feodore. Received a letter from Lord Melbourne in which he said he would wait upon me at a little before 9. At 9 came Lord Melbourne, whom I saw in my room, and of *course quite alone*, as I shall *always* do all my Ministers. He kissed my hand, and I then acquainted him that it had long been my intention to retain him and the rest of the present Ministry at the head of affairs, and that it could not be in better hands than his. He again then kissed my hand. He then read to me the Declaration which I was to read to the Council, which he wrote himself, and which is a very fine one. I then talked with him some little time longer, after which he left me. He was in full dress. I like him very much, and feel confidence in him. He is a very straightforward, honest, clever and good man. I then wrote a letter to the Queen. At about 11 Lord Melbourne came again to me, and spoke to me upon various subjects. At about half-past 11 I went downstairs and held a Council in the red saloon.

I went in of course quite alone and remained seated the whole time. My two Uncles, the Dukes of Cumberland and Sussex, and Lord Melbourne conducted me. The Declaration, the various forms, the swearing in of the Privy Councillors, of which there were a great number present, and the reception of some of the Lords of the Council, previous to the Council, in an adjacent room (likewise alone) I subjoin here. I was not at all nervous and had the satisfaction of hearing that people were satisfied with what I had done and how I had done it. Received after this, audiences of Lord Melbourne, Lord John Russell, Lord Albemarle (Master of the Horse), and the Archbishop of Canterbury, all in my room and alone. Saw Stockmar. Saw Clark, whom I named my physician. Saw Mary. Wrote to Uncle Ernest. Saw Ernest

Hohenlohe, who brought me a kind and very feeling letter from the poor Queen. I feel very much for her, and really feel that the poor good King was always so kind personally to me, that I should be ungrateful were I not to recollect it and feel grieved at his death. The poor Queen is wonderfully composed now, I hear.

Wrote my journal. Took my dinner upstairs alone. Went downstairs. Saw Stockmar. At about twenty minutes to 9 came Lord Melbourne and remained till near 10. I had a very important and a very *comfortable* conversation with him. Each time I see him I feel more confidence in him; I find him very kind in his manner too. Saw Stockmar. Went down and said good-night to Mamma, etc. My *dear* Lehzen will *always* remain with me as my friend, but will take no situation about me, and I think she is right.

Lord John Russell to Queen Victoria

Wilton Crescent, 22nd June 1837

Lord John Russell presents his humble duty to your Majesty, and has the honour to report that he presented to the House of Commons this day your Majesty's gracious Message.

He then moved an Address of Condolence and Congratulation, which was seconded by Sir Robert Peel. Sir Robert Peel very properly took occasion to speak in terms of high admiration of the deportment of your Majesty before the Privy Council on Tuesday. The Address was agreed to be without a dissentient voice, and your Majesty may rest assured that the House of Commons is animated by a feeling of loyalty to the Throne, and of devotion to your Majesty.

The King of the Belgians to Queen Victoria

Laeken, 27th June 1837

MY DEAR CHILD,—. . . I shall add to this a piece of advice. Whenever a question is of some importance, it should not be decided on the day when it is submitted to you. Whenever it is not an urgent one, I make it a rule not to let any question be forced upon my *immediate* decision; it is really not doing oneself justice *de décider des questions sur le pouce.* And even when in my mind I am disposed to accede, still I

Queen Victoria's First Council, 20th June 1837

The Marquess of Lansdowne, the President of the Council, is sitting on the Queen's left and, at the table, stands Lord Melbourne; behind him are Lord John Russell and Lord Palmerston

From a print after the painting by Sir David Wilkie

King Leopold
From an early photograph

Baron Stockmar
From a portrait by F. Winterhalter

always keep the papers with me some little time before I return them. The best mode for you will be, that each Minister should bring his box with him, and when he submits to you the papers, *explain them to you.* Then you will keep the papers, either to think yourself upon it or to consult somebody, and either return them the next time you see the Minister to whom they belong, or send them to him. Good habits formed *now* may for ever afterwards be kept up, and will become so natural to you that you will not find them at all fatiguing.

The King of the Belgians to Queen Victoria

Laeken, 30th June 1837

MY DEAREST CHILD,—... I recommend to your kind attention what Stockmar will think it his duty to tell you; he will never press anything, never plague you with anything, without the thorough conviction that it is indispensable for your welfare. I can guarantee his independence of mind and disinterestedness; nothing makes an impression upon him but what his experience makes him feel to be of importance for you. I am delighted with your plan. You will recollect that I pressed upon you repeatedly how necessary it was for you to continue your studies on a more *extended* scale, more appropriate to the station you were destined once to fill. No one is better qualified to direct those studies for the next few years than Stockmar, few people possess more general information, and very, very few have been like him educated, as it were, by fate itself since 1816. There is no branch of information in which he may not prove useful—(1) History, considered in a practical and philosophical way; (2) International Law and everything connected with it; (3) Political Economy, an important branch nowadays; (4) Classic studies; (5) *belles lettres* in general; (6) Physical Science in all its branches, etc., etc.—the list would be very long if I were to enumerate it all. The *sooner* you do this the better; in all countries and at all times men like Stockmar have filled similar situations, even in the most bigoted and jealous countries, such as Spain, Austria, etc. You will have him in this case *constantly near you without* anybody having the right of finding fault with it, and to be useful to you he should be near you. Stockmar would have the *immense* advantage, for so young a Queen, to be a *living* dictionary of all matters scientific and politic that happened these thirty years, which to you is of the greatest importance, because you *must study* the political history of at least the last thirty-seven years *more particularly*. I had begun something of the sort with you, even so far back as George II; you will do well to go through the reign of George III, and to follow the various circumstances which brought on finally the present state of affairs. ...

LEOPOLD R.

The Earl of Liverpool to Baron Stockmar

5th July 1837

Went about half-past ten o'clock to Apsley House, and told the Duke of Wellington the whole of my communication with the Queen, Duchess of Kent, and Sir John Conroy on 15th June, also of my communication subsequently with Lord Melbourne, all of which he very much approved of. He said that he was quite sure that the Queen would find Lord Melbourne an honourable man, and one in whom Her Majesty might put confidence; that he was a man apt to treat matters too lightly, or, as he expressed it, a *poco curante*, but in the main an honest and an honourable man. Upon my speaking to him of the kind and paternal conduct of King Leopold towards his Niece, he said that he was fully persuaded of this, and should at all and any time be ready to uphold it by his approbation, but that he had no immediate connection with the Press, whose attacks indeed he held very cheap, though they were frequently very offensive. He then asked me whether it was not true that the Queen had thought of some reviews at which she would appear on horseback. I said there had been some talk of it. He desired me to say that he thought this would be very dangerous, that she had much better do this in an open carriage, as no one except such as himself knew how difficult it was to get steady riding horses, and besides that, she could not be attended by any female, and that this would appear indelicate.

The King of the Belgians to Queen Victoria

Neuilly, 12th July 1837

... Having still a few moments before a special messenger sets off, I take advantage of it to add a few words. By all I can hear, there are

many intrigues on foot in England at this moment. Princess Lieven*
and another individual recently imported from her country seem to be
very active in what concerns them not; beware of them. A rule which
I cannot sufficiently recommend is, *never to permit* people to speak on
subjects concerning yourself or your affairs, without your having yourself desired them to do so. The moment a person behaves improperly
on this subject, change the conversation, and make the individual feel
that he has made a mistake.... People will certainly try to speak to
you on your *own personal* affairs; decline it boldly, and they will leave
you alone....   LEOPOLD R.

Lord John Russell to Queen Victoria

Endsleigh, 15th August 1837

Lord John Russell presents his humble duty to your Majesty, and has
the honour to lay before your Majesty a general statement of the result
of the elections, which, with the exception of one or two doubtful
counties in Ireland, may be said to be completed....

Lord John Russell is sorry to add that bribery, intimidation, and
drunkenness have been very prevalent at the late elections, and that in
many cases the disposition to riot has only been checked by the appear-

* The Princess Dorothea de Benckendorff married the Count de Lieven at
fifteen; in 1812, he became Russian Minister (and later Ambassador) in London,
whither she accompanied him. She was a woman of extraordinary cleverness,
enjoying the confidence of George IV, Liverpool, Canning, Castlereagh, and
Wellington. Inspiring the efforts and even composing the despatches of her
husband, she became herself the confidential correspondent of Nesselrode, Ester-
hazy, Posso di Borgo, Guizot, and Lord Aberdeen. In 1834, the Lievens returned
to St Petersburg, where the Emperor Nicholas, though indifferent to the society
of women of talent, showed her special marks of regard. Her husband died at
Rome, in January 1838, and she established herself in Paris, afterwards seeking a
home in England during the troubles of 1848. Returning to Paris, her *salon*
became again the resort of diplomatists, politicians, and men of the world. She
died in January 1857.

Madame de Lieven about this time told Greville that she had had an audience
of the Queen, 'who was very civil and gracious, but timid and embarrassed, and
talked of nothing but commonplaces'; and Greville adds that the Queen 'had
probably been told that the Princess was an *intrigante*, and was afraid of com-
mitting herself.'

ance of the Military, who have in all cases conducted themselves with great temper and judgment.

The King of the Belgians to Queen Victoria

Laeken, 9th October 1837

... I have also told Stockmar to try to settle something for *regular* safe communication; in quiet times like the present, one a week would be sufficient. You know now that all letters are read, and that should not be *always* the case with ours. There is, however, one thing about which I think it right to warn you. This way of reading people's letters is often taken advantage of by the writers of them, who are *not so ignorant of the thing as is imagined* to write the very subject which they wish to convey to the ears of persons without compromising themselves. I will give you an example: we are still plagued by Prussia concerning those fortresses; now, to tell the Prussian Government many things, which we *should not like* to tell them *officially*, the Minister is going to write a despatch to our man at Berlin, sending it *by post*; the Prussians *are sure* to read it, and to learn in this way what we wish them to hear. The diplomats in England may resort to this same mode of proceeding to injure people, to calumniate, and to convey to your knowledge such things as they may hope to have the effect of injuring some people *they may fear*, in your eyes. I tell you the *trick*, that you should be able to guard against it; it is of importance, and I have no doubt will be resorted to by various political people. ...

The King of the Belgians to Queen Victoria*

Laeken, 26th December 1837

MY DEAREST CHILD,—You were *somewhat irritable* when you wrote to me! ... Affairs stand now as follows: the studies at Bonn take the whole of April, and may be concluded at the beginning of May. From May till the end of August, if you approved of the visit, the time should be *utilisé*. A *séjour* at Coburg would *not* be of much use; here

---

* This letter refers to the course of study which Prince Albert was about to pursue.

26

we are generally absent in the summer. To confide therefore the young gentleman to his Uncle Mensdorff for three months, would give him so much time for some *manly accomplishments*, which do no harm to a young man. To make him *enter the Service* would *not* do at all. What you say about his imbibing principles of a political nature, there is no great fear of that. First of all, Prague is not a town where politics are at all agitated; these topics are very rarely touched upon; besides, Albert is clever, and it is not at the eleventh hour that anybody in three months will make him imbibe political principles. Perhaps you will turn in your mind what you think on the subject, and communicate me the result of it. . . .

1838

Queen Victoria to the King of the Belgians

Buckingham Palace, 22nd February 1838

MY DEAR UNCLE,—. . . I had a very brilliant Levée again yesterday, at which O'Connell and all his sons, son-in-law, nephew, etc., appeared. I received him, as you may imagine, with a very smiling face; he has been behaving very well this year.* It was quite a treat for me to see him, as I had for long wished it. . . .

Viscount Palmerston to Queen Victoria

Stanhope Street, 25th February 1838

Viscount Palmerston presents his humble duty to your Majesty, and with reference to your Majesty's question upon the subjects to which Lord William Russell's recent despatch relates, he has the honour to state: that in the Governments of the Continent, and more especially in those which have no representative Assemblies, the second class of persons in the public offices possess and exercise much more power and influence than the corresponding class of persons do in this country.

* Ever since the Accession, O'Connell's speeches had been full of expressions of loyalty, and he had been acting in concert with the Whigs.

In England the Ministers who are at the head of the several departments of the State, are liable any day and every day to defend themselves in Parliament; in order to do this, they must be minutely acquainted with all the details of the business of their offices, and the only way of being constantly armed with such information is to conduct and direct those details themselves.

On the Continent, where Ministers of State are not liable so to be called to account for their conduct, the Ministers are tempted to leave the details of their business much more to their Under-Secretaries and to their chief clerks. Thus it happens that all the routine of business is generally managed by these subordinate agents; and to such an extent is this carried, that Viscount Palmerston believes that the Ministers for Foreign Affairs, in France, Austria, Prussia, and Russia, seldom take the trouble of writing their own despatches, except, perhaps, upon some very particular and important occasion.

Your Majesty will easily see how greatly such a system must place in the hands of the subordinate members of the public departments the power of directing the policy and the measures of the Government; because the value and tendency, and the consequence of a measure, frequently depend as much upon the manner in which that measure is worked out, as upon the intention and spirit with which it was planned.

Another circumstance tends also to give great power to these second-class men, and that is their permanence in office. . . .

This class of subordinate men has, from the fact of its being possessed of so much power, been invested by the jargon of the day with the title of 'Bureaucratic'—a name fabricated in imitation of the words 'aristocratic' and 'democratic,' each being compounded of the word 'cratic,' which is a corruption from the Greek word 'kratos,' which means power; and the prefix, denoting the particular class of society whose power is meant to be expressed. Thus '*aristo*-cratic' is the power of the upper, or, as in Greek it is called, the 'aristos' class of society; '*demo*-cratic' is the power of the people, which in Greek is called the 'demos'; and '*bureau*-cratic' is the power of the public offices or 'bureaus,' for which latter the French name has been taken instead of a Greek word. . . .

The King of the Belgians to Queen Victoria

13th April 1838

... Concerning the education of our friend Albert, it has been the best plan you could have fixed upon, to name Stockmar your commissary-general; it will give *unité d'action et de l'ensemble*, which otherwise we should not have had. I have communicated to him what your uncle and the young gentleman seem to wish, and what strikes me as the best for the moment. Stockmar will make a regular report to you on this subject.... On one thing you can rely, that it is my *great anxiety* to see Albert a *very good* and *distinguished young man*, and *no pains will be thought too much* on my part if this end can be attained....

Queen Victoria to the King of the Belgians

Buckingham Palace, 25th May 1838

MY DEAREST UNCLE,—... Old Talleyrand is at last dead. I hear he showed wonderful composure and firmness to the last. He was one of those people who I thought never would die. Did you know what Pozzo said to somebody here about him? He said he (Talleyrand) would not die yet, *'parce que le Diable ne voulait pas l'avoir.'*

Queen Adelaide to Queen Victoria

Marlboro' House, 28th June 1838
(At a quarter before 12 o'clock on the Coronation Day)

MY DEAREST NIECE,—The guns are just announcing your approach to the Abbey, and as I am not near you, and cannot take part in the sacred ceremony of your Coronation, I must address you in writing to assure you that my thoughts and my whole heart are with you, and my prayers are offered up to Heaven for your happiness, and the prosperity and glory of your reign. May our Heavenly Father bless and preserve you, and His Holy Ghost dwell within you to give you that peace which the world cannot give! Accept of these my best wishes, and the blessing of your most devoted and attached Aunt,

ADELAIDE

1839

8th May 1839

Lord Melbourne presents his humble duty to your Majesty, and is much grieved that he did not answer your Majesty's letter yesterday evening, as your Majesty desired, but he did not get it till late, and he felt much tired and harassed by all that had passed during the day. The situation is very painful, but it is necessary for your Majesty to be prudent and firm. It is of all things necessary not to be suspected of any unfair dealing. Whilst Lord Melbourne holds his office, everything of course may be written to him as usual; but still the resolutions for the formation of the new Government will now commence, and it will never do, whilst they are going on, either for appearance or in reality, that Lord Melbourne should dine with your Majesty, as he did before this disturbance. It would create feeling, possibly lead to remonstrance, and throw a doubt upon the fairness and integrity of your Majesty's conduct. All this is very painful both to do and to say, but it is unavoidable; it must be said, and it must be done. Lord Melbourne will wait upon your Majesty at eleven.

Queen Victoria to Viscount Melbourne

8th May 1839

The Queen told Lord Melbourne she would give him an account of what passed, which she is *very* anxious to do. She saw the Duke for about twenty minutes; the Queen said she supposed he knew why she sent for him, upon which the Duke said, No, he had no idea. The Queen then said that she had had the greatest confidence in her late Ministry, and had parted with them with the greatest reluctance; upon which the Duke observed that he could assure me no one felt more pain in hearing the announcement of their resignation than he did, and that he was deeply grieved at it. The Queen then continued, that as his party had been instrumental in removing them, that she must look to him to form a new Government. The Duke answered that he had no power whatever in the House of Commons, 'that if he was to say black was white, they would say it was not,' and that he advised me to send for Sir Robert Peel, in whom I could place confidence, and who was a gentleman and a man of honour and integrity. The Queen then said she hoped he would at all events have a place in the new Cabinet. The Duke at first rather refused, and said he was so deaf, and so old and unfit for any discussion, that if he were to consult his own feelings he would rather not do it, and remain quite aloof; but that as he was very anxious to do anything that would tend to the Queen's comfort, and would do everything and at all times that could be of use to the Queen, and therefore if she and her Prime Minister urged his accepting office, he would. The Queen said she had more confidence in him than in any of the others of his party. The Queen then mentioned the subject of the Household, and of those who were not in Parliament. The Duke did not give any decisive answer about it, but advised the Queen not to begin with conditions of this sort, and wait till the matter was proposed. The Queen then said that she felt certain he would understand the great friendship she had for Lord Melbourne, who had been to her quite a parent, and the Duke said *no one felt and knew that better than he did, and that no one could still be of greater use to the Queen than Lord Melbourne.* The Duke spoke of his personal friendship for Lord Melbourne, and that he hoped I knew that he had often done all he could to help your (Lord Melbourne's) Government. The Queen then mentioned her intention to prove her great *fairness* to her new Government in telling them, that they might know there was no unfair dealing, that I meant to see you often as a friend, as I owed *so* much to you. The Duke said he quite understood it, and knew I would not exercise this to weaken the Government, and that he would take my part about it, and felt for me. He was very kind, and said he called it 'a misfortune' that you had all left me.

The Queen wrote to Peel, who came after two, embarrassed and put out. The Queen repeated what she had said to the Duke about her former Government, and asked Sir Robert to form a new Ministry.

He does not seem sanguine; says entering the Government in a minority is very difficult; he felt unequal to the task, and far from exulting in what had happened, as he knew what pain it must give; he quite approved that the Duke should take office, and saw the importance of it; meant to offer him the post of Secretary for Foreign Affairs, and if he refused, Lord Aberdeen; Lord Lyndhurst, Chancellor; hoped to secure Stanley and Graham; Goulburn to be the candidate for the Speaker's Chair; he expects a severe conflict then, and if he should be beat must either resign or dissolve Parliament. Before this the Queen said she was against a dissolution, in which he quite agreed, but of course wished no conditions should be made; he felt the task arduous, and that he would require me to demonstrate (*a certain* degree, if *any* I can only feel) confidence in the Government, and that my Household would be one of the marks of that. The Queen mentioned the same thing about her Household, to which he at present would give no answer, and said nothing should be done without my knowledge or approbation. He repeated his surprise at the course you had all taken in resigning, which he did not expect. The Queen talked of her great friendship for, and gratitude to Lord Melbourne, and repeated what she had said to the Duke, in which Peel agreed; but he is such a cold, odd man she can't make out what he means. He said he couldn't expect me to have the confidence in him I had in you (and which he never can have) as he has not deserved it. My impression is, he is not *happy* and sanguine. He comes to me to-morrow at one to report progress in his formation of the new Government. The Queen don't like his manner after—oh! how different, how dreadfully different, to that frank, open, natural and most kind, warm manner of Lord Melbourne. The Duke I like by far better to Peel. The Queen trusts Lord Melbourne will excuse this long letter, but she was so very anxious he should know all. The Queen was very much collected, and betrayed no agitation during these two trying Audiences. But afterwards again *all* gave way. She feels Lord Melbourne will understand it, amongst enemies to those she most relied on and esteemed, and people who seem to have no heart; but what is worst of all is the being deprived of seeing Lord Melbourne as she used to do.

Queen Victoria to Viscount Melbourne

Buckingham Palace, 9th May 1839

The Queen writes one line to prepare Lord Melbourne for what *may* happen in a very few hours. Sir Robert Peel has behaved very ill, and has insisted on my giving up my Ladies, to which I replied that I never would consent, and I never saw a man so frightened. He said he must go to the Duke of Wellington and consult with him, when both would return, and he said this must suspend all further proceedings, and he asked whether I should be ready to receive a decision, which I said I should; he was quite perturbed—but this is *infamous*. I said, besides many other things, that if he or the Duke of Wellington had been at the head of the Government when I came to the Throne, perhaps there might have been a few more Tory Ladies, but that then if you had come into Office you would never have *dreamt* of changing them. I was calm but very decided, and I think you would have been pleased to see my composure and great firmness; the Queen of England will not submit to such trickery. Keep yourself in readiness, for you may soon be wanted.

Queen Victoria to the King of the Belgians

Buckingham Palace, 15th July 1839

MY DEAR UNCLE,—. . . I shall send this letter by a courier, as I am anxious to put several questions to you, and to mention some feelings of mine upon the subject of my cousins' visit, which I am desirous should not transpire. First of all, I wish to know if *Albert* is aware of the wish of his *Father* and *you* relative to *me?* Secondly, if he knows that there is *no engagement* between us? I am anxious that you should acquaint Uncle Ernest, that if I should take Albert, that I can make *no final promise this year*, for, at the *very earliest*, any such event could not take place till *two or three years hence*. For, independent of my youth, and my *great* repugnance to change my present position, there is *no anxiety* evinced in *this country* for such an event, and it would be more prudent, in my opinion, to wait till some such demonstration is shown, —else if it were hurried it might produce discontent.

Though all the reports of Albert are most favourable, and though I have little doubt I shall like him, still one can never answer beforehand for *feelings*, and I may not have the *feeling* for him which is requisite to ensure happiness. I *may* like him as a friend, and as a *cousin*, and as a *brother*, but not *more*; and should this be the case (which is not likely), I am *very* anxious that it should be understood that I am *not* guilty of *any* breach of promise, for *I never gave any*. I am sure you will understand my anxiety, for I should otherwise, were this not completely understood, be in a very painful position. As it is, I am rather nervous about the visit, for the subject I allude to is not an agreeable one to me. I have little else to say, dear Uncle, as I have now spoken open to you, which I was very, *very anxious* to do. . . .

Queen Victoria to Viscount Melbourne

Windsor Castle, 7th October 1839

The Queen sends the little *charm* which she hopes may keep Lord Melbourne from *all evil*, and which it will make her very happy if he will put [? it with] his keys. If the ring is too small Lord Melbourne must send it back to her, and she will have it altered.

Queen Victoria to the King of the Belgians

Windsor Castle, 12th October 1839

MY DEAR UNCLE,—. . . The dear cousins arrived at half-past seven on Thursday, after a very bad and almost dangerous passage, but looking both very well, and much improved. Having no clothes, they could not appear at dinner, but nevertheless *débutéd* after dinner in their *négligé*. Ernest is grown quite handsome; Albert's *beauty* is *most striking*, and he so amiable and unaffected—in short, very *fascinating*; he is excessively admired here. The Granvilles and Lord Clanricarde happened just to be here, but are gone again to-day. We rode out yesterday and danced after dinner. The young men are very amiable, delightful companions, and I am very happy to have them here; they are playing some Symphonies of Haydn *under* me at this very moment; they are passionately fond of music.

Queen Victoria to the King of the Belgians

Windsor Castle, 15th October 1839

MY DEAREST UNCLE,—This letter will, I am sure, give you pleasure, for you have always shown and taken so warm an interest in all that concerns me. My mind is quite made up—and I told Albert this morning of it; the warm affection he showed me on learning this gave me *great* pleasure. He seems *perfection*, and I think that I have the prospect of very great happiness before me. I *love* him *more* than I can say, and I shall do everything in my power to render the sacrifice he has made (for a *sacrifice* in my opinion it is) as small as I can. He seems to have a very great tact—a very necessary thing in his position. These last few days have passed like a dream to me, and I am so much bewildered by it all that I know hardly how to write; but I *do* feel *very, very* happy.

It is absolutely necessary that this determination of mine should be known to *no one* but yourself, and Uncle Ernest—till the meeting of Parliament—as it would be considered otherwise neglectful on my part not to have assembled Parliament at once to have informed them of it. . . . Lord Melbourne, whom I of course have consulted about the whole affair, quite approves my choice, and expresses great satisfaction at the event, which he thinks in every way highly desirable. Lord Melbourne has acted in this business, as he has always done towards me, with the greatest kindness and affection.

We also think it better, and Albert quite approves of it, that we should be married very soon after Parliament meets, about the beginning of February; and indeed, loving Albert as I do, I cannot wish it should be delayed. My feelings are a *little* changed, I must say, since last Spring, when I said I couldn't *think* of marrying for *three or four years*; but seeing Albert has changed all this.

Pray, dearest Uncle, forward these two letters to Uncle Ernest (to whom I beg you will enjoin *strict* secrecy, and explain these details, which I have not time to do) and to faithful Stockmar.

I think you might tell Louise of it, but none of her family. I should wish to keep the dear young gentlemen here till the end of next month. Ernest's sincere pleasure gave me great delight. He does so adore dearest Albert. Ever, dearest Uncle, your devoted Niece,

VICTORIA R.

Viscount Melbourne to Queen Victoria

Windsor Castle, 16th October 1839

Lord Melbourne will be ready to wait upon your Majesty at a little before one.

Lord Melbourne reads with great satisfaction your Majesty's expression of feeling, as your Majesty's happiness must ever be one of Lord Melbourne's first and strongest interests.

The King of the Belgians to Queen Victoria

Wiesbaden, 24th October 1839

MY DEAREST VICTORIA,—Nothing could have given me greater pleasure than your dear letter. I had, when I saw your decision, almost the feeling of old Zacharias—'Now lettest Thou Thy servant depart in peace!' Your choice had been for these last years my conviction of what might and would be *best* for your happiness; and just because I was convinced of it, and knowing how *strangely* fate often *deranges* what one tries to bring about as being the best plan one could fix upon, *the maximum of a good arrangement*, I feared that it would *not* happen. In your position, which may and will, perhaps, become in future even more difficult in a political point of view, *you could not exist* without having a *happy* and an *agreeable intérieur*.

And I am much deceived—which I think I am not—or you will find in Albert just the very qualities and dispositions which are indispensable for your happiness, and *which will suit your own character, temper, and mode of life.* You say most amiably that you consider it a sacrifice on the part of Albert. This is true in many points, because his position will be a difficult one; but much, I may say *all*, will depend on your affection for him. If *you love him, and are kind to him*, he will easily bear the burthen of the position; and there is a steadiness and at the same time cheerfulness in his character which will facilitate this. I think your plans excellent. If Parliament had been called at an unusual time it would make them uncomfortable, and if, therefore, they receive the communication at the opening of the Session, it will be best. The marriage, as you say, might then follow as closely as possible. . . .

Queen Victoria to Prince Albert

Buckingham Palace, 21st November 1839

... It is desired here that the matter should be declared at Coburg as soon as possible, and immediately after that I shall send you the Order.

Your rank will be settled just before you come over, as also your rank in the Army. Everything will be very easily arranged. Lord Melbourne showed me yesterday the *Declaration*, which is very simple and nice. I will send it you as soon as possible. ...

Lord Melbourne told me yesterday, that the whole Cabinet are strongly of opinion that you should NOT *be made a Peer.* I will write that to Uncle. ...

Queen Victoria to the Prince Albert

Windsor Castle, 23rd November 1839

... Just arrived here, 5.30. Everything has gone off very well. The Council was held at two o'clock; more than a hundred persons were present, and *there* I had to read the Declaration. *It was rather an awful moment, to be obliged to announce this to so many people, many of whom were quite strangers, but they told me I did it very well, and I felt so happy to do it.*

Good Lord Melbourne was deeply moved about it, and Uxbridge likewise; it lasted only two or three minutes. *Everybody, they tell me, is very much pleased, and I wish you could have seen the crowds of people who cheered me loudly as I left the Palace for Windsor.* I am so happy to-day! oh, if only *you* could be here! I wish that you were able to participate in all the kindness which is shown to me. To-day I can only send you the Declaration. *The description of the whole* I will send after this. ...

Send me as soon as possible the report of the announcement at Coburg. I wear your dear picture mornings and evenings, and wore it also at the meeting of the *Conseil*.

The King of the Belgians to Queen Victoria

Wiesbaden, 22nd November 1839

MY DEAREST VICTORIA,—. . . Concerning the peerage, that is a matter to be considered at any time; the only reason why I do wish it is, that

Albert's foreignership should disappear as much as possible. I have, in different circumstances to be sure, suffered greatly from my having declined conditionally the peerage when it was offered me in 1816. . . .

Queen Victoria to the King of the Belgians

Windsor Castle, 26th November 1839

MY DEAR UNCLE,—. . . The *whole* Cabinet agree with me in being *strongly* of opinion that Albert should *not* be a Peer; indeed, I see everything against it and *nothing* for it; the English are very jealous at the idea of Albert's having any political power, or meddling with affairs here—which I know from himself he will *not* do. . . .

Queen Victoria to the Prince Albert

Windsor Castle, 27th November 1839

The English are very jealous of any foreigner interfering in the government of this country, and have already in some of the papers (which are friendly to me and you) expressed a hope that you would not interfere. Now, though I know you never would, still, if you were a Peer, they would all say, the Prince meant to play a political part. I am certain you will understand this, but it is much better not to say anything more about it now, and to let the whole matter rest. The Tories make a great disturbance (saying) that you are *a Papist*, because the words *'a Protestant Prince'* have not been put into the Declaration—a thing which would be quite unnecessary, seeing that I *cannot* marry a Papist. . . .

Queen Victoria to the Prince Albert

Windsor Castle, 8th December 1839

As to your wish about your gentlemen, my dear Albert, I must tell you quite honestly that it will not do. You may entirely rely upon me that people who will be about you will be absolutely pleasant people, of high standing and good character. *These gentlemen will not be in continual attendance on you; only on great occasions, and to accompany you when you go anywhere, and to dinners, etc. Seymour is your*

Queen Victoria in 1838

*From a lithograph by Edwin Dalton
after Sir William Ross*

Prince Albert in 1840

*From a sketch by Sir George Hayter for his
painting 'The Royal Marriage'*

Queen Victoria and Prince Albert, *c.* 1840

Both from sketches by John Doyle

'Susannah and the Elders'
The Young Queen riding with Lord Melbourne and Lord John Russell, 1837

*confidential attendant, and also Schenk and Anson, whom Lehzen
has written to you about.*

*Old Sir George Anson has been told of your gracious wish to have
him as Groom of the Bedchamber and is delighted.*

*I can only have Lords, and they will not be Peers, but Lords, the
eldest sons of Dukes or Marquesses, or Earls (Counts), and who as far
as possible are not in Parliament, for then they need not change, but
your people are appointed by you and not by me (nominally), and
therefore, unless they were to vote against my Government (which
would be awkward), they need not change. You may rely upon my
care that you shall have proper people, and not idle and not too young,
and Lord Melbourne has already mentioned several to me who would
be very suitable. . . .*

I have received to-day an ungracious letter from Uncle Leopold. He
appears to me to be nettled because I no longer ask for his advice, but
dear Uncle is given to believe that he must rule the roast everywhere.
However, this is not a necessity. As he has written to Melbourne, Melbourne will reply to him on every point, and will tell him that Stockmar
ought to come here as soon as possible to arrange everything about the
treaty. That will be a very good thing, because Stockmar understands
all English things so well.

The *Second*, as you always called Palmerston, is to be married within
the next few days to Lady Cowper, the sister of my Premier (*Primus*);
I have known this for a long time, but Melbourne asked me not to
tell it to any one. They are, both of them, above fifty, and I think that
they are quite right so to act, because Palmerston, since the death of
his sisters, is quite alone in the world, and *Lady C.* is a very clever
woman, and *much* attached to him; still, I feel sure it will make you
smile. . . .

Queen Victoria to the King of the Belgians

Windsor Castle, 9th December 1839

MY DEAR UNCLE,—. . . I was quite miserable at not hearing from Albert
for *ten* days; such a long silence is quite insupportable for any one in
my position towards Albert, and I was overjoyed on receiving yesterday the *most dear, most* affectionate, delightful long letter from him.
He writes so beautifully, and so simply and unaffectedly. I hope, dear

Uncle, you received my last letter (quite a packet) for Albert, on the 5th or 6th? I send you another now. I fear I am very indiscreet about these letters, but I have so much to tell him, and it will only last two months, so that I trust you will forgive it, and forward them.

1840

Queen Victoria to the Prince Albert

Buckingham Palace, 17th January 1840

... I observe with horror that I have not formally invited your father; though that is a matter of course. My last letter will have set that right. I ought not to have written to you on picture notepaper, seeing that we are in deep mourning for my poor Aunt, the Landgravine, but it was quite impossible for me to write to you on mourning paper. ...

But this will not interfere with our marriage in the least; the mourning will be taken off for that day, and for two or three days after, and then put on again.

Queen Victoria to the Prince Albert

Buckingham Palace, 21st January 1840

... We are all of us very much preoccupied with politics. The Tories really are very astonishing; *as they cannot and dare not attack us in Parliament, they do everything that they can to be personally rude to me. ... The Whigs are the only safe and loyal people, and the Radicals will also rally round their Queen to protect her from the Tories; but it is a curious sight to see those, who as Tories, used to pique themselves upon their excessive loyalty, doing everything to degrade their young Sovereign in the eyes of the people. Of course there are exceptions.*

Queen Victoria to the Prince Albert

Buckingham Palace, 31st January 1840

... You have written to me in one of your letters about our stay at Windsor, but, dear Albert, you have not at all understood the matter.

You forget, my dearest Love, that I am the Sovereign, and that business can stop and wait for nothing. Parliament is sitting, and something occurs almost every day, for which I may be required, and it is quite impossible for me to be absent from London; therefore two or three days is already a long time to be absent. I am never easy a moment, if I am not on the spot, and see and hear what is going on, and everybody, including all my Aunts (who are very knowing in all these things), says I must come out after the second day, for, as I must be surrounded by my Court, I cannot keep alone. This is also my own wish in every way.

Now as to the Arms: *as an English Prince you have no right, and Uncle Leopold had no right to quarter the English Arms, but the Sovereign has the power to allow it by Royal Command: this was done for Uncle Leopold by the Prince Regent, and I will do it again for you. But it can only be done by Royal Command.*

I will, therefore, without delay, have a seal engraved for you.

The King of the Belgians to Queen Victoria

Brussels, 4th February 1840

MY DEAREST VICTORIA,—I have now treated all the questions you wished me to touch upon with Albert, and I was much pleased with his amiable disposition. At a certain distance explanations by letter are next to impossible, and each party in the end thinks the other unreasonable. When he arrived he was rather exasperated about various things, and pretty full of grievances. But our conversations have dissipated these clouds, and now there will only remain the new parliamentary events and consequences, which change a good deal of what one could reasonably have foreseen or arranged. You will best treat these questions now verbally. Albert is quick, not obstinate, in conversation, and open to conviction if good arguments are brought forward. When he thinks himself right he only wishes to have it *proved* that he *misunderstands* the case, to give it up without ill-humour. He is not inclined to be sulky, but I think he may be rendered a little melancholy if he thinks himself unfairly or unjustly treated, but being together and remaining together, there *never* can arise, I hope, any occasion for any disagreement even on trifling subjects. . . . Ever, my dearest Victoria, your devoted Uncle,   LEOPOLD R.

Queen Victoria to the Prince Albert

10th February 1840

DEAREST,—. . . How are you to-day, and have you slept well? I have rested very well, and feel very comfortable to-day. What weather! I believe, however, the rain will cease.

Send one word when you, my most dearly loved bridegroom, will be ready. Thy ever-faithful,   VICTORIA R.

Queen Victoria to the King of the Belgians

Windsor Castle, 11th February 1840

MY DEAREST UNCLE,—I write to you from here, the happiest, happiest Being that ever existed. Really, I do not think it *possible* for any one in the world to be *happier*, or AS happy as I am. He is an Angel, and his kindness and affection for me is really touching. To look in those dear eyes, and that dear sunny face, is enough to make me adore him. What I can do to make him happy will be my greatest delight. Independent of my personal happiness, the reception we both met with yesterday was the most gratifying and enthusiastic I ever experienced; there was no end of the crowds in London, and all along the road. I was a good deal tired last night, but am quite well again to-day, and happy. . . .

My love to dear Louise. Ever your affectionate,   VICTORIA R.

Memorandum by Mr Anson
Minutes of Conversations with Lord Melbourne and Baron Stockmar

28th May 1840

Lord Melbourne.—'I have spoken to the Queen, who says the Prince complains of a want of confidence on trivial matters, and on all matters connected with the politics of this country. She said it proceeded entirely from indolence; she knew it was wrong, but when she was with the Prince she preferred talking upon other subjects. I told Her Majesty that she should try and alter this, and that there was no objection to her conversing with the Prince upon any subject she pleased. My impression is that the chief obstacle in Her Majesty's mind is the fear of difference of opinion, and she thinks that domestic harmony is more likely to follow from avoiding subjects likely to create difference. My own experience leads me to think that subjects between man and wife, even where difference is sure to ensue, are much better discussed than avoided, for the latter course is sure to beget distrust. I do not think that the Baroness is the cause of this want of openness, though her name to me is never mentioned by the Queen.'

Baron Stockmar.—'I wish to have a talk with you. The Prince leans more on you than on any one else, and gives you his entire confidence; you are honest, moral, and religious, and will not belie that trust. The Queen has not started upon a right principle. She should by degrees impart everything to him, but there is danger in his wishing it all at once. A case may be laid before him; he may give some crude and unformed opinion; the opinion may be taken and the result disastrous, and a forcible argument is thus raised against advice being asked for the future. . . .'

The Queen of the Belgians to Queen Victoria

Laeken, 30th November 1840

MY MOST BELOVED VICTORIA,—I have been longing to write to you ever since we got the *joyful* tidings,* but I would not do so before the nine days were at an end. Now that they are over, I hope you are, thank God, so well, I may venture a few lines to express *a part* of my feelings, and to wish you joy on the happy birth of your dear little girl. I need not tell you the *deep, deep* share I took in this most *happy event*, and all I felt for you, for dear Albert, when I heard of it, and since we last met. You know my affection for you, and I will not trouble you with the repetition of what you know. All I will say is that I thanked God

---

* The Princess Royal, afterwards the Empress Frederick of Germany, was born 21st November 1840.

with all my heart, and as I have scarcely thanked Him for any other favour. . . .

Queen Victoria to the King of the Belgians

15th December 1840

MY DEAREST UNCLE,—Many thanks for your kind little letter of the 10th from Ardenne. I am very prosperous, walking about the house like myself again, and we go to Windsor on the 22nd or 23rd, which will quite set me up. I am *very* prudent and careful, you may *rely* upon it. Your little grand-niece is most flourishing; she gains daily in health, strength and, I may add, beauty; I think she will be very like her dearest father; she grows amazingly; I shall be proud to present her to you. . . .

Albert sends his affectionate love, and pray believe me always, your devoted Niece,   VICTORIA R.

The King of the Belgians to Queen Victoria

Laeken, 26th December 1840

. . . I can well understand that you feel quite astonished at finding yourself within a year of your marriage a very respectable mother of a nice little girl, but let us thank Heaven that it is so. Any illness to which, unfortunately, we poor human creatures are very subject, would almost have kept you longer in bed, and make you longer weak and uncomfortable, than an event which in your position as Sovereign is of a very great importance.

Because there is no doubt that a Sovereign without heirs direct, or brothers and sisters, which by their attachment may stand in lieu of them, is much to be pitied, viz., Queen Anne's later years. Moreover, children of our own, besides the affection which one feels for them, have also for their parents sentiments which one rarely obtains from strangers. I flatter myself therefore that you will be a delighted and delightful *Maman au milieu d'une belle et nombreuse famille*. . . .

1841

Queen Victoria to the King of the Belgians

MY DEAREST UNCLE,—I have to thank you for two very kind letters, of the 26th December and 1st January, and for all your very kind and good wishes. I am sorry to hear you have all been plagued with colds; we have as yet escaped them, and I trust will continue to do so. I think, dearest Uncle, you cannot *really* wish me to be the 'Mamma d'une *nombreuse* famille,' for I think you will see with me the great inconvenience a *large* family would be to us all, and particularly to the country, independent of the hardship and inconvenience to myself; men never think, at least seldom think, what a hard task it is for us women to go through this *very often*. God's will be done, and if He decrees that we are to have a great number of children, why we must try to bring them up as useful and exemplary members of society. Our young lady flourishes exceedingly, and I hope the Van der Weyers (who have been here for three days), who have seen her twice, will give you a favourable description of her. I think you would be amused to see Albert dancing her in his arms; he makes a capital nurse (which I do not, and she is much too heavy for me to carry), and she always seems so happy to go to him.

The christening will be at Buckingham Palace on the 10th of February, our dear marriage-day.

Affairs are certainly still precarious, but I feel confident all will come right. . . .

Ever your devoted Niece,   VICTORIA R.

Memorandum—Mr Anson

Windsor Castle, 15th January 1841

Lord Melbourne said, 'The Prince is bored with the sameness of his chess every evening. He would like to bring literary and scientific people about the Court, vary the society, and infuse a more useful tendency into it. The Queen however has no fancy to encourage such people. This arises from a feeling on her part that her education has not fitted her to take part in such conversation; she would not like conversation to be going on in which she could not take her fair share, and she is far too open and candid in her nature to pretend to one atom more knowledge than she really possesses on such subjects; and yet, as the world goes, she would, as any girl, have been considered accomplished, for she speaks German well and writes it; understands Italian, speaks French fluently, and writes it with great elegance. In addition to this old Davys instilled some Latin into her during his tutorship. The rest of her education she owes to her own natural shrewdness and quickness, and this perhaps has not been the proper education for one who was to wear the Crown of England.

'The Queen is very proud of the Prince's utter indifference to the attractions of all ladies. I told Her Majesty that these were early days to boast, which made her rather indignant. I think she is a little jealous of his talking much even to men.'

Viscount Melbourne to Queen Victoria

22nd January 1841

Lord Melbourne presents his humble duty to your Majesty.

Lord Melbourne will be most happy to wait upon your Majesty on Saturday and Sunday.

Lord Melbourne is very sorry that your Majesty is compelled to come to London contrary to your inclinations; but Lord Melbourne much rejoices that your Majesty expresses that reluctance, as there is no surer sign of complete happiness and contentment in the married life than a desire to remain quietly in the country, and there is nothing on the earth Lord Melbourne desires more anxiously than the assurance of your Majesty's happiness.

The King of the Belgians to Queen Victoria

Brussels, 22nd January 1841

MY DEAREST VICTORIA,—I thank you very sincerely for your kind letter of the 19th, which I hasten to answer. I should not have bored you by my presence, but the act of the christening is, in my eyes, a sort of closing of the first cyclus of your dear life. I was shooting at the late Lord Craven's in Berkshire, when I received the messenger who brought me the horrifying news of your poor father's deadly illness. I hastened in bitter cold weather to Sidmouth, about two days before his death. His affairs were so much deranged that your Mother would have had no means even of leaving Sidmouth if I had not taken all this under my care and management. That dreary journey, under-taken, I think, on the 26th of January, in bitter cold and damp weather, I shall not easily forget. I looked very sharp after the poor little baby, then about eight months old. Arrived in London, we were very un-kindly treated by George IV, *whose great wish was to get you and your Mamma out of the country*, and I must say without my assistance you could *not* have remained. . . . I state these facts, because it is useful to remember through what *difficulties* and *hardships* one had to struggle. You will also remember that though there existed the *possibility* of your eventually succeeding to the Crown, that possibility was very doubtful, the then Duchess of Clarence having been confined after your Mother, and there being every reason to think that, though poor little Elizabeth did not live more than some months, other children might appear.

It was a long time from 1820 to 1837! We got over it, however, and, as far as you are concerned, God be praised! safely and happily. You are married, with every prospect of many happy years to come, and your happiness is *crowned*, and *consolidated*, as it were, by the birth of the dear little lady. Having from motives of discretion, perhaps *carried even too far*, not assisted at your coming to the throne, nor at your Coronation, nor afterwards at your marriage, I wished to assist at the christening of the little Princess, an event which is of great impor-tance. . . .

Viscount Melbourne to Queen Victoria

5th February 1841 (6 o'clock)

Lord Melbourne presents his humble duty to your Majesty, and is very sorry to have to acquaint your Majesty that the Duke of Wellington was taken ill in the House of Lords this evening with a seizure, probably paralytic, and of the same nature with those which he has had before. Lord Brougham, who was standing opposite to the Duke and addressing the House, observed the Duke's face to be drawn and distorted, and soon afterwards the Duke rose from his seat and walked staggeringly towards the door. He walked down the gallery, supported on each side, but never spoke. A medical man was procured to attend him; he was placed in his carriage and driven home. . . .

Viscount Melbourne to Queen Victoria

24th April 1841

. . . We have had under our consideration at the Cabinet the unfortunate subject of the conduct of Lord Cardigan.* The public feeling upon it is very strong, and it is almost certain that a Motion will be made in the House of Commons for an Address praying your Majesty to remove him from the command of his regiment. Such a Motion, if made, there is very little chance of resisting with success, and nothing is more to be apprehended and deprecated than such an interference of the House of Commons with the interior discipline and government of the Army. It was also felt that the general order issued by the Horse Guards was not sufficient to meet the case, and in these circumstances it was thought proper that Lord Melbourne should see Lord Hill, and should express to him the opinion of the Cabinet, that it was necessary that he should advise your Majesty to take such measures as should have the effect of removing Lord Cardigan from the command of the 11th Hussars. The repeated acts of imprudence of which Lord Cardigan has been guilty, and the repeated censures which he has drawn down upon himself, form a ground amply sufficient for such a proceeding, and indeed seem imperiously to demand it.

* 'Within the space of a single twelvemonth, one of his [Lord Cardigan's] captains was cashiered for writing him a challenge; he sent a coarse and insulting verbal message to another, and then punished him with prolonged arrest, because he respectfully refused to shake hands with the officer who had been employed to convey the affront; he fought a duel with a lieutenant who had left the corps; and shot him through the body; and he flogged a soldier on Sunday, between the Services, on the very spot where, half an hour before, the man's comrades had been mustered for public worship.'—Sir G. Trevelyan, *Life and Letters of Lord Macaulay*, chap. viii.

Lord Melbourne has seen Lord Hill and made to him this communication, and has left it for his consideration. Lord Hill is deeply chagrined and annoyed, but will consider the matter and confer again with Lord Melbourne upon it to-morrow.

Viscount Melbourne to Queen Victoria

25th April 1841

Lord Melbourne presents his humble duty to your Majesty. He is most anxious upon all subjects to be put in possession of Your Majesty's full and entire opinions. It is true that this question may materially affect the discipline of the Army, by subjecting the interior management of regiments to be brought continually under the inspection and control of the House of Commons upon complaints of officers against their superiors, or even of private men against the officers.

The danger of the whole of Lord Cardigan's proceedings has been lest a precedent of this nature should arise out of them. The whole question is whether it is not more prudent to prevent a question being brought forward in the House of Commons, than to wait for it with the certainty of being obliged to yield to it or of being overpowered by it. But of course this cannot be done unless it is consistent with justice and with the usage and prestige of the Service. . . .

Memorandum by Mr Anson
'The Ministry in jeopardy.' (Heading in the Prince Albert's hand.)

Windsor Castle, 4th May 1841

Lord Melbourne came down from town after the House of Lords. I went with him to his room for an hour after the Queen had retired. He said the main struggle would take place on the Sugar Duties on Friday. His impression was that the Government would be beat, and he must then decide whether to go out or dissolve. He leaned to the former. I said, 'I trusted he would not dissolve unless he thought there was some prospect of increasing his strength, and begged him to remember what was done would not be considered the act of the Government but that of himself and the Queen, and that he individually would be held as the responsible person.'

He said he had not written to the Queen to prepare H.M. for coming events and the course that it would be incumbent upon her to take, for he felt it extremely difficult and delicate, especially as to the use she would make of the Prince, and of her mode of communication when she required it with Lord Melbourne. He thought she ought never to ask his advice direct, but if she required his opinion there would be no objection to her obtaining it through the Prince.

He said H.M. had relied so implicitly upon him upon all affairs, that he felt that she required in this emergency advice upon almost every subject. That he would tell H.M. that she must carefully abstain from playing the part she did, again, on Sir R. Peel's attempt to form a Ministry, for that nothing but the forbearance of the Tories had enabled himself and his colleagues to support H.M. at that time. He feared Peel's doggedness and pertinacity might make him insist, as a point of honour, on having all discretion granted to him in regard to the removal of Ladies. I told him of the Prince's suggestion that before the Queen saw Sir R. Peel some negotiation might be entered into with Sir Robert, so that the subject might be avoided by mutual consent, the terms of which might be that Sir Robert should give up his demand to extort the principle. The Queen, on the other hand, should require the resignation of those Ladies objected to by Sir Robert. Lord Melbourne said, however, that the Prince must not have personal communication with Sir Robert on this subject, but he thought that I might through the medium of a common friend.

Viscount Melbourne to Queen Victoria

South Street, 7th May 1841

Lord Melbourne presents his humble duty to your Majesty, and laments much the prospect that lies before us, more especially as it is so repugnant to your Majesty's feelings. Your Majesty has often observed that these events must come in the course of affairs at some moment or another, but Lord Melbourne knows not whether it is much consolation to reflect that what is very disagreeable is also natural and unavoidable. Lord Melbourne feels certain that your Majesty will consider the situation calmly and impartially, will do that which shall appear the best for your own interests and those of the country, which are identical.

Everything shall be done that can be; the question which may arise shall be considered well, and upon as full information as can be obtained. But Lord Melbourne has little to add to what he wrote to your Majesty yesterday. So many interests are affected by this Sugar question, the West Indian, the East Indian, the opponents of Slavery and others, that no small number of our supporters will be induced either to stay away or to vote against us, and this must place us in a minority upon the main points of our Budget. In this we can hardly acquiesce, nor can we adopt a different policy and propose other taxes, when in our opinion the necessary revenue can be raised without imposing them. This state of things imposes upon us the alternative of dissolution or of resignation, and to try the former without succeeding in it would be to place both your Majesty and ourselves in a worse situation than that in which we are at present.

Memorandum by Mr Anson

NOTES UPON AN INTERVIEW WITH SIR ROBERT PEEL (No. 1)

9th May 1841

Told Sir Robert that I had wished to have sought him through the medium of a common friend, which would have given him a greater confidence than I had now a right to expect at his hands, but I felt upon so delicate a mission it was safer, and would be more in accordance with his wishes, to come direct.

That the Prince had sent me to him, with the object of removing difficulties upon his coming into office.

That Her Majesty was anxious that the question of the removal of the Ladies of the Bedchamber should not be revived, and would wish that in any personal communication with Sir Robert this question might be avoided.

That it might be arranged that if Sir Robert would not insist upon his principle, Her Majesty might procure the resignation of any Ladies whom Sir Robert might object to; that I thought there might be a disposition to yield to the removal of the Mistress of the Robes, Lady

Normanby, and the Duchess of Bedford, as being connected with leading political persons in Government.

Endeavoured to impress upon Sir Robert that if he acts fairly and kindly towards the Queen, he will be met in the same spirit.

Sir Robert said he had considered the probable object of my interview, and thought, from my former position with Lord Melbourne, that Lord Melbourne would be aware of my coming. He must be assured of this before he could speak confidentially to me.

Upon this I admitted that Lord Melbourne had knowledge of my intention, but that I was not authorised to say that he had.

Sir Robert said, 'I shall put aside all form, and treat you frankly and confidentially. You may depend upon every word you say being held as sacred. No part, without further permission, shall be mentioned even to the Duke, much less to any of my other colleagues.

'I would waive every pretension to office, I declare to God! sooner than that my acceptance of it should be attended with any personal humiliation to the Queen.'

He thought that giving in the names of those Ladies whom he considered obnoxious was an offensive course towards the Queen.

For the sake of office, which he did not covet, he could not concede any constitutional principle, but it was necessary that the principle should be mooted.

'It would be repulsive to my feelings that Her Majesty should part with any of her Ladies, as the *result of a forced stipulation on my part*; in a party sense it would doubtless be advantageous to me to say that I had demanded from the Queen, and the Queen had conceded to me the appointments of these three Ladies.'

The mode he would like, and which he considered as least objectionable for Her Majesty, was for Her Majesty to say to him, 'There is no occasion to revive this constitutional question, as those ladies immediately connected with prominent members of the Administration have sent in their resignation.'

The vacancies existing before Sir Robert Peel sees Her Majesty, there is no necessity for discussion.

On the one hand, by this means, there was less appearance of insult to the Queen, and on the other, there was no appearance of concession of principle upon his.

Sir Robert was ready to make any personal sacrifice for Her Majesty's comfort, except that of his honour. 'Can the Queen for an instant suppose that I would permit my party to urge me on to insist upon anything incompatible with Her Majesty's dignity, which it would be my great aim and honour to defend?'

[This was his indignant reply to my remark upon the rumours that his party would press him to coerce and subdue Her Majesty.]

Sir Robert thinks it better for the Queen to avoid anything in the shape of a stipulation. He would like what he would have done upon a former occasion (and upon which, on the honour of a gentleman, his views had undergone no change) to be taken as a test of what he would be ready to concede to.

Nothing but misconception, he said, could in his opinion have led to failure before. *Had the Queen told me* (after the question was mooted, which it never need have been) *that those three ladies immediately connected with the Government had tendered their resignation, I should have been perfectly satisfied*, and should have consulted the Queen's feelings in replacing them.'

Sir Robert said this conversation shall remain sacred, and to all effect, as if it had never happened, until he saw me again to-morrow morning.

There is nothing said, he added, which in any way pledges or compromises the Queen, the Prince, or Lord Melbourne.

Memorandum by Mr Anson
INTERVIEW WITH SIR ROBERT PEEL (No. 2)

10th May 1841

Peel said: 'It is essential to my position with the Queen that Her Majesty should understand that I have the feelings of a gentleman, and where my duty does not interfere, I cannot act against her wishes. Her Majesty doubtless knows how pressed I am as the head of a powerful party, but the impression I wish to create in Her Majesty's mind is, that I am bound to defend her against their encroachments.'

In regard to Household appointments the holders of which are not in Parliament, he had not considered the question, but in the meantime he would in no way commit himself to anyone, or to any understanding upon the subject, without previous communication. He had no personal objects to serve, and the Queen's wishes would always be consulted.

He again repeated, that if the Queen's personal feelings would suffer less by forming an Administration to his exclusion, he should not be offended. Private life satisfied him, and he had no ambition beyond it.

Lord Melbourne might rest assured that *he* fully appreciated his aim, that his only object was to do that which was most for Her Majesty's advantage, and no human being should know that he was privy to this overture. Lord Melbourne might depend upon his honour. If Lord Melbourne was pressed to a dissolution he should still feel the same impression of Lord Melbourne's conduct, that it was honourable and straightforward.

He wished the Prince to send him a list of those Ladies whom it would be agreeable to Her Majesty to have in her Household. Sir Robert must propose it to the Ladies, but will be entirely guided by Her Majesty's wishes. There should be no appearance that Her Majesty has any understanding, as he was bound to his party to make it appear that the appointments emanated from himself.

Memorandum by the Queen

11th May 1841

The Queen considers it her right (and is aware that her predecessors were peculiarly tenacious of this right) to appoint her Household. She, however, gives up the great officers of State and those of her Lords-in-Waiting, Equerries, and Grooms-in-Waiting, who are *in Parliament*, to the appointment of the Prime Minister, subject to her approval.

The Queen has *always* appointed her *Ladies of the Bedchamber herself*, but has generally mentioned their names to the Prime Minister before appointing them, in order to leave him room for objection in case he should deem their appointment injurious to his Government, when the Queen would probably not appoint the Lady.

The Maids of Honour and Women of the Bedchamber are of course not included amongst those who are mentioned to the Prime Minister before their appointment, but are at once appointed by the Queen.

Extract from the Queen's Journal

Saturday, 15th May 1841

'Lord Melbourne came to me at twenty minutes past one, and we talked about this question of dissolution. "We shall have a long debate upon it this morning at the Cabinet," Lord Melbourne said. "The worst thing is, that if we carry the Sugar Duties, we must dissolve. If we were to dissolve," he continued, "and were to have the parties equal as they are now, it would be very bad; if we *were* to have a *majority*, it would be a great thing, *but* if we were to have a minority it would be still worse. . . . We know that Charles I and Charles II, and even Cromwell, appealed to the country, and had a Parliament returned into their very teeth" (so strong an Opposition), "and that produced deposition, and convulsion, and bloodshed and death; but since then the Crown has always had a majority returned in favour of it. Even Queen Anne," he continued, "who removed Marlborough in the midst of his most glorious victories and dissolved Parliament, had an immense majority, though her measures were miserable; William IV," he said, "even though he had a majority against him which prevented him from keeping his Ministers, had a much stronger feeling for him in that Parliament, than he ever had before. But I am afraid," he added, "that for the first time the Crown would have an Opposition returned smack against it; and that would be an affront to which I am very unwilling to expose the Crown." This is very true.'

Queen Victoria to the King of the Belgians

18th May 1841

. . . I was sure you would feel for me. Since last Monday, the 10th, we have lived in the daily expectation of a final event taking place, and the debate *still* continues, and it is not certain whether it will even finish to-night, this being the eighth night, it having begun on Friday the 7th, two Saturdays and two Sundays having intervened! Our plans are so unsettled that I can tell you nothing, only that you may depend upon it nothing will be done without having been duly, properly, and maturely weighed. Lord Melbourne's conduct is as usual perfect; fair, calm, and totally disinterested, and I am certain that in whatever position he is *you* will treat him *just* as you have always done.

My dearest Angel is indeed a great comfort to me. He takes the greatest interest in what goes on, feeling with and for me, and yet abstaining as he ought from biassing me either way, though we talk much on the subject, and his judgment is, as you say, good and mild. . . .

P.S.—Pray let me hear soon *when* you come. You, I know, like me to tell you what I hear, and for me to be frank with you. I therefore tell you that it is believed by some people here, and even by some in the Government, that *you* wish my Government to be *out*. Now, I never for an instant can believe such an assertion, as I know your liberal feelings, and your interest in my welfare and in that of the country too well to think you could wish for such a thing, and I immediately said I was sure this was not so; but I think you would do well to say to Seymour something which might imply interest in my present Government.

I know you will understand my anxiety on your account, lest such a mischievous report should be believed. It comes, you see, from the idea that your feelings are very French.

Queen Victoria to the King of the Belgians

31st May 1841

. . . I beg you *not* to be alarmed about what is to be done; it is *not* for a Party triumph that Parliament (*the* longest that has sat for *many* years) is to be dissolved; it is the fairest and most constitutional mode of proceeding; and you may trust to the moderation and prudence of my whole Government that nothing will be done without due consideration; if the present Government get a majority by the elections they will go on prosperously; if not, the Tories will come in for a short time. The country is quiet and the people very well disposed. I am happy, dearest Uncle, to give you these quieting news, which I assure you are *not* partial. . . .

Queen Victoria to the King of the Belgians

6th June 1841

... As to my letters, dear Uncle, I beg to *assure* you (for Lord Palmerston was *most indignant* at the doubt when I once asked) that *none* of our letters nor any of those *coming* to us, are ever opened at the Foreign Office. My letters to Brussels and Paris are *quite safe,* and all those to Germany, which are of any *real* consequence, I always send through Rothschild, which is perfectly *safe* and very quick. ...

Viscount Melbourne to Queen Victoria

Windsor Castle, 8th June 1841

Lord Melbourne presents his humble duty to your Majesty. He is quite well, and has nothing particular to relate to your Majesty, at least nothing that presses; except that he is commissioned by Lord John Russell respectfully to acquaint your Majesty that his marriage is settled, and will take place shortly.

Queen Victoria to Viscount Melbourne

Does Lord Melbourne *really* mean J. Russell's *marriage?* and to whom?

Viscount Melbourne to Queen Victoria

The Lady Fanny Eliot. Lord Melbourne did not name her before nor does not now, because he did not remember her Christian name.

Queen Victoria to the King of the Belgians

Buckingham Palace, 17th June 1841

MY DEAREST UNCLE,—A few lines I must write to you to express to you my *very great* delight at the certainty, God willing, of seeing you all *three* next week, and to express a hope, and a *great hope,* that you will try and arrive a little earlier on Wednesday. ... I must again repeat I am so sorry you should come when Society is dispersed and at sixes and sevens, and in such a state that naturally I cannot at the moment of the elections invite many Tories, as that *tells* so at the elections. But we shall try and do our best to make it as little dull as we can, and you will kindly take the will for the deed.

We came back from Nuneham yesterday afternoon. Albert came back at half-past five on Tuesday from Oxford, where he had been enthusiastically received, but the students ... had the bad taste to show their party feeling in groans and hisses when the name of a Whig was mentioned, which they ought not to have done in my husband's presence.

I must now conclude, begging you ever to believe me, your devoted Niece, VICTORIA R.

My Coiffeur will be quite at Louise's disposal, and he can *coiffer* in any way she likes, if her dresser tells him how she wishes it.

Lord Brougham to Queen Victoria

Grafton Street, 19th June 1841

MOST GRACIOUS SOVEREIGN,—I crave leave humbly to approach your Majesty and to state in writing what I should have submitted to your Royal consideration at an Audience, because I conceive that this course will be attended with less inconvenience to your Majesty.

In the counsel which I ventured with great humility, but with an entire conviction of its soundness, to tender, I cannot be biassed by any personal interest, for I am not a candidate for office; nor by any Parliamentary interest, for I have no concern with elections; nor by any factious interest, for I am unconnected with party. My only motive is to discharge the duty which I owe to both the Crown and the country. Nor am I under the influence of any prejudice against your Majesty's servants or their measures; for I charge your Majesty's servants with nothing beyond an error, a great error, in judgment, and I entirely approve of the measures which they have lately propounded (with a single exception partially applicable to one of them), while I lament and disapprove of the time and manner of propounding them, both on account of the Government and of the measures themselves.

I feel myself, Madam, under the necessity of stating that the dissolution of the Parliament appears to me wholly without justification, either from principle or from policy. They who advise it must needs proceed upon the supposition that a majority will be returned favourable to the continuance of the present Administration and favourable to their lately announced policy. On no other grounds is it possible that any such advice should be tendered to your Majesty. For no one could ever think of such a proceeding as advising the Crown to dissolve the Parliament in order to increase the force of the Opposition to its own future Ministers, thus perverting to the mere purposes of party the exercise of by far the most eminent of the Royal prerogatives; and I pass over as wholly unworthy of notice the only other supposition which can with any decency be made, when there is no conflict between the two Houses, namely, that of a dissolution in entire ignorance of the national opinion and for the purpose of ascertaining to which side it inclines. Your Majesty's advisers must, therefore, have believed, and they must still believe, that a majority will be returned favourable both to themselves and their late policy. I, on the other hand, have the most entire conviction that there will be a considerable majority against them, and against their policy a majority larger still, many of their supporters having already joined to swell that majority. Whoever examines the details of the case must be satisfied that the very best result which the Government can possibly hope for is a narrow majority against them—an event which must occasion a second dissolution by whatever Ministry may succeed to the confidence of your Majesty. But those best acquainted with the subject have no doubt at all that the majority will be much more considerable.

I beg leave, Madam, humbly to represent to your Majesty, in my own vindication for not having laid my opinion before your Majesty as soon as I returned from the Continent, that when I first heard of the course taken by the Government early in May, I formed the opinion which I now entertain, but conceived that I must have mistaken the facts upon which they were acting; and when I arrived twelve days ago I was confirmed in the belief (seeing the fixed resolution taken to dissolve) that I must have been under an erroneous impression as to the probable results of the elections. But I have since found ample reason for believing that my original conviction was perfectly well founded, and that no grounds whatever exist sufficient to make any one who considers the subject calmly, and without the bias of either interest or prejudice, really believe that this ill-fated proceeding can have any other result than lasting injury to your Majesty's service, to the progress of sound and just views of policy, and to the influence of those in whom the Crown and the country alike should repose confidence.

That a number of short-sighted persons whose judgments are warped by exclusive attention to a single subject, or by personal feelings, or by party views (and these narrow and erroneous), may have been loudly clamorous for the course apparently about to be pursued, is extremely possible, and affords no kind of excuse for it. Many of these will be the slowest to defend what they have so unfortunately called for; some will be among the first to condemn it when a manifest failure shall have taken place, and general discomfiture shall throw a few local successes into the shade.

My advice is humbly offered to your Majesty, as removed far above such confined and factious views; as the parent of all your people; as both bound and willing to watch over their true interests; and as charged by virtue of your exalted office with the preservation of the public peace, the furtherance of the prosperity, and the maintenance of the liberties of your subjects.

I am, with profound respect, Madam, your Majesty's faithful and dutiful Subject,   BROUGHAM *

Memorandum by Mr Anson

Woburn Abbey, 27th July 1841

Arrived here last night with the Prince and the Queen; this is now the second expedition (Nuneham being the first) which Her Majesty has taken, and on neither occasion has the Baroness accompanied us.

* Parliament, however, notwithstanding this rescript of Lord Brougham, was dissolved, and the Ministry went to the country with the cry of a fixed duty on corn, as against a sliding scale, and they attacked, as monopolists, at once the landowner, who enjoyed protection for his wheat, and the West Indian proprietor, who profited by the duty on foreign sugar. The Conservatives impugned the general policy of the Whig Administration. The result, a majority of seventy-six, was an even greater Conservative triumph than the most sanguine of the party anticipated.

The Prince went yesterday through a review of the many steps he had made to his present position—all within eighteen months from the marriage. Those who intended to keep him from being useful to the Queen, from the fear that he might ambitiously touch upon her prerogatives, have been completely foiled; they thought they had prevented Her Majesty from yielding anything of importance to him by creating distrust through imaginary alarm. The Queen's good sense, however, has seen that the Prince has no other object in all he seeks but a means to Her Majesty's good. The Court from highest to lowest is brought to a proper sense of the position of the Queen's husband. The country has marked its confidence in his character by passing the Regency Bill *nem. con.* The Queen finds the value of an active right hand and able head to support her and to resort to for advice in time of need. Cabinet Ministers treat him with deference and respect. Arts and science look up to him as their especial patron, and they find this encouragement supported by a full knowledge of the details of every subject. The good and the wise look up to him with pride and gratitude as giving an example, so rarely shown in such a station, of leading a virtuous and religious life.

Memorandum by Mr Anson

Windsor Castle, 7th August 1841

I went to Lord Melbourne this morning in his room as he had desired me. He said: 'The Prince has been urging me to accept the Blue Riband before I quit office, and I wished to tell you that I am very anxious that this should not be pressed upon me by the Queen; it may be a foolish weakness on my part, but I wish to quit office without having any honour conferred upon me; the Queen's confidence towards me is sufficiently known without any public mark of this nature. I have always disregarded these honours, and there would be an inconsistency in my accepting this. I feel it to be much better for my reputation that I should not have it forced upon me. Mr Pitt never accepted an order, and only the Cinque Ports on being pressed to do so. Lord Grenville accepted a peerage, but never any other honour or advantage, and I wish to be permitted to retire in like manner. If I was a poor man, I should have no hesitation in receiving money in the shape of place or pension; I *only don't wish* for place, because I do not *want* it.'

In the course of conversation Lord Melbourne said that he considered it very improbable that he should ever again form a part of any Administration.

He did not think that a violent course was at all to be apprehended from Lord John Russell; he said Lord John had been far more of a 'finality' man than he had, and in the Cabinet had always been averse to violent change. He added, 'I think you are in error in forming the opinion which you have of him.'

Lord Melbourne thought the Queen very much disliked being talked *at* upon religion; she particularly disliked what Her Majesty termed a *Sunday face*, but yet that it was a subject far more thought of and reflected upon than was [thought to be?] the case.

Viscount Melbourne to Queen Victoria

South Street, 28th August 1841

Lord Melbourne presents his humble duty to your Majesty, and begs to acknowledge gratefully the communication which he has just received from your Majesty. Lord Melbourne feels certain that your Majesty's sense and firmness will enable your Majesty to bear up under this which your Majesty names a severe trial. The kindness of your Majesty's expressions emboldens Lord Melbourne to say that he also feels deeply the pain of separation from a service, which has now for four years and more been no less his pleasure than his pride. . . .

Lord Melbourne is sure that your Majesty will at once perceive that it would not have a good appearance if he were to return to Windsor immediately after having announced his resignation to the House of Lords on Monday next.

It is right that there should be no appearance of delay or of unwillingness to carry into effect the wishes of both Houses of Parliament, and, therefore, your Majesty will forgive Lord Melbourne if he suggests that it would be well if your Majesty could make up your mind to appoint Sir R. Peel on Monday next, so that there might be as little delay as possible in the formation of a new Government. On all accounts, and particularly on account of the lateness of the Season, it is desirable that this should be done as speedily as possible.

Memorandum by Mr Anson

Windsor Castle, 30th August 1841

Directly I got here this morning the Prince sent for me, and said he had been made somewhat uneasy by a conversation he had just had with the Queen. Her Majesty said that after the manner in which the Tories had treated the Prince (relative to annuity) he ought now to keep them at a distance. She said they would try to flatter him, and would all come to see him; this he should resist, and should refuse to see them, at all events for some time.

The Prince wished me to mention this to Lord Melbourne when I went to take leave of him, and to urge Lord Melbourne to set this right with the Queen by his advice before he parted with the Queen, reminding him that his view had always been that from this moment the Prince would take up a new position, and that the Queen, no longer having Lord Melbourne to resort to in case of need, must from this moment consult and advise with the Prince. That Lord Melbourne should urge the Queen to have no scruple in employing the Prince, and showing that unless a proper under-standing existed from the first, he in attempting to do good would be easily misrepresented.

I found Lord Melbourne alone in his dressing-room and put this case before him. He said he had always thought that when he left the service of the Queen the Prince would of necessity be brought forward, and must render great assistance to the Queen; and the Queen's confidence in his judgment having so much increased, this consequence was the more natural. The Prince must, however, be very cautious at first, and in a little time he would fall into it. He must be very careful not to alarm the Queen, by Her Majesty for an instant supposing that the Prince was carrying on business with Peel without her cognisance.

If it were possible for any one to advise Peel, he would recommend that he should write fully to Her Majesty, and *elementarily,* as Her Majesty always liked to have full knowledge upon everything which was going on. He would advise the Queen to be cautious in giving a verbal decision, that she should not allow herself to be *driven into a corner*, and forced to decide where she felt her mind was not made up and required reflection.

Peel should be very careful that intelligence came first from him direct. King William was very particular upon this point, so was the Queen.

I asked Lord Melbourne if he had considered the future position of himself with the Queen, and also of Peel with the Queen. He said he owned he had not and would avoid entering into any discussion—he felt sure that he should be regarded with extreme jealousy, not so much by Peel as by the party. He would be looked upon as Lord Bute had been in his relation to George III,—always suspected of secret intercourse and intrigue. He would make me the medium of any written communication.

With regard to Peel's position with the Queen, he thought that circumstances must make it. He thought the Queen must see him oftener than King William did him, as he thought the present state of things would require more frequent intercourse. The late King used to see him once a week after the Levée, seldom oftener; all the rest of the business was transacted by correspondence, but this mode, though it had its merits in some respect, very much impeded the public business.

The less personal objections the Queen took to any one the better, as any such expression is sure to come out and a personal enemy is made. It was also to be recollected that Peel was in a very different position now, backed by a large majority, to when the other overture was made. He had the power *now* to extort what he pleased, and he fancied he saw the blank faces of the heads of the Party when Peel told them that he had agreed to the dismissal or resignation of only three of the Queen's ladies.

Lord Melbourne said the Queen was afraid she never could be at ease with Peel, because his manner was so embarrassed, and that conveyed embarrassment also to her, which it would be very difficult to get over.

The Queen took leave of Lord Melbourne to-day. Her Majesty was much affected, but soon recovered her calmness.

Peel had his first audience at half-past three o'clock.

Queen Victoria to Viscount Melbourne

Windsor Castle, 30th August 1841

... The first interview with Sir Robert Peel has gone off well, and only lasted twenty minutes; and he sends the Queen to-morrow, in writing, the proposed arrangements, and will only come down on Wednesday morning. He first wished to come to-morrow, but on the Queen's saying that he need not do that, but might send it and only come down Wednesday, he thought the Queen might prefer having it to consider a little, which she said she certainly should, though she meant no want of confidence. The Queen, in the first instance, stated that she concluded he was prepared for her sending for him, and then stated exactly what Lord Melbourne wrote, viz., the resignation having taken place in consequence of the Addresses —the Queen's great regret at parting with her present Ministers— the confidence she had in them, and her only acceding in consequence of the Addresses in Parliament, and then that consequently she looked to him (Sir Robert Peel) as possessing the confidence of both Houses of Parliament to form an Administration. He made many protestations of his sorrow, at what must give pain to the Queen (as she said to him it did), but of course said he accepted the task. The Duke of Wellington's health too uncertain, and himself too prone to sleep coming over him—as Peel expressed it—to admit of his taking an office in which he would have much to do, but to be in the Cabinet, which the Queen expressed her wish he should. He named Lord De Grey as Lord Lieutenant of Ireland, and Lord Eliot as Secretary for Ireland, who, he said, were both moderate people. The Queen said she gave up to him the officers of State and those of her Household who were in Parliament, and he then asked if Lord Liverpool would be agreeable as Lord Steward (the Queen said he would), and if she would object to Lord Jersey as Master of the Horse (she said she would not), as she believed he understood it perfectly. He said he was so anxious to do everything which could be agreeable to the Queen, that he wished her to name whom she should like as Lord Chamberlain; she said he might suggest some one, but as he would not, and pressed the Queen to name whoever she pleased, she said she should like the Duke of

Rutland, and he said he would certainly name it to him. The Queen said that Lord Melbourne had always been very particular to name no one who might be disagreeable to her in the Household, and Sir R. Peel said he felt this, and should be most anxious to do what could be agreeable to me and for my comfort, and that he would even sacrifice any advantage to this. The Queen mentioned the three Ladies' resignation, and her wish not to fill up the three Ladies' places immediately. She mentioned Lady Byron, to which he agreed immediately, and then said, as I had alluded to those communications, he hoped that he had been understood respecting the *other* appointments (meaning the Ladies), that provided I chose some who had a leaning towards the politics of the Administration, I might take any I liked, and that he quite understood that I should notify it to them. The Queen said this was her rule, and that she wished to choose moderate people who should not have scruples to resign in case another Administration should come in, as changing was disagreeable to her. Here it ended, and so far well. He was very anxious the Queen should understand *how* anxious he was to do everything which was agreeable to the Queen. The Queen wishes to know if Lord Melbourne thinks she should name the Duchess of Buccleuch Mistress of the Robes, on Wednesday, and if she shall ask Sir Robert to sound the Duchess, or some one else, and then write to appoint her? She thinks of proposing Lady de la Warr and Lady Abercorn by and by as the two Ladies, but these she will sound herself through other people, or Lady Canning, or Lady Rosslyn, in case these others should not take it. She should say she meant to sound those, and no more. What the Queen felt when she parted from her dear, kind friend, Lord Melbourne, is better imagined than described; she was dreadfully affected for some time after, but is calm now. It is very, very sad; and she cannot quite believe it yet. The Prince felt it very, very much too, and really the Queen cannot say how kind and affectionate he is to her, and how anxious to do everything to lighten this heavy trial; he was quite affected at this sad parting. We do, and shall, miss you so dreadfully; Lord Melbourne will easily understand what a change it is, after these four years when she had the happiness of having Lord Melbourne always about her. But it will not be so long till we meet again. Happier and brighter times will come again. We anxiously hope Lord Melbourne is well, and got up well and safe. The Queen trusts he will take care of his valuable health, now more than ever.

Queen Victoria to Sir Robert Peel

7th September 1841

The Queen wishes that Sir Robert Peel would mention to Lord De la Warr that he should be very particular in always naming to the Queen any appointment he wishes to make in his department, and always to take her pleasure upon an appointment before he settles on them; this is a point upon which the Queen has always laid great stress. This applies in great measure to the appointment of Physicians and Chaplains, which used to be very badly managed formerly, and who were appointed in a very careless manner; but since the Queen's accession the Physicians and Chaplains have been appointed only for merit and abilities, by the Queen herself, which the Queen is certain Sir Robert Peel will at once see is a far better way, and one which must be of use in every way. Sir Robert Peel may also tell Lord De la Warr that it is unnecessary for him to appear in uniform, as the Queen always dispenses with this in the country. This applies also to the Ministers, who the Queen does not expect or wish should appear in uniform at Councils which are held in the country....

Queen Victoria to Sir Robert Peel

9th September 1841

The Queen takes this opportunity of writing to Sir Robert Peel *confidentially* about another person: this is about Lord ——. The Queen is strongly of opinion that Lord —— should *not* be employed in any post of importance, as his being so would, in her opinion, be detrimental to the interests of the country. The Queen wishes Sir Robert to state this to Lord Aberdeen as her opinion. The Queen is certain that Sir Robert will take care that it should not be known generally that this is her opinion, for she is always most anxious to avoid anything that might appear personal towards anybody.

The Queen cannot refrain from saying that she cannot quite approve of Sir Charles Bagot's appointment, as from what she has heard of his qualities she does not think that they are of a character quite to suit in the arduous and difficult position in which he will be placed. At the same time the Queen does not mean to object to his appointment (for she has already formally approved of it), but she feels it her duty to state frankly and at all times her opinion, as she begs Sir Robert also to do unreservedly to her. For the future, it appears to the Queen that it would be best in all appointments of such importance that before a direct communication was entered into with the individual intended to be proposed, that the Queen should be informed of it, so that she might talk to her Ministers fully about it; not because it is likely that she would object to the appointment, but merely that she might have time to be acquainted with the qualities and abilities of the person. The Queen has stated this thus freely to Sir Robert as she feels certain that he will understand and appreciate the motives which prompt her to do so. The Queen would wish the Council to be at two on Tuesday, and she begs Sir Robert would inform her which of the Ministers besides him will attend.

Memorandum by Mr Anson

Royal Lodge, 21st September 1841

Saw Baron Stockmar this morning at the Castle, and had a good deal of conversation with him on various matters. He is very apprehensive that evil will spring out of the correspondence now carried on between the Queen and Lord Melbourne. He thinks it is productive of the greatest possible danger, and especially to Lord Melbourne; he thought no Government could stand such undermining influence. I might tell this to Lord Melbourne, and say that if he was totally disconnected from his Party, instead of being the acknowledged head, there would not be the same objection. He said, Remind Lord Melbourne of the time immediately after the Queen's accession, when he had promised the King of the Belgians to write to him from time to time an account of all that was going on in this country; and upon Lord Melbourne telling him of this promise, he replied, This will not do. It cannot be kept a secret that you keep up this correspondence, and jealousy and distrust will be the fruit of a knowledge of it. 'Leave it to me,' he said, 'to arrange with the King; you cease to write, and I will put it straight with the King.'

The Baron seemed to expect Lord Melbourne to draw the inference from this that a correspondence between Lord Melbourne and the Queen was fraught with the same danger, and would, when known, be followed by distrust and jealousy on the part of Sir Robert Peel. I said I reconciled it to myself because I felt that it had been productive of much good and no harm—and that, feeling that it was conducted on such honourable terms, I should not, if it were necessary, scruple to acquaint Sir Robert Peel of its existence. The Baron said, 'Ask Lord Melbourne whether he would object to it.' He said Peel, when he heard of it, would not, on the first impression, at all approve of it; but prudence and caution would be immediately summoned to his aid, and he would see that it was his policy to play the generous part—and would say he felt all was honourably intended, and he had no objection to offer—'but,' said the Baron, 'look to the result. Distrust being implanted from the first, whenever the first misunderstanding arose, or things took a wrong turn, all would, in Peel's mind, be immediately attributed to this cause.'

Sir Robert Peel to Queen Victoria

26th September 1841

Sir Robert Peel presents his humble duty to your Majesty, and begs to be permitted to submit for your Majesty's consideration a suggestion which has occurred to Sir Robert Peel, and which has reference to the communication which he recently addressed to your Majesty on the subject of the promotion of the Fine Arts in connection with the building of the new Houses of Parliament.

Sir Robert Peel would humbly enquire from your Majesty whether (in the event of your Majesty's being graciously pleased to approve of the appointment of a Royal Commission for the further investigation and consideration of a subject of such deep importance and interest to the encouragement of art in this country) your Majesty would deem it desirable that the Prince should be invited in the name of your Majesty to place himself at the head of this Commission, and to give to it the authority and influence of his high name, and the advantage of his taste and knowledge.

Sir Robert Peel will not of course mention this subject to any one, until he has had the honour of receiving from your Majesty an intimation of your Majesty's opinions and wishes on this subject.

Queen Victoria to Sir James Graham

Windsor Castle, 3rd October 1841

The Queen has received Sir James Graham's communication with the enclosures. She thinks that it would be extremely inconvenient if Audiences were to be granted to Peers for the purpose of presenting Petitions or Addresses. The Queen knows that it has always been considered a sort of right of theirs to ask for and receive an Audience of the King or Queen. But the Queen knows that upon several occasions Lord Melbourne and Lord John Russell wrote to the Peers who requested Audiences, stating that it would be very inconvenient for the Queen, particularly in the country, and that they had better either put off asking for it, till the Queen came to town, or send what they had to say; communicate in writing—which was complied with. If, therefore, Sir James Graham would state this to Lord Radnor, he may probably give up pressing for an Audience. Should he, however, urge his wish very strongly, the Queen will see him in the manner proposed by Sir James. The Queen would wish to hear from Sir James again before she gives a final answer.

Memorandum by Mr Anson

Windsor Castle, 3rd October 1841

Sat by the Queen last night at dinner. Her Majesty alluded to Sir Robert Peel's awkward manner, which she felt she could not get over. I asked if Her Majesty had yet made any effort, which I was good-humouredly assured Her Majesty 'thought she really had done.'

Sir Robert's ignorance of character was most striking and unaccountable; feeling this, made it difficult for Her Majesty to place reliance upon his judgment in recommendations.

Memorandum by Mr Anson

Windsor Castle, 6th October 1841

...Her Majesty asked Dr Hawtrey the evening before who was the cleverest boy at Eton.

Dr Hawtrey made a profound bow to the Queen and said, 'I trust your Majesty will excuse my answering, for if I did I make 600 enemies at once.'

Memorandum: Baron Stockmar to Viscount Melbourne

23rd November 1841

The apprehension which haunts me since my return to England is well known to you. It was my intention to have written to you upon it some time hereafter, but the contents of a certain letter, sent by you just before your departure, accelerates the execution of my design. From your own expressions used some time back, I was led to expect that you would be glad to take advantage *of any fair opportunity* which might contribute towards that devoutly to be wished for object, viz., to let a certain correspondence die a natural death. You may easily conceive how much I felt disappointed when I heard that you had written again, without a challenge, and that, without apparent cause, you had volunteered the promise to write from time to time. This happens at a moment when *your* harassing apprehension received new life and strength from two incidents which I think it my duty to make known to you, and of which the one came to pass *before,* the other after, your departure from here. Some weeks back I was walking in the streets with Dr Prætorius, when, finding myself opposite the house of one of my friends, it came across my mind to give him a call. Prætorius wanted to leave me, on a conception that, as a stranger, he might obstruct the freedom of our conversation. I insisted, however, on his remaining with me, and we were shown into the drawing-room, where in all there were five of us. For some minutes the conversation had turned on insignificant things, when the person talking to me said quite abruptly: 'So I find the Queen is in daily correspondence with Lord Melbourne.' I replied, 'Who told you this?' The answer was, 'Mrs Norton; she told me the other

71

evening. Don't you believe that Lord Melbourne has lost his influence over the Queen's mind; he daily writes to her, and receives as many answers, in which she communicates everything to him.' Without betraying much emotion I said, 'I don't believe a word of it; the Queen may have written once or twice on private matters, but the daily correspondence on all matters is certainly the amplification of a thoughtless and imprudent person, who is not aware of such exaggerated assertions.' My speech was followed by a general silence, after which we talked of other things, and soon took our leave. When we were fairly in the open air, Prætorius expressed to me his amazement at what he had heard, and he remained for some time at a loss to comprehend the character of the person who, from mere giddiness, let out so momentous a secret.

The other fact took place the day after you had left. From the late events at Brussels, it had become desirable that I should see Sir Robert Peel. From Belgium we travelled over to Home politics. I expressed my delight at seeing the Queen so happy, and added a hope that more and more she would seek and find her real happiness in her domestic relations only. He evidently caught at this, and assured me that he should at all times be too happy to have a share in anything which might be thought conducive to the welfare of Her Majesty. That no consideration of personal inconvenience would ever prevent him from indulging the Queen in all her wishes relating to matters of a private nature, and that the only return for his sincere endeavours to please Her Majesty he looked to, was honesty in public affairs. Becoming then suddenly emphatic, he continued, 'But on this I must insist, and I do assure you, that that moment I was to learn that the Queen takes advice upon public matters in another place, I shall throw up; for such a thing I conceive the country could not stand, and I would not remain an hour, whatever the consequences of my resignation may be.'...

Approaching the conclusion of this letter, I beg to remind you of a conversation I had with you on the same subject in South Street, the 25th of last month. Though you did not avow it then in direct words, I could read from your countenance and manner that you assented in your head and heart to all I had said, and in particular to the advice I volunteered at the end of my speech. At that time I pointed out to you a period when I thought a decisive step ought to be taken on your part. This period seems to me to have arrived. Placing unreserved confidence into your candour and manliness, I remain, for ever, very faithfully yours,   STOCKMAR

Viscount Melbourne to Baron Stockmar

24th November 1841
(Half-past 10 p.m.)

MY DEAR BARON,—I have just received your letter; I think it unnecessary to detain your messenger. I will write to you upon the subject and send it through Anson. Yours faithfully,   MELBOURNE

Queen Victoria to the King of the Belgians

Buckingham Palace, 29th November 1841

MY DEAREST UNCLE,— . . . Our little boy* is a wonderfully strong and large child, with very large dark blue eyes, a finely formed but somewhat large nose, and a pretty little mouth; I *hope* and *pray* he may be like his dearest Papa. He is to be called *Albert*, and Edward is to be his second name. Pussy, dear child, is still *the* great pet amongst us all, and is getting so fat and strong again.

Queen Victoria to the King of the Belgians

Windsor Castle, 7th December 1841

MY DEAREST UNCLE,—We arrived here *sains et saufs* with our awfully large Nursery Establishment yesterday morning. It was a nasty warm and very rainy day, but to-day is very bright, clear and dry, and we walked out early and felt like prisoners freed from some dungeon. Many thanks for your kind letter of the 2nd, by which I grieve to see that you are not quite well. But let me repeat again, you *must* not despond so; you must not be so out of spirits. I have likewise been suffering so from *lowness* that it made me quite miserable, and I know how difficult it is to fight against it. I am delighted to hear

---

* His Majesty King Edward VII, born 9th November.

73

that all the children are so well. I wonder very much who our little boy will be like. You will understand *how* fervent my prayers and I am [sure] *everybody's* must be, to see him resemble his angelic dearest Father in *every, every* respect, both in body and mind. Oh! my dearest Uncle, I am sure if you knew *how* happy, how blessed I feel, and how *proud* I feel in possessing *such* a perfect being as my husband, as he is, and if you think that you have been instrumental in bringing about this union, it must gladden your heart! How happy should I be to see our child grow up *just* like him! Dear Pussy travelled with us and behaved like a grown-up person, so quiet and looking about and coquetting with the Hussars on either side of the carriage. Now adieu! Ever your devoted Niece,

VICTORIA R.

Memorandum by Mr Anson

Windsor Castle, 26th December 1841

Christmas has brought its usual routine of festivity and its agreeable accompaniment of Christmas presents. The Queen was not at all well again yesterday, being again troubled with lowness. The Melbourne correspondence still is carried on, but I think not in its pristine vigour by any means. He has taken no notice of the Baron's remonstrance to him, and we are in the dark in what manner, if at all, he means to deal with it.

I have sat by Her Majesty at dinner several times lately. I should say that Her Majesty interests herself less and less about politics, and that her dislike is less than it was to her present Ministers, though she would not be prepared to acknowledge it. Her Majesty is a good deal occupied with the little Princess Royal, who begins to assume companionable qualities. In the evening, instead of her usual conversation with her old Prime Minister, some round game at cards is substituted, which always terminates at eleven. The Prince, to amuse the Queen at this, has nearly left off his chess; his amusements—shooting or hunting—always commence and terminate between eleven and two, not to interfere with Her Majesty's arrangements, in which he is included as her companion.

1842

Queen Victoria to the King of the Belgians

Pavilion, 7th March 1842

MY DEAR UNCLE,— ... You will have heard how well our Portsmouth
expedition went off; the sea was quite smooth on Tuesday, and we
had a delightful visit to the *Queen,* which is a splendid ship. I think
it is in these immense wooden walls that our real greatness exists,
and I am proud to think that no *other* nation *can* equal us in *this*. ...
Now *addio!* Ever your most affectionate Niece,   VICTORIA R.

Viscount Melbourne to Queen Victoria

South Street, 21st March 1842

Lord Melbourne presents his humble duty to your Majesty. A letter
from Charles Fox to Lady Holland, and which she has sent to me,
informs me of the shocking end of Munster,* which your Majesty
will have heard long before you receive this. Charles Fox attributes
it entirely to the vexatious and uneasy life which he led with Lady
Munster, but he was always, as your Majesty knows, an unhappy
and discontented man, and there is something in that unfortunate
condition of illegitimacy which seems to distort the mind and feelings
and render them incapable of justice or contentment.

It is not impossible that upon this event application may be made
to your Majesty for the continuance of the pension upon the Privy
Purse to his son. As Lord Melbourne advised your Majesty to continue
these pensions upon the late King's death, perhaps it may not be
improper that he should now say that it is his strong opinion that
they should not be continued further. There is no reason for it.
They are not very rich, but neither are they poor, and they have
very opulent connections and relations. It appears to me that the first
opportunity should be taken to show that it is not your Majesty's

* The Earl of Munster, son of William IV and Mrs. Jordan, shot himself,
20th March. His wife was a daughter of the Earl of Egremont.

intention to charge the Crown with the maintenance and support of all these families, which will otherwise be the case. Lord Melbourne thinks it not improper to mention this matter thus early, as otherwise the [compassionate] feelings naturally raised by such an event might lead to a different determination.

Queen Victoria to Sir Robert Peel

Buckingham Palace, 20th April 1842

The Queen encloses the Prince's letter to Sir Robert Peel, containing his acceptance of the Guards. At the same time, both the Prince and Queen feel much regret at the Prince's leaving the 11th, which is, if possible, enhanced by seeing the Regiment out to-day, which is in beautiful order. It was, besides, the Regiment which escorted the Prince from Dover to Canterbury on his arrival in England in February '40. The Queen fears, indeed knows, that Lord Cardigan will be deeply mortified at the Prince's leaving the Regiment, and that it will have the effect of appearing like another slight to him; therefore, the Queen much wishes that at some fit opportunity a mark of favour should be bestowed upon him. . . .

The Queen hopes Sir Robert will think of this.

Viscount Melbourne to Queen Victoria

Brocket Hall, 15th May 1842

. . . Lord Melbourne is come down here again, being determined to see this spring thoroughly and completely. His feelings are like those, so beautifully described by Schiller, of Max Piccolomini, when, after a youth passed entirely in war, he for the first time sees a country which has enjoyed the blessings of peace. The Germans seem to Lord Melbourne generally to prefer Goethe to Schiller, a decision which surprises him, although he feels that he has no right to dictate to a people, of whose language he does not understand a word, their judgment upon their own authors. But the one, Schiller, seems to him to be all truth, clearness, nature and beauty; the other, principally mysticism, obscurity, and unintelligibility.

76

The Earl of Aberdeen to Queen Victoria

Foreign Office, 28th June 1842

Lord Aberdeen, with his humble duty, begs to enclose for your Majesty's information a list of the presents brought by the Envoy of the Imam of Muscat for your Majesty.

Lord Aberdeen will attend to-morrow with the Envoy, at the hour your Majesty has been pleased to command; and he will suggest that the presents should be sent previously to the Palace, in order to be laid before your Majesty.

[List of Articles sent for Her Most Gracious Majesty, The Mighty Queen, a trifling Gift scarce worth being mentioned.]

Two Pearl Necklaces,
Two Emeralds,
An Ornament made like a Crown,
Ten Cashmere Shawls,
One Box containing four Bottles Otto of Roses.

Four Horses, before mentioned in a former letter, but for the transmission of which no opportunity offered in Bombay, but now sent in my own ship. Through your kindness have those things taken from Ali bin Nassur, and make an excuse for me to Her Most Gracious Majesty, and peace be on you!

Queen Victoria to Sir Robert Peel

Claremont, 16th July 1842

The Queen is anxious to draw Sir Robert Peel's attention to a circumstance which she has already some months ago mentioned to him: this is relative to Sir Edward Disbrowe.* The Queen knows that Sir Robert Peel shares her opinion as to Sir Edward Disbrowe's abilities not being of the first order, but this is not the only thing; what she chiefly complains of is his decided unfairness towards Belgium, which she thinks has always shown itself, and again most strongly in his last despatches. The King of the Belgians has never dropped a word on the subject, but the Queen really feels it her duty by her Uncle to state this frankly to Sir Robert Peel, and to say that she thinks it

* Then British Minister at the Hague.

highly important that Sir Edward Disbrowe should be removed to some other Mission. Of course she wishes that this should be done quietly, but she thinks that with a man like the present King of the Netherlands, who is continually intriguing in Belgium and making her Uncle's position very painful, it is of the utmost importance that our Minister there should be totally *unbiassed*—which Sir Edward Disbrowe most decidedly is not. Could not Sir T. Cartwright be sent there, and Sir Edward Disbrowe go to Stockholm? The Queen merely suggests this; but, of course, as long as the man sent to the Hague is sensible and *fair*, it is indifferent to her who goes there. . . .

Sir Robert Peel to Queen Victoria

Cabinet Room, Downing Street,
13th August 1842

. . . The accounts received this morning from Manchester with regard to the state of the country in that neighbourhood are very unsatisfactory, and they are confirmed by the personal testimony of magistrates who have arrived in London for the purpose of making representations to your Majesty's servants on the subject.

A Cabinet has just been held, and it is proposed to send a battalion of Guards by the railway this evening. The 16th of August (Tuesday next) is the anniversary of a conflict which took place in Manchester in the year 1819 between the Yeomanry Cavalry and the populace, and it is feared that there may be a great assemblage of persons riotously disposed on that day.

Under these circumstances it appears desirable to your Majesty's confidential advisers that a proclamation should be immediately issued, warning all persons against attendance on tumultuous meetings, and against all acts calculated to disturb the public peace. It is necessary that a Council should be held for the issue of this proclamation, and important that it should arrive in Manchester on Monday. . . .

Sir James Graham to Queen Victoria

Whitehall, 15th August 1842

Sir James Graham, with humble duty, begs to lay before your Majesty the enclosed letter from Major-General Sir William Warre in command of the Northern District.

From this report it is evident that a strong and salutary moral impression had been produced by the arrival of a reinforcement of 1,400 men in the disturbed district in the short time of six-and-thirty hours after the first requisition for assistance had been sent from Manchester; and the General has now at his disposal a force quite adequate to cope with the vast assemblage of people who are expected to meet to-morrow at Manchester.

Some symptoms of this disposition forcibly to suspend labour have appeared in the West Riding of Yorkshire; but on the whole the accounts, both from Scotland and the disturbed district, which have been received this morning, may be considered favourable. The railroad communications as yet are uninterrupted; no collision has taken place between the troops and the multitude, except at Preston; and Sir James Graham is willing to hope that this insurrectionary movement may be suppressed without recourse to extreme measures. Every precaution, however, has been taken, and arrangements are made for augmenting the force under the command of Sir William Warre, if it should become necessary.

The character of these riots has assumed more decidedly a political aspect. It is no longer a strike for higher wages, but the Delegates, who direct the movement, avow that labour shall not be resumed until the people's Charter be granted....

Sir Robert Peel to Queen Victoria

Whitehall, 18th August 1842
(Thursday morning)

... It appears to Sir Robert Peel that the general tenor of the reports is *satisfactory*. From Manchester, from Wigan, from Preston, the reports are very good.

The movement is not one caused by distress. The demand for employment has increased, and the price of provisions—and particularly of potatoes, bread, and bacon—has rapidly fallen within the last fortnight or three weeks.

People of property and the Magistrates (notwithstanding their political dissensions) are now acting in harmony, and with more energy.

Orders have been sent to apprehend the Delegates assembled in Manchester, *the very moment* that the law will warrant their apprehension, and Sir Robert Peel should not be surprised to hear of their committal to Lancaster Castle in the course of to-day.

Every vigilance will be exerted with reference to *Cooper* (whom your Majesty names) and all other itinerant agitators. . . .

Viscount Melbourne to Queen Victoria

South Street, 17th August 1842

. . . There is a great mass of discontented feeling in the country arising from the actual state of society. It arises from the distress and destitution which will fall at times upon a great manufacturing population, and from the wild and extravagant opinions which are naturally generated in an advanced and speculative state of society.

This discontent has been aggravated and fermented by the language of every party in the state. Lord Melbourne can exempt no party from this blame, nor hardly any individual except himself. . . .

Sir James Graham to Queen Victoria

20th August 1842

. . . An attempt to hold a meeting at dusk in the suburbs of London was resisted by the police yesterday evening in pursuance of orders issued by the Government in conjunction with the Lord Mayor, and the peace of the metropolis was preserved.

The above is humbly submitted by your Majesty's dutiful Subject and Servant,   J. R. G. GRAHAM

Queen Victoria to the King of the Belgians

Taymouth, 8th September 1842

MY DEAREST UNCLE,— . . . Albert has told you already how successfully everything had gone off hitherto, and how much pleased we were with Edinburgh, which is an unique town in its way. We left Dalkeith on Monday, and lunched at Dupplin, Lord Kinnoul's, a pretty place with quite a new house, and which poor Lord Kinnoul displayed so well as to fall head over heels down a steep bank, and was proceeding down another, if Albert had not caught him; I did not see it, but Albert and I have nearly died with laughing at the *relation* of it. From Dalkeith we went through Perth (which is *most beautifully* situated on the Tay) to Scone Palace, Lord Mansfield's, where we slept; fine but rather gloomy. Yesterday morning (Tuesday) we left Scone and lunched at Dunkeld, the beginning of the Highlands, in a tent; *all* the Highlanders in their fine dress, being encamped there, and with their old shields and swords, looked very romantic; they were chiefly Lord Glenlyon's men. *He,* poor man! is suddenly become *totally* blind, and it was very melancholy to see him do the *honours, not* seeing *anything*. The situation of Dunkeld, down in a valley surrounded by wooded hills, is very, very pretty. From thence we proceeded to this enchanting and princely place; the whole drive here was beautiful. All Lord Breadalbane's Highlanders, with himself at their head, and a battalion of the 92nd Highlanders, were drawn up in front of the House. In the evening the grounds were splendidly illuminated, and bonfires burning on the hills; and a number of Highlanders danced reels by torchlight, to the bagpipes, which was very wild and pretty. . . .

Sir Robert Peel to Queen Victoria

Whitehall, 22nd September 1842

Sir Robert Peel presents his humble duty to your Majesty, and begs leave, with reference to your Majesty's note of yesterday, to state to your Majesty that the *first* act of Sir Robert Peel on his return from Scotland was to write to Lord Haddington and strongly urge upon the Admiralty the necessity of providing a steam yacht for your Majesty's accommodation.

Sir Robert Peel trusts that your Majesty may entirely depend upon being enabled to make any excursions your Majesty may resolve upon in the early part of next summer, in a steam vessel belonging to your Majesty, and suitable in every respect for your Majesty's accommodation. . . .

He finds that the Admiralty is now building a large vessel to be worked by steam power, applied by means of a revolving screw instead of paddles. It may be doubtful whether the same degree of velocity can be attained by means of the screw, particularly in a very large vessel. Of this a full trial will be made.

Sir John Barrow assures Sir Robert Peel that he has been on board a steam-boat moved by the screw, and that the working of the engine is scarcely perceptible; that there is none of the tremulous motion which accompanies the beats of the paddles, and that it will be possible to apply an apparatus by means of which the smoke can be consumed, and the disagreeable smell in great measure prevented.

Sir Robert Peel will leave nothing undone to ensure your Majesty's comfort and safety in any future naval excursions that your Majesty may be pleased to make.

Viscount Melbourne to Queen Victoria

Brocket Hall, 29th September 1842

... Lord Melbourne greatly congratulates your Majesty upon the happy progress and termination of the expedition to Scotland. He is very glad of three things—that your Majesty returned by sea, in the steamer, and that the passage was a good one. . . .

The country is indeed most interesting, full of real picturesque beauty and of historical and poetical associations and recollections. There is nothing to detract from it, except the very high opinion that the Scotch themselves entertain of it. Edinburgh is magnificent— situation, buildings, and all—but the boasting of the articles in the newspapers respecting it almost inclined one to deny its superiority. It is also, as your Majesty says, most striking to contemplate in the Clans the remains of feudal times and institutions. It is quite as well, however, particularly for Monarchy, that they are but remains, and that no more of them have been left. . . .

1843

Sir Robert Peel to the Prince Albert

Whitehall, 20th January (1843)

SIR,—I have the painful duty of acquainting your Royal Highness that Mr Drummond, my Private Secretary, was shot at this day about quarter past three o'clock, in the neighbourhood of Charing Cross.

Two pistols were discharged, the first close to Mr Drummond's back, the second after the assassin had been seized by a policeman.

The ball entered in the back and has been extracted, after passing round the ribs. I have just left Mr Drummond's house. No vital part appears to have been injured, and there is no unfavourable symptom whatever.

The assassin gives his name *MacNaghten*, and appears to be a Glasgow man.

Two five-pound notes were, I understand, found upon his person, and a receipt for £750 given to Daniel MacNaghten, confirming, therefore, the man's account of his name.

We have not hitherto been able to discover that this man had any alleged grievance or complaint against the Treasury or any public office.

He has been loitering about the public offices for the last fortnight, and being questioned, I understand, some days since by the Office Keeper of the Council office, said he was a policeman. This, of course, for the purpose of evading further enquiry.

The policeman who apprehended the man, says that he heard the man exclaim after firing the shots: 'He or she (the policeman is uncertain which) shall not disturb my peace of mind any more.'

These are all the particulars I have heard or learned. I am afraid I have given them to your Royal Highness in a hurried manner. I have thought it better to convey this information to Her Majesty, through the kind intervention of your Royal Highness, than by a direct communication to the Queen.

I have the honour to be, Sir with sincere respect, your Royal Highness's most faithful and humble Servant,

ROBERT PEEL

Sir Robert Peel to Queen Victoria

Whitehall, 21st January 1843

Sir Robert Peel begs leave to mention to your Majesty a fact *which has not hitherto transpired*—and of which he was not aware until he had an interview this morning with Sir James Graham.

On the Inspector Tierney going into the cell of MacNaghten this morning, he said to MacNaghten: 'I suppose you are aware who is the person whom you have shot?'

He (MacNaghten) said: 'Yes—Sir Robert Peel.'

From this it would appear that he had mistaken Mr Drummond for Sir Robert Peel.

The Magistrate thought it better not to have this evidence at present placed on record.

Sir Robert Peel to Queen Victoria

Whitehall, 18th February (1843)
(Saturday morning)

Sir Robert Peel presents his humble duty to your Majesty, and begs leave to acquaint your Majesty that the debate was brought to a close this morning about half-past three o'clock. . . .

In the course of the evening there was much excitement and animated discussion, in consequence of the speech of Mr Cobden, who is the chief patron of the Anti-Corn Law League.

Mr Cobden with great vehemence of manner observed more than once that Sir Robert Peel ought to be held *individually responsible* for the distress of the country.

Coupling these expressions with the language frequently held at the meetings of the Anti-Corn Law League, and by the press in connection with it, Sir Robert Peel in replying to Mr Cobden charged him with holding language calculated to excite to personal violence.

Sir Robert Peel to Queen Victoria

Whitehall (4th March 1843)
(Sunday morning)

Sir Robert Peel presents his humble duty to your Majesty, and begs leave to acquaint your Majesty that the prisoner MacNaghten was acquitted last night, after a trial which lasted two days, upon the ground of insanity.

The fuller account of the evidence which Sir Robert Peel has seen is on the accompanying newspaper.

The only other information which has reached Sir Robert Peel is contained in a note (enclosed) from Mr Maule, the solicitor to the Treasury, who conducted the prosecution. The three Judges appear to have concurred in opinion, that the evidence of insanity was so strong as to require a verdict of acquittal—and the Chief Justice advised the Jury to find that verdict without summing up the evidence or delivering any detailed charge upon the facts of the case and the law bearing upon them.

It is a lamentable reflection that a man may be at the same time so insane as to be reckless of his own life and the lives of others, and to be pronounced free from moral responsibility, and yet capable of preparing for the commission of murder with the utmost caution and deliberation, and of taking every step which shall enable him to commit it with certainty.

Queen Victoria to Sir Robert Peel

Buckingham Palace, 12th March 1843

The Queen returns the paper of the Lord Chancellor's to Sir Robert Peel with her best thanks.

The law may be perfect, but how is it that whenever a case for its application arises, it proves to be of no avail? We have seen the trials of Oxford and MacNaghten conducted by the ablest lawyers of the day—Lord Denman, Chief Justice Tindal, and Sir Wm. Follett, —and *they allow* and *advise* the Jury to pronounce the verdict of *Not Guilty* on account of *Insanity,*—whilst *everybody* is morally *convinced* that both malefactors were perfectly conscious and aware of what they did! It appears from this, that the force of the law is entirely put into the Judge's hands, and that it depends merely upon his charge whether the law is to be applied or not. Could not the Legislature lay down that rule which the Lord Chancellor does in his paper, and which Chief Justice Mansfield did in the case of Bellingham; and why could not the Judges be *bound* to interpret the law in *this* and *no other* sense in their charges to the Juries?

Sir Robert Peel to Queen Victoria

Whitehall, 27th March 1843

Sir Robert Peel presents his humble duty to your Majesty, and hastens to reply to your Majesty's note of this date.

Sir Robert Peel assures your Majesty that he does not think that there is the slightest ground for apprehension on the occasion of the Levée, but Sir Robert Peel, will, without the slightest allusion to your Majesty's communication to him, make personal enquiries into the police arrangements, and see that every precaution possible shall be taken.

He begs, however, humbly to assure your Majesty that there never has reached him any indication of a hostile feeling towards the Prince. It could only proceed from some person of deranged intellect, and he thinks it would be almost impossible for such a person to act upon it on the occasion of a Levée.

It may tend to remove or diminish your Majesty's anxiety to know that Sir Robert Peel has *walked* home every night from the House of Commons, and, notwithstanding frequent menaces and intimations of danger, he has not met with any obstruction.

He earnestly hopes that your Majesty will dismiss from your mind any apprehension, and sincerely believes that your Majesty may do so with entire confidence. But nothing shall be neglected.

Viscount Melbourne to Queen Victoria

Brocket Hall, 2nd April 1843

Lord Melbourne presents his humble duty to your Majesty. He received yesterday morning your Majesty's letter of the 30th ult., for which he sincerely thanks your Majesty. Lord Melbourne is delighted to find that your Majesty was pleased with the bouquet. The daphnes are neither so numerous nor so fine as they were, but there are still enough left to make another bouquet, which Lord Melbourne will take care is sent up by his cart to-morrow, and left at Buckingham Palace. Lord Melbourne is very much touched and obliged by your Majesty's very kind advice, which he will try his utmost to follow, as he himself believes that his health entirely depends upon his keeping up his stomach in good order and free from derangement. He owns that he is very incredulous about the unwholesomeness of dry champagne, and he does not think that the united opinion of the whole College of Physicians and of Surgeons would persuade him upon these points—he cannot think that a 'Hohenlohe' glass of dry champagne, i.e. half a *schoppen*, can be prejudicial. Lord and Lady Errol and Lord Auckland and Miss Eden are coming in the course of the week, and they would be much surprised not to get a glass of champagne with their dinner. . . .

Sir Robert Peel to Queen Victoria

Whitehall, 6th April 1843

Sir Robert Peel, with his humble duty to your Majesty, hastens to make a communication to your Majesty, on the subject of your Majesty's letter of this morning, which he hopes will remove from your Majesty's mind any unfavourable impression with regard to the *toasts* at the theatrical dinner, or to the conduct of the Duke of Cambridge in reference to them.

Sir Robert Peel, since he addressed your Majesty, has made enquiry from Colonel Wood, the member for Brecon, who was present at the meeting.

In order to have the real statement of the case, Sir Robert Peel did not mention the object of the enquiry. The following were the questions and the answers:

Q. What were the toasts at the theatrical dinner last night?

Colonel Wood. The first was *The Queen and the Prince*. The Duke said he thought he could not give the health of the Queen in a manner more satisfactory than by coupling with the name of Her Majesty that of her illustrious Consort.

Colonel Wood said that his impression was that the Duke meant to do that which would be most respectful to the Prince, and that he had in his mind when he united the name of the Prince with that of your Majesty, the circumstances of the Prince having recently held the Levée on behalf of your Majesty.

It might perhaps have been better had His Royal Highness adhered to the usual custom, and proposed the health of the Prince distinctly and separately, but he humbly submits to your Majesty that the *intention* of His Royal Highness must have been to show respect to the Prince.

The reports of public dinners are frequently incorrect, the reporters being sometimes placed at a great distance from the chairman.

Extract from the Will of his late Royal Highness the Duke of Sussex, dated the 11th August 1840 (sent at the Queen's request by Sir Robert Peel to the Duke of Wellington for his advice).

'I desire that on my death my body may be opened, and should the examination present anything useful or interesting to science, I empower my executors to make it public. And I desire to be buried in the public cemetery at Kensal Green in the Parish of Harrow, in the County of Middlesex, and not at Windsor.'

The Duke of Wellington to Sir Robert Peel

Strathfieldsaye, 21st April 1843

MY DEAR PEEL,—I have just now received your letter of this day, and I return the enclosure in the box. It appears to me that the whole case must be considered as hanging together; that is, the desire to be buried at Kensal Green, that of Freemasons to pay Masonic Honours, that the body of the Duchess of Inverness should be interred near to his when she dies.

Parties still alive have an interest in the attainment of the two last objects, which are quite incompatible with the interment of a Prince of the Blood, a Knight of the Garter, in St George's Chapel at Windsor.

The Queen's Royal Command might overrule the Duke's desire

to be buried at Kensal Green. Nobody would complain of or contend against it.

But there will be no end of the complaints of interference by authority on the part of Freemasons, and of those who will take part with the Duchess of Inverness: and it is a curious fact that there are persons in Society who are interested in making out that she was really married to the Duke. Against this we must observe that it will be urged that the omission to insist that the interment should take place in the Collegiate Chapel of St George's, Windsor, and thus to set aside the will, lowers the Royal Family in the opinion of the public, and is a concession to Radicalism. But it is my opinion that the reasons will justify that which will be done in conformity with the will.

I confess that I don't like to decide upon cases in such haste; and I cannot consider it necessary that a decision should be made on the course to be taken in respect to the Duke's funeral, on the morrow of the day on which he died.

It would be desirable to know the opinion of the Lord Chancellor, the Archbishop, and others.

I can't think of anything likely to occur, which might alter me: and I'll abide by that which I have above given.

It will be absolutely necessary to take effective measures for the preservation of the peace at this funeral at Kensal Green: and even that the magistrates should superintend the procession of the Freemasons. Believe me, ever yours most sincerely,   WELLINGTON

Viscount Melbourne to Queen Victoria

South Street, 22nd June 1843

Lord Melbourne presents his humble duty to your Majesty. He was infinitely obliged to your Majesty for coming into the room the other evening when he was with the Prince, and very much delighted to have an opportunity of seeing your Majesty, especially in such good health and spirits.

. . . Lord Melbourne is very glad that your Majesty has seen *As You Like It*. It is indeed a most gay, lively, and beautiful play. To see or to read it is quite like passing an hour or two in a forest of fairyland. It is so lively, and at the same time so romantic. All depends upon Rosalind, which was an excellent part of Mrs. Jordan. Jacques is also a very particular character and difficult to play.

Lord Melbourne feels himself better, but still weak. He does not like to say much about politics, but he cannot refrain from observing that they seem to him to have permitted these lawless riotings in South Wales* to go on with success and impunity a great deal too long. When such things begin nobody can say how far they will go or how much they will spread. There are many who expect and predict a general rising against property, and this is invariably the way in which such things begin.

Queen Victoria to Sir James Graham

Buckingham Palace, 23rd June 1843

The Queen returns these communications to Sir James Graham, which are of a very unpleasant nature. The Queen trusts that measures of the greatest severity will be taken, as well to suppress the revolutionary spirit as to bring the culprits to immediate trial and punishment. The Queen thinks this of the greatest importance with respect to the effect it may have in Ireland, likewise as proving that the Government is willing to show great forbearance, and to trust to the good sense of the people; but that if outrages are committed and it is called upon to act, it is not to be trifled with, but will visit wrong-doers with the utmost severity.

Queen Victoria to the Duke of Wellington

(July 1843)

The Queen having attentively perused the proposed General Order for the more efficient repression of the practice of duelling in the Army, approves of the same, but recommends that the Duke of Wellington should submit to the Cabinet the propriety of consider-

---

* The agitation against the turnpike system which had broken out in South Wales.

ing of a general measure applicable to *all branches* of the Naval and Military Service.*

Queen Victoria to Sir Robert Peel

Windsor Castle, 3rd August 1843

The Queen returns the enclosed papers, and gives her sanction to the bringing in of the Bill for Enrolling and Arming the Out-Pensioners of Chelsea Hospital with great pleasure, as she thinks it a very good measure at the present crisis, calculated to relieve the troops which are rather overworked, and to secure a valuable force to the service of the Government. The Queen hopes that in bringing in the Bill Sir Robert Peel will make as little of it as possible, in order not to make it appear a larger measure than it is.

The Regulations strike the Queen as very judicious, and she has little doubt that they will raise the military spirit in the Pensioners, and will make the measure popular with them, which cannot fail to attach them more to the Crown.

Sir Robert Peel to the Prince Albert

Whitehall, Sunday, 12th November 1843

SIR,—I send to your Royal Highness a little book which is published every month, giving very useful information as to distances, or at least times, on all the railways. Possibly your Royal Highness has this book regularly sent to you.

I think, before Her Majesty promises a visit to Witley Court, there are one or two points worthy of consideration which are in favour of proposing to the Queen Dowager to meet the Queen at Drayton Manor first. The Queen would have to go and to return in the same day. The Queen Dowager might remain either one night or two nights at Drayton. Secondly, the Birmingham and Derby line

---

* An influential anti-duelling association had been formed this year, and subsequently public attention was drawn to the question by a duel on 1st July, at Camden Town, in which Colonel Fawcett was shot by his brother-in-law, Lieutenant Munro, who had reluctantly gone out, after enduring much provocation. Mainly owing to Prince Albert's efforts, the Articles of War were so amended as to put a stop to the practice.

is not on the same level with the line which goes to Droitwich (eleven miles from Witley Court), and there is a little delay in posting a carriage, or in passing from the lower line of railway to the upper.

Thirdly, there is the passage for Her Majesty, though not through Birmingham as in an ordinary travelling carriage, yet in the immediate outskirts of the town, and this twice in the same day.

The Corporation (which is a completely Radical one) might solicit permission to present an Address to Her Majesty at the station.

There would, I am sure, be nothing but demonstrations of the greatest loyalty and attachment to Her Majesty, but there would probably be a great concourse of people, and some delay, if the Addresses were received.

Perhaps your Royal Highness will think of these suggestions, which I am induced to offer by the desire to foresee everything which may have a bearing upon the personal comfort of the Queen.

I have the honour to be, Sir, with sincere respect, your Royal Highness's most faithful and humble Servant, ROBERT PEEL

Memorandum enclosed from Sir Robert Peel to Prince Albert, about the political condition of Birmingham, which the Prince was intending to visit.

The Mayor is a hosier—of *extreme* political opinions—*in fact, a Chartist.*

The contest for the office of Mayor was between him and a man of Radical opinions, but Chartism prevailed.

The Mayor has taken a violent part, before his Mayoralty, against Church Rates, and in reference to the state of Ireland.

The Conservative party took no part whatever in the Municipal Elections, and would not vote.

They would, if invited or permitted by the Mayor and Town Council, cordially co-operate with men of opposite opinions in any mark of respect to the Prince.

No probability of any tumult or of any demonstration but one of respect personally towards the Prince, if his visit be clearly and manifestly unconnected with politics.

An immense concourse of people must be expected, not only from Birmingham, but Wolverhampton, Walsall, and all the neighbouring towns, and previous police arrangements must be very carefully made.

There may be a proposal of a collation and of an Address, to be received in the Town Hall.

Should not the Lord Lieutenant (Lord Warwick) have notice?

Is the Mayor to accompany the Prince in the same carriage?

The Mayor has no carriage.

No communication should be made to any party in Birmingham, except to the municipal authorities, notwithstanding their political bias and *extreme* opinions.

The late Mayor, Mr James, though a Radical, would have summoned the leading men of different parties.

Doubts as to whether the present Mayor would, or whether he would not, place the whole arrangement in the hands of the party with which he is connected.

This risk must be incurred, as communications to other parties would not be advisable.

Queen Victoria to the King of the Belgians

Windsor Castle, 12th December 1843

MY DEAREST UNCLE,—I thank you much for your kind letter of the 7th, which I received as usual on Sunday. Louise will be able to tell you *how* well the remainder of our journey went off, and how well Albert's hunting answered. One can hardly credit the absurdity of people here, but Albert's riding so boldly and hard has made such a sensation that it has been written all over the country, and they make much more of it than if he had done some great act!

It rather disgusts one, but still it had done, and does, good, for it has put an end to all impertinent sneering for the future about Albert's riding. This journey has done great good, and my beloved Angel in particular has had *the greatest success*; for instance, at Birmingham the good his visit has done has been immense, for Albert spoke to all these manufacturers *in their own language,* which they did not expect, and these poor people have only been accustomed to hear demagogues and Chartists.

The King of the Belgians to Queen Victoria

Laeken, 15th December 1843

My DEAREST VICTORIA,— ... I am glad also that the Birmingham course succeeded so well; the theme had been for some years, particularly amongst manufacturers, that Royalty was useless and ignorant, and that the greatest blessing would be, to manufacture beyond measure, and to have an American form of Government, with an elective head of State.

Fortunately, there has always hitherto been in England a very aristocratic feeling freely accepted by the people, who like it, and show that they like it.... I was much amused, some time ago, by a very rich and influential American from New York assuring me that they stood in great need of a Government which was able to grant protection to property, and that the feeling of many was for Monarchy instead of the misrule of mobs, as they had it, and that he wished very much *some branch of the Coburg family might be disposable* for such a place. *Qu'en dites-vous*, is not this flattering? ...

1844

Queen Victoria to the King of the Belgians

Windsor Castle, 4th June 1844

My BELOVED UNCLE,—I gave Louise a long and detailed description of the Emperor,* etc. The papers are full of the details. A great event and a great compliment *his* visit certainly is, and the people *here* are extremely flattered at it. He is certainly a *very striking* man; still very handsome; his profile is *beautiful*, and his manners *most* dignified and graceful; extremely civil—quite alarmingly so, as he is so full of attentions and *politesses*. But the expression of the *eyes* is *formidable*, and unlike anything I ever saw before. He gives me and Albert the impression of a man who is *not* happy, and on

---

* The Emperor Nicholas of Russia had just arrived on a visit to England.

whom the weight of his immense power and position weighs heavily and painfully; he seldom smiles, and when he does the expression is *not* a happy one. He is very easy to get on with. Really, it seems like a dream when I think that we breakfast and walk out with *this* greatest of all earthly Potentates as quietly as if we walked, etc., with Charles or any one. We took him, with the dear good King of Saxony, who is a great contrast to the *Czar* (and with whom I am *quite* at my ease), to Adelaide Cottage after breakfast. The grass here is just as if it had been burned with fire. *How* many different Princes have we not gone the same round with! ! The children are much admired by the *Sovereigns*—(how *grand* this sounds!)—and Alice allowed the Emperor to take her in his arms, and kissed him *de son propre accord*. We are always so thankful that they are *not* shy. Both the Emperor and the King are *quite* enchanted with Windsor. The Emperor said very *poliment:* 'C'est digne de vous, Madame.' I must say the Waterloo Room lit up with that entire service of gold looks splendid; and the Reception Room, beautiful to sit in afterwards. The Emperor praised *my* Angel very much, saying: 'C'est impossible de voir un plus joli garçon; il a l'air si noble et si bon'; which I must say *is very* true. The Emperor amused the King and me by saying he was so *embarrassé* when people were presented to him, and that he felt so *'gauche' en frac*, which certainly he is quite *unaccustomed* to wear. If we can do anything to get him to do what is right by you, we shall be most happy, and Peel and Aberdeen are very anxious for it. I believe he leaves on Sunday again. To-morrow there is to be a great review, and on Thursday *I* shall probably go with them to the races; *they* are gone there with Albert to-day, but I have remained at home.

I think it is time to conclude my long letter.

If the French are angry at this visit, let their dear King and their Princes come; *they* will be sure of a *truly affectionate* reception on our part. The one which Emperor Nicholas has received is cordial and civil, *mais ne vient pas du cœur.*

I humbly beg that any remarks which may *not* be favourable to our great visitor may *not go beyond* you and Louise, and *not* to *Paris*. Ever your devoted Niece,   VICTORIA R.

Queen Victoria to the King of the Belgians

Buckingham Palace, 11th June 1844

MY DEAREST UNCLE,—I received your very kind and long letter of the 7th on Sunday, and thank you very much for it. I am delighted that my accounts interested you, and I shall try and give you some more to-day, which you will see come from an unbiassed and impartial mind, and which I trust therefore *will* be relied upon. The excitement has ceased as suddenly as it had begun, and I am still confused about it. I will go back to where I last left you. The *Revue* on the 5th was really very interesting, and our reception as well as that of the Emperor *most* enthusiastic. Louise tells me you had a review the same day, and that it also was so hot. Our children were there, and charmed. On the 6th we went with the Emperor and King to the races, and I never saw such a crowd; again *here* the reception was *most brilliant*. Every evening a large dinner in the Waterloo Room, and the two last evenings in uniforms, as the Emperor disliked so being *en frac*, and was quite embarrassed in it. On the 7th we took him and the King back here, and in the evening had a party of 260 about. On Saturday (8th) my Angel took the Emperor and King to a very elegant breakfast at Chiswick, which I for prudence' sake did *not* go to, but was very sorry for it. In the evening we went to the Opera (*not* in State), but they recognised us, and we were most brilliantly received. I had to force the Emperor forward, as he never would come forward when I was there, and I was obliged to take him by the hand to make him appear; it was impossible to be better bred or more respectful than he was towards me. Well, on Sunday afternoon at five, he left us (my Angel accompanied him to Woolwich), and he was much affected at going, and really unaffectedly touched at his reception and stay, the simplicity and quietness of which told upon his love of domestic life, which is very great. I will now (having told *all* that has passed) give you *my* opinion and feelings on the subject, which I may say are Albert's also. I was extremely against the visit, fearing the *gêne* and bustle, and even at first, I did not feel at *all* to like it, but by living in the same house together quietly and unrestrainedly (and this Albert, and with great truth, says is the great advantage of these visits, that I not only *see* these great people but *know* them), I got to know the Emperor and he to know me. There is much about him which I cannot help liking, and I think his character is *one* which should be understood, and looked upon for *once* as it is. He is stern and severe—with fixed principles of *duty* which *nothing* on earth will make him change; very *clever* I do *not* think him, and his mind is an uncivilised one; his education has been neglected; politics and military concerns are the only things he takes great interest in; the arts and all softer occupations he is insensible to, but he is sincere, I am certain, *sincere* even in his most despotic acts, from a sense that that *is* the *only* way to govern; he is not, I am sure, aware of the dreadful cases of individual misery which he so often causes, for I can see by various instances that he is kept in utter ignorance of *many* things, which his people carry out in most corrupt ways, while he thinks that he is extremely just. He thinks of general measures, but does not look into detail. And I am sure *much* never reaches his ears, and (as you observed), how can it? He asked for *nothing* whatever, has merely expressed his great anxiety to be upon the best terms with us, but *not* to the *exclusion of others*, only let things remain as they are. . . . He is, I should say, too frank, for he talks so openly before people, which he should not do, and with difficulty restrains himself. His anxiety *to be believed* is *very* great, and I must say his personal promises I *am inclined* to believe; then his feelings are very strong; he *feels* kindness deeply—and his love for his wife and children, and for all children, is *very* great. He has a strong feeling for domestic life, saying to me, when our children were in the room: 'Voilà les doux moments de notre vie.' He was not only civil, but extremely kind *to us both*, and spoke in the highest praise of dearest Albert to Sir Robert Peel, saying he wished any Prince in Germany had that ability and sense; he showed Albert great confidence, and I *think* it will do great good, as if *he* praises him abroad it will have great weight. He is *not* happy, and that melancholy which is visible in the countenance made me sad at times; the sternness of the eyes goes very much off when you know him, and changes according to his being put out (and he *can* be much embarrassed) or not, and also from his being heated, as he suffers with congestions to the head. My Angel thinks that he is a man inclined too much to give way to impulse and feeling, which makes him act wrongly often. His admiration for beauty is very great, and put me much in mind of you, when he drove out with us, looking out for pretty people. But he remains very faithful to those he admired *twenty-eight* years ago; for instance, Lady Peel, who has hardly any remains left. Respecting Belgium he did not speak to *me*, but to Albert and the Ministers. As for unkindly feeling towards *you*, he disclaims positively any, saying he knew you well, and that you had served in the Russian Army, etc., but he says those *unfortunate* Poles are the *only* obstacle, and that he positively cannot enter into direct communication *with Belgium* as long as they are *employed*. If you could only somehow or other get rid of them, I am sure the thing would be done at once. We all think he *need* not mind this, but I fear he has pledged himself. He admired Charlotte's picture. *Pour finir*, I must say one more word or two about his personal appearance. He puts us much in mind of his and our cousins the Würtembergs, and has altogether much of the Würtemberg family about him. He is bald now, but in his Chevalier Garde Uniform he is *magnificent* still, and very *striking*. I cannot deny that we were in great anxiety when we took him out lest some Pole might make an attempt, and I always felt thankful when we got him safe home again. His poor daughter is very ill, I fear.

The good King of Saxony remains another week with us, and we like him much. He is *so* unassuming. He is out sight-seeing *all* day, and enchanted with everything. I hope that you will persuade the King to come all the same in September. Our *motives* and politics are *not* to be exclusive, but to be on good terms with *all*, and why should we not? We make no secret of it.

Now I must end this very long letter. Ever your devoted Niece,

VICTORIA R.

You will kindly not *speak* of these details, but only in *allgemein* say the visit went off very satisfactorily on *both sides*, and that it was *highly pacific*.

Queen Victoria to the King of the Belgians

Buckingham Palace, 18th June 1844

MY DEAREST UNCLE,— ... I can write to you with a light heart, thank goodness, to-day, for the Government obtained a majority, which *up* to the *last* moment last night we feared they would not have, and we have been in sad trouble for the last four or five days about it. It is the more marvellous, as, if the Government asked for a *Vote* of Confidence, they would have a *Majority* of 100; but this very strength makes the supporters of the Government act in a *most* unjustifiable manner by continually acting and voting against them, *not* listening to the debates, but coming down and voting against the Government. So that we were generally in the greatest *possible* danger of having a resignation of the Government *without knowing to whom to turn*, and this from the recklessness of a handful of foolish *half* 'Puseyite' half 'Young England' people! I am sure you will agree with me that Peel's resignation would not only be for us (for *we cannot* have a better and a *safer* Minister), but for the whole country, and for the peace of Europe—a *great calamity*. Our present people are all *safe*, and not led away by impulses and reckless passions. We must, however, take care and not get into another crisis; for I assure you we have been quite miserable and *quite* alarmed ever since Saturday.

Since I last wrote to you, I spoke to Aberdeen (whom I should be equally sorry to lose, as he is *so very fair*, and has served *us personally*, so kindly and truly), and he told me that the Emperor has *positively pledged* himself to send a Minister to Brussels the moment those Poles are no longer employed; that he is quite aware of the importance of the measure, and would be disposed to make the arrangement easy, and that he spoke very kindly of *you* personally. Aberdeen says it is not necessary to disgrace them in any way, but only for the present *de les éloigner*. The Emperor has evidently some time ago made some strong declaration on the subject which he feels he cannot get over, and, as I said before, he will not give up what he has once pledged his word to. *Then, no one* on earth *can* move him. *Au fond*, it is a fine *trait*, but he carries it too far. He wrote me a *very* kind and affectionate letter from the Hague.

The Emperor has given Bertie the Grand Cross of St Andrew, which the boy was quite proud of. . . .   VICTORIA R.

The Queen of the Belgians to Queen Victoria

Laeken, 5th October 1844

MY DEARLY BELOVED VICTORIA,— . . . I have not much to say about my father's *lodging habits* and *likings*.* My father is one of the beings *most easy* to *please, satisfy,* and to *accommodate.* His eventful life has used him to everything, and makes any kind of arrangements acceptable to him; there is only *one thing* which he *cannot easily do,* it is to be *ready very early.* He means notwithstanding to try to come to your breakfast, but you *must insist upon his not doing it.* It would disturb him in all his habits, and be bad for him, as he would certainly eat, a thing he is not used to do in the morning. He generally takes hardly what may be called a *breakfast,* and eats *only twice* in the day. It would be also *much better* for him if he only appeared to luncheon and dinner, and if you kindly dispensed him altogether of the breakfast. You must not tell him that I wrote you *this,* but you must manage it with Montpensier, and kindly order for him a bowl of *chicken broth.* It is the only thing he takes generally in the morning, and between his meals. I have also no observation to make, but I have told Montpensier to speak openly to Albert whenever he thought something ought to be done for my father, or might hurt and inconvenience him, and you may consult him when you are in doubt. He is entrusted with all the recommendations of my mother, for my father is naturally *so imprudent* and *so little accustomed to caution and care,* that he must in some measure be *watched* to prevent his catching cold or doing what may be injurious to him. About his *rooms,* a hard bed and a large table for his papers are the only things he requires. He generally sleeps on a horse-hair mattress with a plank of wood under it: but *any*

* The difficulty with France as to Tahiti having been satisfactorily disposed of, King Louis Philippe was enabled to visit England, the first French King to come on a visit to the Sovereign of England. The King was enthusiastically received in England, visited Claremont (which he was destined to occupy in exile), was installed as a Knight of the Garter at Windsor with great magnificence, and visited Eton College and Woolwich Arsenal.

kind of bed will do, if it is not *too soft*. His liking will be to be entirely at *your commands* and to do *all you like*. You know he can take a great deal of exercise, and *everything* will *interest* and *delight* him, to see, as to do: this is not a compliment, but a *mere fact*. His only wish is, that you should not go out of your way for him, and change your habits on his account. Lord Aberdeen will be, of course, at Windsor, and I suppose you will ask, as you told me, the Royal Family. My father hopes to see also Sir Robert Peel, Lord Stanley, and your other Ministers. You will probably ask most of them during his stay. He wishes very much to see again those he already knows, and to make the acquaintance of those he does not know yet. In writing all this I think I *dream*, I *cannot believe* yet that in a few days my dear father will have, God willing, the *unspeakable happiness* to see you again and at *Windsor,* a thing he had *so much wished* for and which for a *long time* seemed *so improbable*. You have *no notion* of the *satisfaction* it gives him, and *how delighted* he will be to see you again, and to be once more in England. God grant he may have a good passage, and arrive to you *safely* and *well. Unberufen,* as you will soon, I trust, be able to see, he is, notwithstanding the usual talk of the papers, *perfectly well*. . . . Yours most devotedly,

LOUISE

The Queen of the Belgians to Queen Victoria

Laeken, 7th October 1844

MY DEARLY BELOVED VICTORIA,— . . . I wrote to my mother, to quiet her, all you kindly tell me about my dear father. We are *quite sure,* I assure you, that you and Albert will *take care of him,* and that he is with you *in safe hand.* And what makes my mother *uneasy* is the fear that, being at liberty and without control, he will make *too much,* as she says, *le jeune homme,* ride, go about, and do everything as if he was still twenty years old. If I must tell you *all the truth,* she is afraid also he will *eat too much.* I am sure he will tell it to you himself, as he was so much amused with *this fear*; but to do her pleasure, being well assured by me that you would allow it, and that it was even *customary,* he has given up, of himself, all thought of attending your early breakfast: but I perceive I write as if *he was not already* under *your* roof. I will also only say, that though he has sent over his horses in case they should be wanted, my mother begs you to *prevent, if possible, his riding at all.* I wrote to her already that I supposed there would be *no occasion* for riding, and that your *promenades* would be either on foot or in carriage. I entrusted Montpensier with all my messages for you, my beloved Victoria and your dear children. He hopes you will permit him, during his stay at Windsor, to make *two* excursions—one to London, and one to Woolwich—he is very curious to see, as an artillery officer. I mention it as he would be, perhaps, *too shy* or *too discreet* to mention it himself. He might very well do those two trips by the railroad and be back for dinner-time, and I am sure you will have no objection to them. . . . Yours most devotedly,   LOUISE

I am very glad that Lord Charles Wellesley is one of those who will attend my father. Montpensier and him will have surely capital fun together, and he was, you know, a great favourite with every one at Eu. If by chance Lord Hardwicke was in waiting during my father's stay, you must kindly put my father in mind to thank him for the famous cheese, which arrived safely, and was found very good. . . .

Sir Henry Hardinge to Queen Victoria

23rd November 1844

Sir Henry Hardinge * with his most humble duty to your Majesty, humbly submits for your Majesty's consideration the following observations on the state of affairs in this large portion of your Majesty's dominions.

The return of peace has also increased the desire of the native population to receive the advantages of English education. The literature of the West is the most favourite study amongst the Hindoos in their schools and colleges. They will discuss with accuracy the most important events in British History. Boys of fifteen years of age, black in colour, will recite the most favourite passages from Shakespeare, ably quoting the notes of the English and German com-

* Governor-General of India, in succession to Lord Ellenborough.

mentators. They excel in mathematics, and in legal subtleties their acuteness is most extraordinary.

In order to reward native talent and render it practically useful to the State, Sir Henry Hardinge, after due deliberation, has issued a resolution, by which the most meritorious students will be appointed to fill the public offices which fall vacant throughout Bengal.

This encouragement has been received by the Hindoo population with the greatest gratitude. The studies in the Mohammedan schools and colleges have hitherto been confined to Arabic, the Koran, and abstruse studies relating to their religion, having always shown a marked aversion to English literature. Since the publication of the Resolution they have at once determined to change their system in order to participate in the benefits held out to native merit of every sect.

It is impossible throughout your Majesty's immense Empire to employ the number of highly paid European civil servants which the public service requires. This deficiency is the great evil of British Administration. By dispersing annually a proportion of well-educated natives throughout the provinces, under British superintendence, well-founded hopes are entertained that prejudices may gradually disappear, the public service be improved, and attachment to British institutions increased. . . .

Sir Henry Hardinge, in closing these observations, most humbly ventures to assure your Majesty that he anticipates no occurrence as probable, by which the tranquillity of this portion of your Majesty's dominions is likely to be disturbed.   H. HARDINGE

1845

Queen Victoria to the King of the Belgians

Windsor Castle, 28th January 1845

. . . The feeling of loyalty in this country is happily *very* strong, and wherever we show ourselves we are most heartily and warmly received, and the civilities and respect shown to us by those we visit is *most* satisfactory. I mention merely a trifling instance to show *how* respectful they are—the Duke of Buckingham, who is immensely proud, bringing the cup of coffee after dinner on a waiter to Albert himself. And everywhere my dearest Angel receives the respect and honours I receive.

Many thanks for returning the list; it was not Albert but *Tatane* who made the black crosses. Are not 'Les 3 Mousquetaires,' by Dumas, and 'Arthur,' by Eugène Sue, *readable* for *me?*

Now adieu, dearest, best Uncle. Ever your truly devoted Niece,

VICTORIA R.

Queen Victoria to Sir Robert Peel

Pavilion, 10th February 1845

Though the Queen knows that Sir Robert Peel has already turned his attention to the urgent necessity of doing something to Buckingham Palace, the Queen thinks it right to recommend this subject herself to his serious consideration. Sir Robert is acquainted with the state of the Palace and the total want of accommodation for our little family, which is fast growing up. Any building must necessarily take some years before it can be safely inhabited. If it were to be begun this autumn, it could hardly be occupied before the spring of 1848, when the Prince of Wales would be nearly seven, and the Princess Royal nearly eight years old, and they cannot possibly be kept in the nursery any longer. A provision for this purpose ought, therefore, to be made this year. Independent of this, most parts of the Palace are in a sad state, and will ere long require a further outlay to render them *decent* for the occupation of the Royal Family or any visitors the Queen may have to receive. A room, capable of containing a large number of those persons whom the Queen has to invite in the course of the season to balls, concerts, etc., than any of the present apartments can at once hold, is much wanted. Equally so, improved offices and servants' rooms, the want of which puts the departments of the household to great expense yearly. It will be for Sir Robert to consider whether it would not be best to remedy all these deficiencies at once, and to make use of this opportunity to render the exterior of the Palace such as no longer to be a *disgrace* to the country, which it certainly now is. The Queen thinks the country would be better pleased to have the question of the Sovereign's residence in London so finally disposed of, than to have it so repeatedly brought before it.

Queen Victoria to Sir Robert Peel

Pavilion, 18th February 1845

The Queen has received Sir Robert Peel's letter, and is glad that the progress in the House of Commons was so satisfactory.

The Queen was much hurt at Mr Borthwick's most impertinent manner of putting the question with respect to the title of King Consort, and much satisfied with Sir Robert's answer. The title of King is open assuredly to many difficulties, and would perhaps be no *real* advantage to the Prince, but the Queen is positive that something must at once be done to place the Prince's position on a constitutionally recognised footing, and to give him a title adequate to that position. *How* and *when,* are difficult questions. . . .

Queen Victoria to the King of the Belgians

Windsor Castle, 25th March 1845

. . . I copied what you wrote me about Peel in a letter I wrote him, which I am sure will please him much, and a Minister in these days *does* require a little encouragement, for the abuse and difficulties they have to contend with are dreadful. Peel works so hard and has so much to do, that sometimes he says he does not know *how* he is to get through it all!

You will, I am sure, be pleased to hear that we have succeeded in purchasing *Osborne* in the Isle of Wight, and if we can manage it, we shall probably run down there before we return to Town, for three nights. It sounds so snug and nice to have a place of *one's own,* quiet and retired, and free from all Woods and Forests, and other charming Departments who really are the plague of one's life.

Now, dearest Uncle, adieu. Ever your truly devoted Niece,

VICTORIA R.

Queen Victoria to Viscount Melbourne

Buckingham Palace, 3rd April 1845

... The Queen refers Lord Melbourne to Mr Anson for particulars of the property, which is very extensive, as she is not at all competent to explain about acres, etc. But she thinks it is impossible to imagine a prettier spot—valleys and woods which would be beautiful anywhere; but all this near the sea (the woods grow into the sea) is quite perfection; we have a charming beach quite to ourselves. The sea was so blue and calm that the Prince said it was like Naples. And then we can walk about anywhere by ourselves without being followed and mobbed, which Lord Melbourne will easily understand is delightful. And last, not least, we have Portsmouth and Spithead so close at hand, that we shall be able to watch what is going on, which will please the Navy and be hereafter very useful for our boys. ....

Queen Victoria to the King of the Belgians

Buckingham Palace, 23rd April 1845

MY DEAREST UNCLE,—Our Maynooth Bill is through the second reading. I think, if you read Sir Robert's admirable speeches, you will see how good his plan is. The *Catholics* are quite delighted at it—full of gratitude, and behave extremely well; but the Protestants behave shockingly, and display a narrow-mindedness and want of sense on the subject of religion which is quite a disgrace to the nation. The case of Austria, France, etc., cannot be compared to this, as *this* is a *Protestant* country, while the others are Catholic; and I think it would never do to support a Roman Catholic Church with money belonging to the Protestant Church. The Protestant Establishment in Ireland must remain untouched, but let the Roman Catholic Clergy be well and handsomely educated. ....

Sir James Graham to Queen Victoria

Whitehall, 13th May 1845

Sir James Graham, with humble duty, begs to lay before your Majesty the enclosed Memorial.

The proceedings in Newgate on the occasion of the last condemned sermon and on the morning of the execution have been fully investigated; and the report established the necessity of legislative interference to prevent the recurrence of scenes so disgraceful and demoralising. The policy of depriving capital executions of their present publicity is well worthy of careful revision; and Sir James Graham, in obedience to your Majesty's desire, will bring the subject under the notice of his colleagues. He is disposed to think that the sentence might be carried into execution in the presence of a Jury to be summoned by the Sheriff with good effect; and that the great body of idle spectators might be excluded, without diminishing the salutary terror and awful warning which this extreme punishment is intended to produce on the public mind. In dealing, however, with a matter in which the community has so deep an interest, it is prudent not to violate public opinion, and caution is necessary before a change of the long-established usage is proposed.

Sir James Graham deeply regrets the part taken by the newspapers in seeking to indulge the general curiosity with respect to all details of the conduct, habits, and demeanour of these wretched criminals in their last moments; but he fears that the license of the Press cannot be checked by any act of authority; if the public be excluded from witnessing the executions, they will probably become still more anxious to obtain a printed report of all that has taken place; and Sir James Graham is so thoroughly convinced that the punishment of death in certain cases must be maintained, that he would consider any course inexpedient which was likely to lead the public to desire the remission of capital executions in all cases without exception. . . .

J. R. G. GRAHAM

Lord Stanley to Queen Victoria

Downing Street, 10th July 1845

Lord Stanley, with his humble duty, submits to your Majesty a despatch just received from the Governor of South Australia, enclosing the letter of a settler in the province, Mr Walter Duffield, who is anxious to be allowed the honour of offering for your Majesty's acceptance a case of the first wine which has been made in the colony.

Lord Stanley will not venture to answer for the quality of the vintage; but as the wine has been sent over with a loyal and dutiful feeling, and the importer, as well as the colonists in general, might feel hurt by a refusal of his humble offering, he ventures to hope that he may be permitted to signify, through the Governor, your Majesty's gracious acceptance of the first sample of a manufacture which, if successful, may add greatly to the resources of this young but now thriving colony.

The above is humbly submitted by your Majesty's most dutiful Servant and Subject, STANLEY

Sir Robert Peel to Queen Victoria

Osborne, 15th September 1845

Sir Robert Peel, with his humble duty to your Majesty, begs leave to acquaint your Majesty that there remains the sum of £700 to be applied in the current year to the grant of Civil List Pensions.

Sir Robert Peel humbly recommends to your Majesty that another sum of £200 should be offered to Mr Tennyson, a poet of whose powers of imagination and expression many competent judges think most highly.

He was brought under the notice of Sir Robert Peel by Mr Hallam. His pecuniary circumstances are far from being prosperous. . . .

The King of the Belgians to Queen Victoria

St Cloud, 10th October 1845

MY DEAREST VICTORIA,— . . . All you say about our dear Albert, whom I love like my own child, is perfectly true. The attacks, however unjust, have but one advantage, that of showing the points the enemy thinks *weakest* and best calculated to hurt. This, being the case, Anson, without boring A. with *daily* accounts which in the end become very irksome, should pay attention to these very points, and contribute to avoid what may be turned to account by the enemy. To hope to *escape* censure and calumny is next to impossible, but whatever is considered by the enemy as a fit subject for attack is better modified or avoided. The dealings with artists, for instance, require great prudence; they are acquainted with all classes of society, and for that very reason dangerous; they are hardly *ever satisfied*, and when you have too much to do with them, you are sure to have *des ennuis*. . . . Your devoted Uncle, LEOPOLD R.

Queen Victoria to Sir Robert Peel

Osborne, 28th November 1845

The Queen is very sorry to hear that Sir Robert Peel apprehends further differences of opinion in the Cabinet, at a moment of impending calamity; it is more than ever necessary that the Government should be strong and united.

The Queen thinks the time is come when a removal of the restrictions upon the importation of food cannot be successfully resisted. Should this be Sir Robert's own opinion, the Queen very much hopes that none of his colleagues will prevent him from doing what it is *right* to do.

Sir Robert Peel to Queen Victoria

Whitehall, 4th December 1845

Sir Robert Peel, with his humble duty to your Majesty, begs leave to acquaint your Majesty that a leading paragraph in the *Times* of to-day, asserting that your Majesty's servants had unanimously agreed to an immediate and total repeal of the Corn Laws, is quite without foundation.*

Memorandum by the Prince Albert

. . . Yesterday Sir Robert Peel arrived here and explained the condition of affairs.

On 1st November he had called his Cabinet, and placed before its members the reports of the Irish Commissioners, Dr Buckland, Dr

---

* See *Memoirs of the Life of Henry Reeve*, vol. i, p. 175, for Lord Dufferin's refutation of the story that Sidney Herbert confided the secret to Mrs Norton, and that she sold it to the *Times*. The story has obtained a wide currency through Mr Meredith's *Diana of the Crossways*. Lord Stanmore, in his *Life of Sidney Herbert*, substantially attributes the communication to Lord Aberdeen, but does not give the details.

Playfair and Dr Lindley, on the condition of the potato crop, which was to the effect that the half of the potatoes were ruined by the rot, and that no one could guarantee the remainder. Belgium, Holland, Sweden, and Denmark, in which states the potato disease had likewise deprived the poorer class of its usual food, have immediately taken energetic means, and have opened the harbours, bought corn, and provided for the case of a rise of prices. Sir Robert proposed the same thing for England, and, by opening the ports, a preparation for the abolition of the Corn Laws. His colleagues refused, and of the whole Cabinet only Lord Aberdeen, Sir James Graham, and Mr Sidney Herbert voted with him. Sir Robert hoped that in time the opinions of the others would change, and therefore postponed a final decision. In the meanwhile the agitation of the Anti-Corn Law League began; in every town addresses were voted, meetings were held, the *Times* —barometer of public feeling—became suddenly *violently* Anti-Corn Law, the meetings of the Cabinet roused attention, a general panic seized on the mass of the public. Sir Robert called anew his Cabinet. In the midst of their deliberation Lord John Russell issues from Edinburgh an address to the City of London.

The whole country cries out: the Corn Laws are doomed.

Thereon Sir Robert declared to his Cabinet that nothing but unanimity could save the cause, and pressed for a decision.

The Duke of Buccleuch and Lord Stanley declared they could not take a part in a measure abolishing the Corn Laws, and would therefore have to resign. The other members, including the Duke of Wellington, showed themselves ready to support Sir Robert, yet, as the latter says, 'apparently not willingly and against their feelings.' Thereupon Sir Robert resolved to lay down his office as Minister.

When he arrived here he was visibly much moved, and said to me, that it was one of the most painful moments of his life to separate himself from us, 'but it is necessary, and if I have erred it was from loyalty and too great an anxiety not to leave Her Majesty in a moment of such great difficulty. I ought to have gone when I was first left by my colleagues in a minority in my own Cabinet. I was anxious, however, to try my utmost, but it is impossible to retrieve lost time. As soon as I saw Lord John's letter I felt that the ground was slipping away from under me, and that whatever I might now propose would appear as dictated by the Opposition, as taking Lord John's measure. On the 1st of November the whole country was prepared for the thing; there had been no agitation, everybody looking to the Government, as soon as they saw this wavering and hesitating, the country decided for itself, and Lord John has the merit, owing to his most dexterous move and our want of unanimity.'

On my observing that Sir Robert has a majority of one hundred in the House of Commons, and asking whether it was not possible for him to continue the Government, he said:

'The Duke of Buccleuch will carry half Scotland with him, and Lord Stanley, leading the Protectionists in the House of Lords, would lead to great and immediate defections even in Her Majesty's household. The Duchess of Buccleuch, Lord Hardwicke, Lord Exeter, Lord Rivers, Lord Beverley, etc., would resign, and we should not be able to find successors; in the House of Commons I am sure I should be beat, the Tories, agriculturists, etc., in rage would turn round upon me and be joined by the Whigs and Radicals, who would say, "This is *our* measure and we will not allow you to carry it." It is better that I should go now, when *nobody has committed himself* in the heat of party contest, when no factions have been formed, no imprudent declarations been made; it is better for Her Majesty and for the country that it should be so.'

After we had examined what possibilities were open for the Crown, the conclusion was come to that Lord John was the only man who could be charged with forming a Cabinet. Lord Stanley, with the aristocracy as his base, would bring about an insurrection [or riots], and the ground on which one would have to fight would be this: to want to force the mass of the people, amidst their great poverty, to pay for their bread a high price, in favour of the landlords.

It is a matter of the utmost importance not to place the House of Lords into direct antagonism with the Commons and with the masses of the people. Sir Robert says very correctly:

'I am afraid of other interests getting damaged in the struggle about the Corn Laws; already the system of promotion in the Army, the Game Laws, the Church, are getting attacked with the aid of the League.'

After Victoria had in consequence [of the foregoing] decided in favour of Lord John, and asked Sir Robert: 'But how is it possible for him to govern with so exceedingly small a minority?' Sir Robert said: 'He will have difficulties and perhaps did not consider what he was doing when he wrote that letter; but *I will support him*. I feel it my duty to your Majesty not to leave you without a Government. Even if Lord John goes to the full extent of his declaration in that letter (which I think goes too far), I will support him in Parliament and use all my influence with the House of Lords to prevent their impeding his progress. I will do more, if he likes it. I will say that the increase of the estimates which will become necessary are my work, and I alone am responsible for it.'

Sir Robert intends to give me a memorandum in which he is to make this promise in writing.

He was greatly moved, and said it was not 'the loss of power (for I hate power) nor of office,' which was nothing but a plague for him, but 'the breaking up of those relations in which he stood to the Queen and me, and the loss of our society,' which was for him a loss, for which there was no equivalent; we might, however, rely on his being always ready to serve us, in what manner and in what place it might be. Lord Aberdeen is said to feel the same, and very deeply so; and on our side the loss of two so estimable men, who possess our whole and perfect confidence in public as well as in private affairs, and have always proved themselves true friends, leaves *a great gap*.   ALBERT

Memorandum by the Prince Albert

Windsor Castle, 20th December 1845
(4 o'clock p.m.)

We saw Sir Robert Peel, who had been apprised by Sir James Graham (to whom Lord John Russell had written) of what had passed. He was much affected, and expressed his concern at the failure of Lord John to form a Government, seemed hurt at Lord John's not having shown more confidence in the integrity of his (Sir Robert Peel's) motives. He would have supported Lord John in *any* measure which he should have thought fit to introduce, and many would have followed his example. He blamed the want of deference shown to the Queen, by not answering her call with more readiness; he said it was quite new and unconstitutional for a man to take a week before he undertook to form a Government, and to pass that time in discussion with other people, to whom the Sovereign had not yet committed the task; and he had been certain it would end so, when so many people were consulted. He in 1834 had been called from Italy, had travelled with all haste and had gone straight to the King, had told him that he had seen nobody, consulted nobody, but immediately kissed the King's hand as his Minister.

He was now prepared to stand by the Queen, all other considerations he had thrown aside, he would undertake to deal with the difficulties, and should have to go down alone to the House of Commons. He had written to his colleagues that he would serve the Queen if she called upon him to do so, that he expected them to meet him at nine o'clock that evening, and that he would tell them what he meant to do. Those who would not go with him, he would dismiss at once. He did not wish to avail himself of any undue advantage, and therefore would not advise an Order in Council, but go at once to Parliament, laying his measure before it: 'Reject it, if you please; there it is!'

He called the crisis an alarming one, which determination alone could overcome.

We showed him Lord John Russell's statement, with which he declared himself very much satisfied. He advised the Queen to write a letter to Lord John, announcing to him Sir Robert's consent to go on with the Government, and wrote a draft of it, which follows here.

He had heard strange instances of disagreement amongst the men whom Lord John had assembled in town.

Sir Robert seemed throughout much moved, and said with much warmth: 'There is no sacrifice that I will not make for your Majesty, except that of my honour.'

Queen Victoria to Lord John Russell

Windsor Castle, 20th December 1845

Sir Robert Peel has just been here. He expressed great regret that Lord John Russell had felt it necessary to decline the formation of a Government.

He said he should have acted towards Lord John Russell with the most scrupulous good faith, and that he should have done everything in his power to give Lord John support.

He thinks many would have been induced to follow his example.

Sir Robert Peel did not hesitate a moment in withdrawing his offer of resignation. He said he felt it his duty at once to resume his office, though he is deeply sensible to the difficulties with which he has to contend.

Sir Robert Peel to Queen Victoria

Whitehall, 21st December 1845

Sir Robert Peel presents his humble duty to your Majesty, and proceeds to give your Majesty an account of what has passed since he left your Majesty at four o'clock yesterday.

The Cabinet met at Sir Robert Peel's house in Downing Street at half-past nine.

Sir Robert Peel informed them that he had not summoned them for the purpose of deliberating on what was to be done, but for the purpose of announcing to them that he was your Majesty's Minister, and whether supported or not, was firmly resolved to meet Parliament as your Majesty's Minister, and to propose such measures as the public exigencies required.

Failure or success must depend upon their decision, but nothing could shake Sir Robert Peel's determination to meet Parliament and to advise the Speech from the Throne.

There was a dead silence, at length interrupted by Lord Stanley's declaring that he must persevere in resigning, that he thought the Corn Law ought to be adhered to, and might have been maintained.

The Duke of Wellington said he thought the Corn Law was a subordinate consideration. He was *delighted* when he received Sir Robert Peel's letter that day, announcing to the Duke that his mind was made up to place his services at your Majesty's disposal.

The Duke of Buccleuch behaved admirably—was much agitated—thought new circumstances had arisen—would not then decide on resigning.

Sir Robert Peel has received this morning the enclosed note from the Duke.

He has written a reply very strongly to the Duke, stating that the present question is not one of Corn Law, but whether your Majesty's former servants or Lord Grey and Mr Cobden shall constitute your Majesty's Government. Sir Robert Peel defied the wit of man to suggest now another alternative to your Majesty.

Lord Aberdeen will see the Duke to-day.

All the other members of the Government cordially approved of Sir Robert Peel's determination not to abandon your Majesty's service.

There was no question about details, but if there is any, it shall not alter Sir Robert Peel's course.

Sir Robert Peel to Queen Victoria

Whitehall, 22nd December 1845

Sir Robert Peel presents his humble duty to your Majesty, and has the utmost satisfaction in informing your Majesty that Mr Gladstone is willing to accept the Seals of the Colonial Office should your Majesty be pleased to confide them to him.

Sir Robert Peel thinks this of great importance, and that immediate decision in filling up so eminent a post will have a good effect.

Queen Victoria to the King of the Belgians

Windsor Castle, 23rd December 1845

MY DEAREST UNCLE,—Many thanks for your two kind letters of the 17th and 19th, which gave me much pleasure. I have little to add to Albert's letter of yesterday, except my *extreme* admiration of our worthy Peel, who shows himself a man of unbounded *loyalty, courage,* patriotism, and *high-mindedness,* and his conduct towards me has been *chivalrous* almost, I might say. I never have seen him so excited or so determined, and *such* a good cause must succeed. We have indeed had an escape, for though Lord John's *own notions* were *very* good and moderate, he let himself be entirely twisted and twirled about by his *violent* friends, and *all* the moderate ones were crushed. . . .

VICTORIA R.

Memorandum by the Prince Albert

Windsor Castle, 25th December 1845

We had a Council yesterday, at which Parliament was prorogued to the 22nd January, then to meet for the despatch of business. Lord Stanley had an audience of the Queen before, and delivered up the Seals of his office. He was much agitated, and had told Sir Robert that he dreaded this interview very much. The Queen thanked him for his services, and begged he would do his best out of office to smooth down the difficulties her Government would have to contend with. At the Council Lord Dalhousie took his seat, and Mr Gladstone received the Colonial Seals. The Queen saw the Duke of Buccleuch and thanked him for the devotion he had shown her during these trying circumstances; the same to the Duke of Wellington, who is in excellent spirits. On my saying, 'You have such an influence over the House of Lords, that you will be able to keep them straight,' he answered: 'I'll do anything; I am now beginning to write to them and to convince them singly of what their duty is.'

We saw afterwards Sir Robert Peel, who stayed more than three hours. He is in the highest spirits at having got Mr Gladstone and kept the Duke of Buccleuch; he proposed that the Duke should be made President, and Lord Haddington Privy Seal in his stead. (Lord Haddington had behaved very well, had given up his place to Sir Robert, and told him he should do with him just as he liked— leave him out of the Cabinet, shift him to another place, or leave him at the Admiralty, as would suit him best.)

Sir Robert hinted to Lord Ripon that Lord Haddington had behaved so well, but got no more out of him, but 'that he would *almost* have done the same.' Sir Robert proposes to see Lord Ellenborough in order to offer him the Admiralty, received the Queen's sanction like-wise to Lord St Germans (the Postmaster-General) being put into the Cabinet. I said: 'With your Government that has no inconvenience, and even if you had a hundred members in the Cabinet, as you don't tell them but what is absolutely necessary, and follow your own course.' He said in reply, that he should be very sorry if he had to have told his Cabinet that he meant to send for Lord Ellenborough. We could not help contrasting this conduct with the subjection Lord

John has shown to his people. It is to his *own* talent and firmness that Sir Robert will owe his success, which cannot fail. He said he had been determined not to go to a general election with the fetters the last election had imposed upon him, and he had meant at the end of the next Session to call the whole Conservative Party together and to declare this to them, that he would not meet another Parliament pledged to the maintenance of the Corn Laws, which could be maintained no longer, and that he would make a public declaration to this effect before another general election came on. This had been defeated by events coming too suddenly upon him, and he had no alternative but to deal with the Corn Laws before a national calamity would *force* it on. The league had made immense progress, and had enormous means at their disposal. If he had resigned in November, Lord Stanley and the Protectionists would have been prepared to form a Government, and a Revolution might have been the consequence of it. Now they felt that it was too late.

Sir Robert has *an immense scheme in view*; he thinks he shall be able to remove the contest entirely from the dangerous ground upon which it has got—that of a war between the manufacturers, the hungry and the poor against the landed proprietors, the aristocracy, which can only end in the ruin of the latter; he will not bring forward a measure upon the Corn Laws, but a much more comprehensive one. He will deal with the whole commercial system of the country. He will adopt the principle of the League, *that of removing all protection and abolishing all monopoly,* but not in favour of one class and as a triumph over another, but to the benefit of the nation, farmers as well as manufacturers. He would begin with cotton, and take in all the necessaries of life and corn amongst them. The experiments he had made in 1842 and 1845 with boldness but with caution had borne out the correctness of the principle: the wool duty was taken off, and wool sold higher than ever before; foreign cattle were let in, and the cattle of England stood better in the market than ever. He would not ask for compensation to the land, but wherever he could give it, and at the same time promote the social development, there he would do it, but on that ground. For instance, one of the greatest benefits to the country would be the establishment of a rural police on the same principle as the metropolitan police. By taking this on the Consolidated Fund, the landowners would be immensely relieved in all those counties which kept a police. One of the heaviest charges on the land was the present administration of law and the carrying on of prosecutions. Sir Robert could fancy this to be very much improved by the appointment of a *public* prosecutor by the State, which would give the State a power to prevent vexatious, illegal and immoral prosecutions, and reduce the expenses in an extraordinary degree. Part of the maintenance of the poor, according to the Poor Law, might be undertaken by the State. A great calamity must be foreseen, when the innumerable railroads now in progress shall have been terminated, which will be the case in a few years. This will throw an enormous labouring population suddenly out of employment. There might be a law passed which would provide employment for them, and improve the agriculture and production of the country, by enabling the State to advance money to the great proprietors for the improvements of their estates, which they could not obtain otherwise without charging their estates beyond what they already have to bear.

Sir Robert means to go with Mr Gladstone into all these details.

ALBERT

1846

Queen Victoria to Sir Robert Peel

Buckingham Palace, 23rd January 1846

THE Queen must compliment Sir Robert Peel on his beautiful and indeed *unanswerable* speech of last night, which we have been reading with the greatest attention.* The concluding part we also greatly

---

* The Queen had opened Parliament in person; the Prime Minister took the unusual course of speaking immediately after the seconder of the Address, and in his peroration, after laying stress on the responsibilities he was incurring, proceeded: 'I do not desire to be Minister of England; but while I am Minister of England I will hold office by no servile tenure; I will hold office unshackled by any other obligation than that of consulting the public interests and providing for the public safety.'

The Duke of Wellington and Sir Robert Peel
From the painting by F. Winterhalter

Lord Palmerston

From an engraving after an early photograph

Lord John Russell

From an engraving by D. J. Pound after a photograph by Mayall

admire. Sir R. Peel has made a very strong case. Surely the impression which it has made must have been a good one. Lord John's explanation is a fair one; the Queen has *not* a doubt that he will support Sir Robert Peel. . . .

What does Sir Robert think of the temper of the House of Commons, and of the debate in the House of Lords? The debates not being adjourned is a good thing. The crowd was immense out-of-doors yesterday, and we were never better received.

Memorandum by the Prince Albert

Buckingham Palace, 1st April 1846

I saw this day Sir R. Peel, and showed him a memorandum, which I had drawn up respecting our conversation of the 30th.

It filled six sheets, and contained, as minutely as I could render it, the whole of the arguments we had gone through. Sir Robert read it through and over again, and, after a long pause, said: 'I was not aware when I spoke to your Royal Highness that my words would be taken down, and don't acknowledge that this is a fair representation of my opinion.' He was visibly uneasy, and added, if he knew that what he said should be committed to paper, he would speak differently, and give his opinion with all the circumspection and reserve which a Minister ought to employ when he gave responsible advice; but he had in this instance spoken quite unreservedly, like an advocate defending a point in debate, and then he had taken another and tried to carry this as far as it would go, in order to give me an opportunity of judging of the different bearings of the question. He did so often in the Cabinet, when they discussed important questions, and was often asked: 'Well, then, you are quite against this measure?' 'Not at all, but I want that the counter argument should be gone into to the fullest extent, in order that the Cabinet should not take a one-sided view.'. . .

I said that I felt it to be of the greatest importance to possess his views on the question, but that I thought I would not have been justified in keeping a record of our conversation without showing it to him, and asking him whether I had rightly understood him; but if he felt a moment's uneasiness about this memorandum, I would at once destroy it, as I was anxious that nothing should prevent his speaking without the slightest reserve to me in future as he had done heretofore. I felt that these open discussions were of the greatest use to me in my endeavour to investigate the different political questions of the day and to form a conclusive opinion upon them. As Sir Robert did not say a word to dissuade me, I took it as an affirmative, and threw the memorandum into the fire, which, I could see, relieved Sir Robert.   ALBERT

Mr Gladstone to Queen Victoria

13 Carlton House Terrace, 1st April 1846

Mr William Gladstone presents his humble duty to your Majesty, and prays that he may be honoured with your Majesty's permission to direct that the Park and Tower Guns may be fired forthwith in celebration of the victory which was achieved by your Majesty's forces over the Sikh army in Sobraon on the 10th of February.

Sir Robert Peel to Queen Victoria

Whitehall, 22nd June 1846

Sir Robert Peel presents his humble duty to your Majesty, and assures your Majesty that he is penetrated with a deep sense of your Majesty's great kindness and your Majesty's generous sympathy with himself and Lady Peel.

Sir Robert Peel firmly believes that the recent attack made upon him was the result of a foul conspiracy concocted by Mr Disraeli and Lord George Bentinck, in the hope and belief that from the lapse of time or want of leisure in Sir Robert Peel to collect materials for his defence, or the destruction of documents and papers, the means of complete refutation might be wanting. . . .

He hopes, however, he had sufficient proof to demonstrate the falseness of the accusation, and the malignant motives of the accusers.

He is deeply grateful to your Majesty and to the Prince for the kind interest you have manifested during the progress of this arduous struggle, which now he trusts is approaching to a successful termination.

Sir Robert Peel to Queen Victoria

House of Commons, 29th June 1846

Sir Robert Peel, with his humble duty to your Majesty, begs leave to acquaint your Majesty that he has just concluded his speech notifying to the House the resignation of the Government.

He thinks it was very well received. Lord Palmerston spoke after Sir Robert Peel, but not very effectively, but no other person spoke. Sir Robert Peel is to see Lord John Russell at ten to-morrow morning.

Sir Robert Peel humbly congratulates your Majesty on the intelligence received *this* day from America. The defeat of the Government on the day on which they carried the Corn Bill, and the receipt of the intelligence from America on the day on which they resign, are singular coincidences.

The Bishop of Oxford* to Mr Anson

61 Eaton Place, 29th June 1846
(Midnight)

MY DEAR ANSON,—Your kind letter reached me half an hour ago whilst Sir T. Acland was sitting with me; and I must say a few words in reply by the early post. I went down to hear Peel in the House of Commons, and very fine it was. The House crowded, Peers and Ambassadors filled every seat and overflowing into the House. Soon after six all private business was over; Peel not come in, all waiting, no one rose for anything; for ten minutes this lasted: then Peel came in, walked up the House: colder, dryer, more introverted than ever, yet to a close gaze showing the fullest working of a smothered volcano of emotions. He was out of breath with walking and sat down on the Treasury Bench (placing a small despatch box with the Oregon despatches on the table) as he would be fully himself before he rose. By-and-by he rose, amidst a breathless silence, and made the speech you will have read long ere this. It was very fine: very effective: really almost solemn: to fall at such a moment. He spoke as if it was his last political scene: as if he felt that between alienated friends and unwon foes he could have no party again; and

* Dr Samuel Wilberforce.

121

could only as a shrewd bystander observe and advise others. There was but one point in the Speech which I thought doubtful: the apostrophe to 'Richard Cobden.' I think it was wrong, though there is very much to be said for it. The opening of the American peace was noble; but for the future, what have we to look to? Already there are whispers of Palmerston and War; the Whig budget and deficiency. The first great question all men ask is: does Lord John come in, leaning on Radical or Conservative aid? Is Hawes to be in the Cabinet? the first Dissenter? the first tradesman? the Irish Church? I wish you were near enough to talk to, though even then you would know too much that must not be known for a comfortable talk. But I shall hope soon to see you; and am always, my dear Anson, very sincerely and affectionately yours,   S. Oxon

Memorandum by the Prince Albert

Osborne House, 30th June 1846

Lord John Russell arrived here this afternoon; he has seen Sir Robert Peel this morning, and is prepared to undertake the formation of a Government which he thinks will stand; at least, for the present session he anticipates no difficulty, as Sir R. Peel has professed himself ready not to obstruct its progress, and as the Protectionists have held a meeting on Saturday at which Lord Stanley has declared that he would let this Government go on smoothly unless the word 'Irish Church' was pronounced. About men and offices, Lord John has consulted with Lord Lansdowne, Palmerston, Clarendon, and Cottenham, who were of opinion that the Liberal members of Sir Robert's Cabinet ought to be induced to retain office under Lord John, viz. Lord Dalhousie, Lord Lincoln, and Mr Sidney Herbert. Sir Robert Peel at the interview of this morning had stated to Lord John that he would not consider it as an attempt to draw his supporters away from him (it not being his intention to form a party), and that he would not dissuade them from accepting the offer, but that he feared that they would not accept. We concurred in this opinion, but Lord John was authorised by Victoria to make the offer. Mr F. Baring, the Chancellor of the Exchequer under the late Whig Government, has intimated to Lord John that he would prefer if no offer of office was made to him; Lord John would therefore recommend Mr Charles Wood for this office. Lord Grey was still a difficulty; in or out of office he seemed to be made a difficulty. It would be desirable to have him in the Cabinet if he could waive his opinions upon the Irish Church. His speech in the House of Lords at the beginning of the session had done much harm, had been very extreme, and Lord John was decidedly against him in that. Lord Grey knew that everybody blamed it, but said everybody would be of those (his) opinions ten years hence, and therefore he might just as well hold them now. Mr Wood having great influence with him might keep him quiet, and so would the Colonial seals, as he would get work enough. About Lord Palmerston, he is satisfied, and would no more make any difficulty.

Lord John Russell told me in the evening that he had forgotten to mention one subject to the Queen: it was that Sir Robert Peel by his speech and his special mention of Mr Cobden as the person who had carried the great measure, had made it very difficult for Lord John not to offer office to Mr Cobden. The Whigs were already accused of being exclusive, and reaping the harvest of other people's work. The only thing he could offer would be a *Cabinet* office. Now this would affront a great many people whom he (Lord J.) had to conciliate, and create even possibly dissension in his Cabinet. As Mr Cobden was going on the Continent for a year, Lord John was advised by Lord Clarendon to write to Mr C., and tell him that he had heard he was going abroad, that he would not make any offer to him therefore, but that he considered him as entitled once to be recommended for office to the Queen. This he would do, with the Queen's permission. . . .

Memorandum by Prince Albert

Buckingham Palace, 6th July 1846

Yesterday the new Ministry were installed at a Privy Council, and the Seals of Office transferred to them. We had a long conversation with Sir Robert Peel, who took leave. I mentioned to him that his word of 'Richard Cobden' had created an immense sensation, but he was not inclined to enter upon the subject. When we begged him to do nothing which could widen the breach between him and his party, he said, 'I don't think that we can ever get together again.' He repeated that he was anxious not to undertake a Government again, that his health would not stand it, that it was better likewise for the Queen's service that other men should be brought forward. Sir Robert, Lord Aberdeen, and Sir James Graham parted with great emotion, and had tears in their eyes when they thanked the Queen for her confidence and support. Lord Aberdeen means to have an interview with Lord Palmerston, and says that when he (Lord A.) came into office, Lord Palmerston and the *Chronicle* assailed him most bitterly as an imbecile Minister, a traitor to his country, etc., etc. He means now to show Lord P. the contrast by declaring his readiness to assist him in every way he can by his advice, that he would at all times speak to him as if he was his colleague if he wished it.

The new Court is nearly completed, and we have succeeded in obtaining a very respectable and proper one, notwithstanding the run which the Party made upon it which had been formerly used to settle these matters, to *their* liking only. The Government is not a united one, however, by any means. Mr Wood and Lord Clarendon take the greatest credit in having induced Lord Grey to join the Government, and are responsible to Lord John to keep him quiet, which they think they will be able to do, as he had been convinced of the folly of his former line of conduct. Still, they say Lord Lansdowne will have the lead only nominally, that Lord Grey is to take it really in the House of Lords. There is the *Grey Party,* consisting of Lord Grey, Lord Clarendon, Sir George Grey, and Mr Wood; they are against Lord Lansdowne, Lord Minto, Lord Auckland, and Sir John Hobhouse, stigmatising them as old women. Lord John leans entirely to the last-named gentlemen. There is no cordiality between Lord John and Lord Palmerston, who, if he had to make a choice, would even forget what passed in December last, and join the Grey Party in preference to Lord John personally. The curious part of all this is that they cannot keep a secret, and speak of all their differences. They got the *Times* over by giving it exclusive information, and the leading articles are sent in and praise the new Cabinet, but the wicked paper added immediately a furious attack upon Sir John Hobhouse, which alarmed them so much that they sent to Sir John, sounding him, whether he would be hereafter prepared to relinquish the Board of Control. (This, however, is a mere personal matter of Mr Walter, who stood against Sir John at Nottingham in 1841 and was unseated.) Sir John Easthope, the proprietor of the *Morning Chronicle,* complains bitterly of the subserviency of the *Times* and treason to him. He says he knows that the information was sent from Lord John's house, and threatens revenge. 'If you will be ruled by the *Times*,' he said to one of the Cabinet, 'the *Times* has shown you already by a specimen that you will be ruled by a rod of iron.'

A Brevet for the Army and Navy is proposed, in order to satisfy Lord Anglesey with the dignity of Field-Marshal.   ALBERT

Queen Victoria to the King of the Belgians

Buckingham Palace, 7th July 1846

MY DEAREST UNCLE,—I have to thank you for your kind letter of the 3rd. It arrived yesterday, which was a very hard day for me. I had to part with Sir R. Peel and Lord Aberdeen, who are irreparable losses to us and the Country; they were both so much overcome that it quite overset me, and we have in them two devoted friends. We felt so safe with them. Never, during the five years that they were with me, did they *ever* recommend a *person* or a thing which was not for my or the Country's best, and never for the Party's advantage only; and the contrast *now* is very striking; there is much less respect and much less high and pure feeling. Then the discretion of Peel, I believe, is unexampled.

Stockmar has, I know, explained to you the state of affairs, which is unexampled, and I think the present Government *very* weak and extremely disunited. What may appear to you as a mistake in November was an inevitable evil. Aberdeen very truly explained it yesterday. 'We had ill luck,' he said; 'if it had not been for this famine in Ireland, which rendered immediate measures necessary, Sir Robert would have prepared them gradually for the change.' Then, besides, the Corn Law Agitation was such that if Peel had not wisely made this change (for which the *whole* Country blesses him), a convulsion would shortly have taken place, and we should have been *forced* to yield what has been granted as a boon. No doubt the breaking up of the Party (which *will* come together again, whether under Peel or some one else) is a very distressing thing. The only thing to be regretted, and I do not know exactly *why* he did it (though we *can* guess), was his praise of *Cobden,* which has shocked people a good deal.

But I can't tell you how sad I am to lose Aberdeen; you can't think what a delightful companion he was; the breaking up of all this intercourse during our journeys, etc., is deplorable.

We have contrived to get a *very* respectable Court.

Albert's use to me, and I may say to the *Country,* by his firmness and sagacity, is beyond all belief in these moments of trial.

We are all well, but I am, of course, a good deal overset by all these tribulations.

Ever your devoted Niece,   VICTORIA R.

I was much touched to see Graham so very much overcome at taking leave of us.

Queen Victoria to Lord John Russell

Osborne, 10th July 1846

... The Queen approves of the pensions proposed by Lord J. Russell, though she cannot conceal from him that she thinks the one to Father Mathew a doubtful proceeding. It is quite true that he has done much good by preaching temperance, but by the aid of superstition, which can hardly be patronised by the Crown.

The Queen is sure that Lord John will like her at all times to speak out her mind, and has, therefore, done so without reserve.

Queen Victoria to Lord John Russell

Buckingham Palace, 3rd August 1846

The Queen has just seen Lord Bessborough, who presses very much for her going to Ireland; she thinks it right to put Lord John Russell in possession of her views on this subject.

It is a journey which must one day or other be undertaken, and

126

which the Queen would be glad to have accomplished, because it must be disagreeable to her that people should speculate whether she *dare* visit one part of her dominions. Much will depend on the proper moment, for, after those speculations, it ought to succeed if undertaken.

The Queen is anxious that when undertaken it should be a National thing, and the good which it is to do must be a permanent and not a transitory advantage to a particular Government, having the appearance of a party move.

As this is not a journey of pleasure like the Queen's former ones, but a State act, it will have to be done with a certain degree of State, and ought to be done handsomely. It cannot be expected that the main expenses of it should fall upon the Civil List, nor would this be able to bear it.

Lord John Russell to Queen Victoria

Chesham Place, 4th August 1846

Lord John Russell presents his humble duty to your Majesty, and is greatly obliged to your Majesty for your Majesty's communication respecting a Royal visit to Ireland. He concurs in your Majesty's observations on that subject. He is of opinion that if the visit partook in any way of a party character, its effects would be mischievous, and not beneficial.

He is also doubtful of the propriety of either incurring very large expense on the part of the public, or of encouraging Irish proprietors to lay out money in show and ceremony at a time when the accounts of the potato crop exhibit the misery and distress of the people in an aggravated shape.

Queen Victoria to Lord John Russell

7th August 1846

With regard to the Statue on the arch of Constitution Hill, the Queen is of opinion that if she is considered individually she is bound by her word, and must allow the Statue to go up, however bad the appearance of it will be. If the constitutional fiction is applied to the case, the Queen acts by the advice of her *responsible* advisers. One Government advised her to give her assent, another advises the withdrawal of that assent. This latter position has been taken in Lord Morpeth's former letter to the Committee, and in the debate in the House of Commons; it must therefore now be adhered to, and whatever is decided must be the act of the Government. It would accordingly be better to keep the word 'Government' at the conclusion of Lord Morpeth's proposed letter, and that the Prince should not go to Town to give an opinion upon the appearance of the figure, when up.

Queen Victoria to the Duke of Wellington

Osborne, 25th November 1846

The Queen has learned from various quarters that there still exists a great anxiety amongst the officers and men who served under the Duke of Wellington's orders in the Peninsula to receive and wear a medal as a testimony that they assisted the Duke in his great undertaking. The Queen not only thinks this wish very reasonable, considering that for recent exploits of infinitely inferior importance such distinctions have been granted by her, but she would feel personally a great satisfaction in being enabled publicly to mark in this way her sense of the great services the Duke of Wellington has rendered to his country and to empower many a brave soldier to wear this token in remembrance of the Duke.

Queen Victoria to Viscount Palmerston

Osborne, 28th November 1846

The Queen has just received Lord Palmerston's draft to Mr Southern,* and must observe that she does not quite approve the tone of it, as it will be likely only to irritate without producing any effect. If our advice is to be taken, it must be given in a spirit of impartiality and fairness. Lord Palmerston's despatch must give the impression that we entirely espouse the cause of the rebels, whose conduct is, to say the least, illegal and very reprehensible. Lord Palmerston like-

---

* Secretary of Legation at Lisbon.

wise takes the nation and the Opposition to be one and the same thing. What we must insist upon is a return to Constitutional Government. And what we may advise is a compromise with the Opposition. What Ministry is to be formed ought to be left to the Portuguese themselves. It being the 28th to-day, the Queen is afraid the despatch went already yesterday. The Queen hopes in future that Lord Palmerston will not put it out of her power to state her opinion in good time.

1847

The Duke of Wellington to Queen Victoria

London, 12th July 1847
(Five in the afternoon)

Field-Marshal the Duke of Wellington presents his humble duty to your Majesty. He submits to your Majesty the expression of his sorrow and shame that your Majesty should be troubled for a moment by anything so insignificant as a statue of himself.

When he first heard of the intention to remove the statue from the pedestal on which it had been placed, he was apprehensive that the measure might be misconstrued and misrepresented in this country as well as abroad.

That feeling was increased when the probable existence of such misconstruction was adverted to in one of the printed papers circulated by the Committee for the erection of the statue; and still farther when the removal became the subject of repeated discussions in Parliament. His daily experience of your Majesty's gracious reception of his endeavours to serve your Majesty; and the events of every day, and the repeated marks which he received of your Majesty's consideration and favour proved clearly, as the Duke stated in his letter to Lord John Russell, that there was no foundation for the misconstruction of the intended act—which undoubtedly existed. The apprehension of such misconstruction had from the first moment created an anxious wish in the mind of the Duke that the removal should be regulated and should be attended by such circumstances as would tend to relieve

QUEEN VICTORIA'S EARLY LETTERS 1847

the transaction from the erroneous but inconvenient impression which had been created.

The Duke apprehended that he might find it impossible to perform the duties with which he had been entrusted, and therefore, when Lord John Russell wrote to him, he deprecated the measure in contemplation; and he rejoices sincerely that your Majesty has been most graciously pleased to countermand the order for the removal of the statue.

All of which is most humbly submitted to your Majesty by your Majesty's most dutiful Subject and most devoted Servant,

WELLINGTON *

Queen Victoria to Lord Palmerston

Buckingham Palace, 12th July 1847

The Queen has been informed by Lord John Russell that the Duke of Wellington is apprehensive that the removal of his statue from the Arch to another pedestal might be constructed as a mark of displeasure on her part. Although the Queen had hoped that her esteem and friendship for the Duke was so well known to the public in general as not to render such a construction possible, and although she had thought that another pedestal would have been more suitable

* The Duke of Wellington wrote to Croker, 19th December 1846: 'I should desire never to move from my principles of indifference and non-interference on the subject of a statue of myself to commemorate my own actions.'
And again, on 14th June 1847, the Duke wrote to Croker: 'It has always been my practice, and is my invariable habit, to say nothing about myself and my own actions.
'More than forty years ago Mr Pitt observed that I talked as little of myself or of my own acts as if I had been an assistant-surgeon of the army....
'I follow the habit of avoiding to talk of myself and of what I have done; with the exception only of occasions when I am urging upon modern contemporaries measures which they don't like, and when I tell them I have some experience, and have had some success in these affairs, and feel they would experience the benefit of attending to my advice, I never talk of myself.
'These are the reasons for which they think that I don't care what they do with the statue.
'But they must be idiots to suppose it possible that a man who is working day and night, without any object in view excepting the public benefit, will not be sensible of a disgrace inflicted upon him by the Sovereign and Government whom he is serving. The ridicule will be felt, if nothing else is!' ...

for *this* statue, and that the Arch might have been more becomingly ornamented in honour of the Duke than by the statue *now* upon it, she has given immediate direction that the Statue should remain in its present situation, and only regrets that this monument should be so unworthy of the great personage to whose honour it has been erected.

Queen Victoria to Lord John Russell

Windsor Castle, 14th October 1847

The Queen has received Lord John Russell's letter, bringing several very important subjects before her. She regrets that the state of the Money Market should still be so uncomfortable, but is sure that the Government cannot by any interference do much to mend matters, though it might easily render them still more complicated, and make itself responsible for a crisis, which it has in no way either brought on or been able to avert.

As to Mr Cobden's appointment to the Poor Law Board, the Queen thinks that he will be well qualified for the place in many respects, and that it will be advantageous to the Government and the Country that his talents should be secured to the service of the State, but the elevation to the Cabinet directly from Covent Garden* strikes her as a very sudden step, calculated to cause much dissatisfaction in many quarters, and setting a dangerous example to agitators in general (for his main reputation Mr Cobden gained as a successful agitator). The Queen therefore thinks it best that Mr Cobden should first enter the service of the Crown, serve as a public functionary in Parliament, and be promoted subsequently to the Cabinet, which step will then become a very natural one. . . .

Viscount Palmerston to Queen Victoria

Foreign Office, 30th October 1847

Viscount Palmerston presents his humble duty to your Majesty, and has many apologies to make for not having attended your Majesty's Council to-day, and the more so as his absence arose from an in-

---

* Free Trade meetings had taken place in Covent Garden Theatre.

advertence which he is almost ashamed to mention. But having got on horseback to ride to the station, with his thoughts occupied with some matters which he was thinking of, he rode mechanically and in a fit of absence to the Nine Elms Station and did not recollect his mistake till he had got there; and although he made the best of his way afterwards to the Paddington Station, he could not get there in time for any train that would have taken him early enough to Windsor. . . .

Viscount Melbourne to Queen Victoria

Brocket Hall, 30th December 1847

Lord Melbourne presents his humble duty to your Majesty. He has received with great pleasure your Majesty's letter of this morning, and reciprocates with the most cordial heartiness your Majesty's good wishes of the season, both for your Majesty and His Royal Highness. Lord Melbourne is pretty well in health, perhaps rather better than he has been, but low and depressed, in spirits for a cause which has long pressed upon his mind, but which he has never before communicated to your Majesty. Lord Melbourne has for a long time found himself much straitened in his pecuniary circumstances, and these embarrassments are growing now every day more and more urgent, so that he dreads before long that he shall be obliged to add another to the list of failures and bankruptcies of which there have lately been so many. This is the true reason why Lord Melbourne has always avoided the honour of the Garter, when pressed upon him by his late Majesty and also by your Majesty. Lord Melbourne knows that the expense of accepting the blue ribbon amounts to £1000, and there has been of late years no period at which it would not have been seriously inconvenient to Lord Melbourne to lay down such a sum.*

* The Queen, through the agency of Mr Anson, advanced Lord Melbourne a considerable sum of money, which seems to have been repaid at his death. Apparently Lord Melbourne's declining health caused him to magnify his difficulties. The report which Mr Anson made shows that he was in no sense seriously embarrassed.

1848

The King of Prussia to Queen Victoria
[*Translation*]

27th February 1848

MOST GRACIOUS QUEEN AND SISTER,—Even at this midnight hour of the day, on the evening of which the awful news from Paris has arrived, I venture to address these lines to your Majesty. God has permitted events which decisively threaten the peace of Europe.

It is an attempt to 'spread the principles of the Revolution by *every* means throughout the whole of Europe.' This programme binds together both these individuals and their parties. The consequences for the peace of the world are *clear* and *certain*. If the revolutionary party carries out its programme, 'The sovereignty of the people,' my minor crown will be broken, no less certainly than the mighty crowns of your Majesty, and a fearful scourge will be laid upon the nations; a century [will follow] of rebellion, of lawlessness, and of godlessness. The late King did not dare to write 'by the Grace of God.' *We*, however, call ourselves King 'by the Grace of God,' because it is true. Well, then, most gracious Queen, let us now show to men, to the peoples threatened with disruption and nameless misery, both *that* we understand our sacred office and *how* we understand it. God has placed in your Majesty's hands, in the hands of the two Emperors, in those of the German Federation, and in mine, a power, which, if it now acts in union and harmony, with reliance on Heaven, is able humanly speaking, to enforce, with certainty, the maintenance of the peace of the world. This power is *not that of arms,* for these, more than ever, must only afford the *ultima ratio.*

The power I mean is 'the power of united speech.' In the year 1830 the use of this immeasurable power was criminally neglected. But now I think the danger is much more pressing than it was then. This power is divided among *us* in equal portions. I possess the smallest portion of it, and your Majesty has by far the greatest share. That share is so great that your Majesty, by your powerful word, might alone carry out the task. But the certainty of victory lies, subject to the Divine blessing, solely in our utterance being united. This must be our message to France; 'that all of us are cordial well-wishers to France; we do not grudge her all possible welfare and glory; we mean never to encroach on it, and we will stand by the new Government as by the old, *foi de gentils-hommes.* But the first breach of the peace, be it with reference to Italy, Belgium, or Germany would be, undoubtedly and at the same time, a breach with 'all of us,' and we should, with all the power that God has given us, let France feel by *sea* and by *land*, as in the years '13, '14, and '15, what our union may mean.'

Now I bless Providence for having placed Lord Palmerston at the head of your Foreign Office, and keeping him there at this very moment. During the last quarter of the past year I could not always cordially agree with him. His genuine British disposition will honour this open confession. All the more frankly may I now express the hopes which rise in me, from the very fact of *his* holding that office at the present moment; for a more active, more vivid, more energetic Minister of foreign affairs, a man that would more indefatigably pursue great aims, your Majesty could probably never have. If at this grave hour he sets himself to proclaim that our forces are united; if he himself utters his message as befits St George, he will earn the blessings of millions, and the blessing of God and of the world will rest on your Majesty's sacred head. That I am your Majesty's and *Old England's* most faithful and most devoted brother and companion, you are aware, and I mean to prove it. On both knees I adjure you, use, for the welfare of Europe, *'Engellands England.'*

With these words I fall at your Majesty's feet, most gracious Queen, and remain your Majesty's most faithfully devoted, most attached Servant and good Brother,   FREDERIC WILLIAM

Post scriptum, 28th, in the evening

I venture to open my letter again, for this day has brought us news from France, which one can only call *horrible.* According to what we hear, there is no longer left a King in France. A regency, a government, and the most complete anarchy has ensued, under the

Buckingham Palace: the Princess Royal sitting for a portrait by Winterhalter
From an engraving by William Radclyffe after Sir John Gilbert

The State Visit of the Emperor Napoleon III (see pp. 210–14): the Queen and Prince Albert with the Emperor and Empress at Covent Garden, 19th April 1855

From a lithograph by G. H. Thomas after Louis Haghe

name of the Republic—a condition of things in which, at first, there will be no possibility of communicating with the people, infuriated with crime. In case a Government should evolve itself out of this chaos, I conscientiously hold that the 'united word' of the great Powers, such as I have indicated in the preceding pages, should be made known, *without any modification, to the new holders of power.* Your Majesty's gracious friendship will certainly not take amiss this addition to my letter, though it be not conformable to strict etiquette.

The fate of the poor old King, of the Duchess of Orleans, of the whole honourable and amiable family, cuts me to the heart, for up to this time we do not know what has become of any of them. We owe Louis Philippe eighteen happy years of peace. No noble heart must forget that. And yet—who would not recognise the avenging hand of the King of kings in all this?

I kiss your Majesty's hands.

Mr Featherstonhaugh to Viscount Palmerston*

Havre, 3rd March 1848

MY DEAR LORD PALMERSTON,—It was a hair-trigger affair altogether, but thanks be to God everything has gone off admirably. I was obliged to abandon the plan of trusting the King in a fishing-boat from Trouville. The weather was very stormy; had he attempted to find the steamer, he might have failed; for the sea was in a furious state and the wind ahead. There was also the danger of the fishing-boat being lost, a contingency the very idea of which made me miserable.

I therefore abandoned the plan altogether, and after much and careful reflection determined to execute one more within my control, and the boldness of which, though trying to the nerves, was its very essence for success. It was to bring the King and Queen into Havre itself before anybody could suspect such a dangerous intention, and have everything ready for their embarkation to a minute. To carry out the plan, I wanted vigilant, intelligent, and firm agents, and I found them as it turned out. It was known to me that the

* British Consul at Havre. This letter was submitted to the Queen by Lord Palmerston.

lower classes suspected it was M. Guizot concealed at Trouville, and as some sinister occurrence might reasonably be expected there, I sent a faithful person into Calvados. It was high time. The mob had assembled at the place where the King was, who had to slip out at the back door and walk two leagues on foot. At length he reached a small cottage belonging to a gardener at Honfleur, where the Queen was. This was half-past six o'clock a.m. yesterday. My agent saw the King and Queen, who, after some conversation, sent him back with this message, that they 'would wait where they were until they again heard from me, and would carry out my final arrangements with exactitude, as far as it depended upon them.' I now instructed Captain Paul to be ready at half-past seven p.m., when it would be dark, to have his water hot, ready to get up steam; to have only a rope moored to the quay with an anchor astern; to expect me with a party a little before eight p.m., and as soon as I had got on board with my party and told him to push off, he was to let me go on shore, cut his rope and cable, get into the middle of the Basin, up with his steam and jib and push for England. Not a word was to be spoken on board.

To get the King here from Honfleur the following method was adopted: M. Bresson, a loyal and intelligent officer in the French Navy and well known to the King, and Mr Jones, my Vice-Consul and principal Clerk, went in the steam ferry-boat a quarter before five p.m. to Honfleur. From the landing-place it is three-quarters of a mile to the place where the King and Queen were concealed. The ferry-boat was to leave Honfleur for Havre a quarter before seven o'clock. I had given M. Bresson a passport for Mr and Mrs Smith, and with this passport the King was to walk to the landing-place, where he was to be met by my Vice-Consul and be governed by him.

If the *gens d'armes* disputed his passport Mr Jones was to vouch for its regularity, and say that he was sent by me to conduct Mr Smith to Havre, who was my Uncle. M. Bresson was to follow with the Queen, and the rest of the suite were to come to the ferry-boat one after another, but none of the party were to know each other. The ferry-boat was to arrive in Havre about half-past seven, and I was to do the rest. A white pocket-handkerchief was to be twice exhibited as a signal that all was right so far. The difficulty of the

gens d'armes being infinitely more to be provided against and apprehended here, I first confidentially communicated to the greatest gossips
in the town that I had seen a written statement from an official
person that the King had reached England in a fishing-boat from
the neighbourhood of Tréport, and then got some persons whom I
could rely upon, sons of my tradesmen here who are in the National
Guard, to be near the steamer that was to receive the King, to give
me their assistance if it should be necessary, on account of the
turbulence of the crowd, to embark some friends of mine who were
going to England. And if an extraordinary number of *gens d'armes*
were stationed at the steamer, and they hesitated about letting my
Uncle go on board, then about one hundred yards off I had two
persons who were to pretend a quarrel and a fight, to which I knew
the *gens d'armes* would all go as well as the crowd. In the meantime
I hoped that as Captain Paul made no noise with his steam that
the crowd would not assemble, and that we might find no *gens
d'armes*. The anxiously expected moment at length arrived. The
ferry-boat steamer came to the quay; it was almost dark, but I
saw the white pocket-handkerchief. There was a great number of
passengers, which favoured the debarkation. When half of them
were out, the trembling Queen came up the ladder. I took her hand,
told her it was me, and M. Bresson walked with her towards our
steamer. At last came the King, disguised, his whiskers shaved off,
a sort of casquette on his head, and a coarse overcoat, and immense
goggles over his eyes. Not being able to see well, he stumbled, when
I advanced, took his hand and said, 'Ah, dear Uncle, I am delighted
to see you.' Upon which he answered, 'My dear George, I am glad
you are here.' The English about me now opened the crowd for
their Consul, and I moved off to a quiet and shaded part of the
quay. But my dear Uncle talked so loud and so much that I had
the greatest difficulty to make him keep silence. At length we reached
the steamer; it was like a clock-work movement. The crowd was
again opened for me. I conducted the King to a state-room below,
gave him some information, and having personally ascertained that
the Queen was in her cabin, and being very much touched with her
tears and her grateful acknowledgments, I respectfully took my leave,
gave the Captain the word to cut loose, and scrambled ashore. In

twenty minutes the steamer was outside, steaming away for England. I drove down to the jetty, and had that last satisfaction of seeing her beyond all possibility of recall, and then drove home. Much has been said this morning about the mysterious departure of Captain Paul, and I have been obliged to confess that the gentleman I was seen conducting on board was a brother of the King of Naples, who was immensely frightened without cause, and that I had engaged the steamer for him and his family. Many think, however, that it was the King, but then again that could not be if he crossed over from Tréport in a fishing-boat. We have got everybody completely mystified, and there are only four persons in the secret, who will all remain in the same story.

I have scribbled amidst the most hurried engagements, this little narrative, believing that it would interest your Lordship. It has the interest of romance and the support of truth. I have the honour to be, etc.   G. W. FEATHERSTONHAUGH

Information has just reached me that one hour after the King and Queen left their hiding-place last night, and just when I was embarking them, an officer and three *gens d'armes* came to the place to arrest him. They were sent by the new Republican *Préfet*. It appears that the man who gave him refuge had confessed who he was as soon as the King had left Trouville, and had betrayed the King's hiding-place at Honfleur. What an escape! Your Lordship will see a paragraph in the enclosed newspaper not altogether false. We in the secret know nothing about Louis Philippe; we know something about the Count of Syracuse and something about Mr William Smith. If it leaks out, it must come from England. Here no one has any proof. In the meantime almost everybody here is delighted to think that he may have escaped.

Lord John Russell to Queen Victoria

House of Commons, 3rd March 1848

Lord John Russell presents his humble duty to your Majesty: he has read with deep interest the affecting letter of the fallen King.

After the vicissitudes of a long life, it may be no irremediable calamity if a Prince of great powers of mind and warm domestic affections is permitted by Providence to end his days in peace and tranquillity.

Of course all enmity to his projects as a King ceases with his deposition.

M. Guizot came to London from Dover at half-past six.

Viscount Palmerston to Queen Victoria

Carlton Gardens, 5th March 1848

Viscount Palmerston presents his humble duty to your Majesty, and cannot see that there could be any objection to the King and Queen of the French coming to town to visit your Majesty, and indeed, on the contrary, it would seem under all the circumstances of the case natural that they should be anxious to see your Majesty, and that your Majesty should be desirous of receiving them.

Viscount Palmerston was sure that your Majesty would read with interest Mr Featherstonhaugh's account of the manner in which he managed the escape of the King and Queen of the French. It is like one of Walter Scott's best tales, and the arrangements and the execution of them do great credit to Mr Featherstonhaugh, who will be highly gratified to learn, as Viscount Palmerston proposes to inform him, that your Majesty has approved his conduct. Mr Featherstonhaugh has also probably rendered a good service to the Provisional Government, who would have been much embarrassed if their Commissioner had arrested the King and Queen.

Queen Victoria to the King of the Belgians

Buckingham Palace, 4th April 1848

MY DEAREST UNCLE,—I have to thank you for three most kind letters, of the 18th and 25th March, and of the 1st. Thank God, I am *particularly strong* and *well* in *every possible respect,* which is a blessing in these *awful, sad, heart-breaking* times. From the first I heard all that passed, and my only thoughts and talk were—Politics; but I never was calmer and quieter or less nervous. *Great* events make me quiet and calm, and little trifles fidget me and irritate my nerves. But *I feel* grown old and serious, and the future is very dark. God, however, will come to help and protect us, and we must keep up our spirits. *Germany* makes me so sad; on the other hand, Belgium is a real pride and happiness. ....

Lord John Russell to the Prince Albert

Chesham Palace, 9th April 1848

SIR,—The Cabinet have had the assistance of the Duke of Wellington in framing their plans for to-morrow.

Colonel Rowan* advised that the procession should be formed, and allowed to come as far as the bridge they may choose to pass, and should there be stopped. He thinks this is the only way to avoid a fight. If, however, the Chartists fire and draw their swords and use their daggers, the Military are to be called out.

I have no doubt of their easy triumph over a London mob.

But any loss of life will cause a deep and rankling resentment. I trust, for this and every reason, that all may pass off quietly. I have the honour to be, your Royal Highness's most obedient Servant,

J. RUSSELL

The Prince Albert to Lord John Russell

Osborne, 10th April 1848

MY DEAR LORD JOHN,—To-day the strength of the Chartists and all evil-disposed people in the country will be brought to the test against the force of the law, the Government, and the good sense of the country. I don't feel doubtful for a moment who will be found the stronger, but should be exceedingly mortified if anything like a commotion was to take place, as it would shake *that* confidence which the whole of Europe reposes in our stability at this moment, and upon which will depend the prosperity of the country. I have enquired a good deal into the state of employment about London, and I find, to my great regret, that the number of workmen of all trades out of employment is *very* large, and that it has been increased by the

* Chief Commissioner of Police, afterwards Sir C. Rowan, K.C.B. The Chartist meeting had been fixed for the 10th.

reduction of all the works under Government, owing to the clamour for economy in the House of Commons. Several hundred workmen have been discharged at Westminster Palace; at Buckingham Palace much fewer hands are employed than are really wanted; the formation of Battersea Park has been suspended, etc., etc. Surely this is not the moment for the tax-payers to economise upon the working classes! And though I don't wish our Government to follow Louis Blanc in his system of *organisation du travail,* I think the Government is bound to do what it can to help the working classes over the present moment of distress. It may do this consistently with real economy in its own works, whilst the reductions on the part of the Government are followed by all private individuals as a sign of the times. I have before this spoken to Lord Morpeth upon this subject, but I wish to bring it specially under your consideration at the present moment. Ever yours truly,   ALBERT

Lord John Russell to Queen Victoria

Downing Street, 10th April 1848
(2 p.m.)

Lord John Russell presents his humble duty to your Majesty, and has the honour to state that the Kennington Common Meeting has proved a complete failure.

About 12,000 or 15,000 persons met in good order. Feargus O'Connor, upon arriving upon the ground in a car, was ordered by Mr Mayne to come and speak to him. He immediately left the car and came, looking pale and frightened, to Mr Mayne. Upon being told that the meeting would not be prevented, but that no procession would be allowed to pass the bridges, he expressed the utmost thanks, and begged to shake Mr Mayne by the hand. He then addressed the crowd, advising them to disperse, and after rebuking them for their folly he went off in a cab to the Home Office, where he repeated to Sir George Grey his thanks, his fears, and his assurances that the crowd should disperse quietly. Sir George Grey said he had done very rightly, but that the force at the bridges should not be diminished.

Mr F. O'Connor—'Not a man should be taken away. The Government have been quite right. I told the Convention that if they had been the Government they never would have allowed such a meeting.'

The last account gave the numbers as about 5,000 rapidly dispersing.

The mob was in good humour, and any mischief that now takes place will be the act of individuals; but it is to be hoped the preparations made will daunt those wicked but not brave men.

The accounts from the country are good. Scotland is quiet. At Manchester, however, the Chartists are armed, and have bad designs.

A quiet termination of the present ferment will greatly raise us in foreign countries.

Lord John Russell trusts your Majesty has profited by the sea air.

Lord John Russell to Queen Victoria

Chesham Place, 15th April 1848

Lord John Russell has a letter from Lord Clarendon to-day in better spirits, but somewhat fearing an outbreak in Dublin tonight. He speaks confidently of the disposition of the troops.

Lord John Russell cannot wonder that your Majesty has felt deeply the events of the last six weeks. The King of the French has brought upon his own family, upon France, and upon Europe a great calamity. A moderate and constitutional Government at home, coupled with an abstinence from ambitious projects for his family abroad, might have laid the foundation of permanent peace, order, and freedom in Europe. Selfishness and cunning have destroyed that which honesty and wisdom might have maintained. It is impossible not to pity the innocent victims of the misconduct of Louis Philippe. Still less can one refrain from regarding with dread the fearful state of Germany, of her princes, her nobles, and her tempest-tossed people.

The example of Great Britain, may, however, secure an interval of reflection for Europe. The next six months will be very trying, but they may end with better prospects than we can now behold. It was impossible that the exclusion of free speaking and writing which formed the essence of Prince Metternich's system could continue. It might have been reformed quietly; it has fallen with a crash which spreads ruin and death around.

Lady John is deeply grateful for the congratulations of your Majesty and the Prince. She is going on well to-day.

Queen Victoria to Lord John Russell

Osborne, 16th April 1848

The Queen has received Lord John Russell's letter. The state of Ireland is most alarming and most anxious; altogether, there is so much inflammable matter all around us that it makes one tremble. Still, the events of Monday must have a calming and salutary effect. Lord John Russell's remarks about Europe, and the unfortunate and calamitous policy of the Government of the poor King of the French are most true. But is he not even most to be pitied for being the cause of such misery? (Though perhaps he does not attribute it to himself), for, to see all his hopes thus destroyed, his pride humbled, his children—whom he loves dearly—ruined—is not this enough to make a man wretched? and indeed much to be pitied; for *he* cannot feel *he* could *not* have prevented all this. Still Guizot is more to blame; *he* was the responsible adviser of all this policy: he is *no* Bourbon, and he ought to have behaved differently. Had the poor King died in 1844 after he came here, and before that most unfortunate Spanish marriages question was started, he would have deservedly gone down to posterity as a great monarch. *Now,* what will be his name in history? His fate is a great *moral!*

With regard to Germany, Prince Metternich is the cause of half the misfortune. His advice was taken by almost all the sovereigns of that country, and it has kept them from doing in time what has now been torn from them with the loss of many rights which they need not have sacrificed. We heard yesterday that the Archduke John had arrived at Frankfort. This is a wise measure, and may do much good and prevent much evil, as he is a popular and most distinguished prince. . . .

Queen Victoria to Viscount Palmerston

Osborne, 1st May 1848

The Queen has this morning received Lord Palmerston's letter.* She cannot see any reason for deviating from the established rules,

---

* M. de Tallenay had arrived in London with a letter from M. Lamartine, accrediting him as provisional *chargé d'affaires* of the French Government, and Lord Palmerston had suggested to the Queen that etiquette would not be violated by inviting him to a Court Ball.

and inviting to Court Frenchmen who are not recognised in their official capacity, and have no natural representatives to present them as private individuals. As an invitation cannot be claimed by them, the omission of it ought not to lead to any misrepresentation; whilst the contrary, under the fiction of their being private individuals, might lead to misconstruction and to most inconvenient precedents.

Queen Victoria to the King of the Belgians

Buckingham Palace, 16th May 1848

MY DEAREST UNCLE,—I have just heard the news of the extraordinary confusion at Paris, which must end in a *Blutbad*. Lamartine has quite lost all influence by yielding to and supporting Ledru Rollin! It seems inexplicable! In Germany, too, everything looks most anxious, and I *tremble* for the result of the Parliament at Frankfort. I am *so* anxious for the fate of the poor smaller Sovereigns, which it would be infamous to sacrifice. I feel it *much* more than Albert, as it would break my heart to see Coburg *reduced*.

Many thanks for your kind and dear letter of the 13th. Thank God! that with you everything goes on so well. I will take care and let Lord Normanby know your kind expressions. The visit to old Claremont was a touching one, and it seemed an incomprehensible dream to see them all there. They bear up wonderfully. Nothing can be kinder than the Queen-Dowager's behaviour towards them all. The poor Duchess of Gloster is again in one of her nervous states, and gave us a dreadful fright at the Christening by quite forgetting where she was, and coming and kneeling at my feet in the midst of the service. Imagine our horror!

I must now conclude. The weather is beautiful, but too hot for me. Ever your devoted Niece, VICTORIA R.

Viscount Palmerston to Queen Victoria

Carlton Gardens, 26th June 1848

Viscount Palmerston presents his humble duty to your Majesty, and is sorry he is not able to submit to your Majesty the proposed draft to Sir Hamilton Seymour to go by to-night's mail, as he has not succeeded in settling the wording of it with Lord John Russell, and is therefore obliged to defer it till the next mail.

Queen Victoria to Lord John Russell

Buckingham Palace, 26th June 1848

The Queen sends this letter, which she has just received from Lord Palmerston. No remonstrance has any effect with Lord Palmerston. Lord John Russell should ask the Duke of Bedford to tell him of the conversation the Queen had with the Duke the other night about Lord Palmerston.

Queen Victoria to Viscount Palmerston

Buckingham Palace, 1st July 1848

The Queen has not yet answered Lord Palmerston's letter of the 29th. She cannot conceal from him that she is ashamed of the policy which we are pursuing in this Italian controversy in abetting wrong, and this for the object of gaining *influence* in Italy. The Queen does not consider influence so gained as an advantage, and though this influence is to be acquired in order to do good, she is afraid that the fear of losing it again will always stand in the way of them. At least in the countries where the greatest stress has been laid on that influence, and the greatest exertions made for it, the *least good* has been done —the Queen means in Spain, Portugal, and Greece. Neither is there any kind of consistency in the line we take about Italy and that we follow with regard to Schleswig; both cases are perfectly alike (with the difference perhaps that there is a question of right mixed up in that of Schleswig); whilst we upbraid Prussia, caution her, etc., etc., we say nothing to Charles Albert except that if he did not wish to take *all* the Emperor of Austria's Italian Dominions, we would not lay any *obstacles* in the way of his moderation. The Queen finds in Lord Palmerston's last despatch to Chevalier Bunsen the following passage: 'And it is manifest and indisputable that no territory or state, which is not now according to the Treaty of 1815 included in the German Confederation, can be added to that territory without the consent of the Sovereign of that territory or state.' How does this agree with our position relative to the incorporation of Lombardy into the states of the King of Sardinia?

Queen Victoria to the King of the Belgians

Buckingham Palace, 11th July 1848

MY DEAREST UNCLE,—For another kind and dear letter of the 8th, I have much to thank you. The prosperity of dear little Belgium is a bright star in the stormy night all around. May God bless and prosper you all, for ever and ever!

Since the 24th February I feel an uncertainty in everything existing, which (uncertain as all human affairs must be) one never felt before. When one thinks of one's children, their education, their future—and prays for them—I always think and say to myself, 'Let them grow up fit for *whatever station* they may be placed in—*high or low.*' This one never thought of before, but I *do* always now. Altogether one's whole disposition is so changed—*bores* and trifles which one would have complained of bitterly a few months ago, one looks upon as good things and quite a blessing—provided one can *keep one's position in quiet!* ...

Queen Victoria to Sir George Grey

Buckingham Palace, 14th July 1848

The Queen has received Sir George Grey's letter of yesterday, and has considered the proposed alteration in the mode of preparing Commissions for Officers in the Army. The Queen does not at all object to the amount of trouble which the signature of so many Commissions has hitherto entailed upon her, as she feels amply compensated by the advantage of keeping up a personal connection between the Sovereign and the Army, and she very much doubts whether the Officers generally would not feel it as a slight if, instead of their Commissions bearing the Queen's sign-manual, they were in future only to receive a certificate from the Secretary of War that they have been commissioned.

She therefore prefers matters to remain on their old footing. ...

Queen Victoria to Lord John Russell

Osborne, 25th July 1848

The Queen sends Lord John Russell the enclosed Despatch from Lord Normanby, with a draft in answer to it which was sent for her approval, but which she really cannot approve. The Queen must tell Lord John what she has repeatedly told Lord Palmerston, but without apparent effect, that the establishment of an *entente cordiale with the French Republic*, for the purpose of driving the Austrians out of *their dominions* in Italy, would be a *disgrace* to this country. That the French would attach the greatest importance to it and gain the greatest advantage by it there can be no doubt of; but how will England appear before the world *at the moment* when she is struggling to maintain her supremacy in Ireland, and boasts to stand by treaties with regard to her European relations, having declined all this time to interfere in Italy or to address one word of caution to the Sardinian Government on account of its attack on Austria, and having refused to mediate when called upon to do so by Austria, because the terms were not good enough for Sardinia, if she should now ally herself with the arch-enemy of Austria to interfere *against her* at the moment when she has recovered in some degree her position in the Venetian territory?

The notion of establishing a Venetian State under French guarantee is too absurd. Lord Palmerston in his draft says that we believe that the French plan would be agreed to by Austria. Now this is completely at variance with every account, report, or despatch we have received from Verona, Innspruck, or Vienna; however, Lord Palmerston hints that the King of Sardinia might expect still better terms. . . .

Queen Victoria to Viscount Palmerston

Osborne, 20th August 1848

The Queen has received an *autograph* letter from the Archduke John (in answer to the private letter she had written to him through Lord Cowley), which has been cut open at the Foreign Office. The Queen wishes Lord Palmerston to take care that this does not happen again. The opening of official letters even, addressed to the Queen, which she has *of late* observed, is really not becoming, and ought to be discontinued, as it used never to be the case formerly.

Queen Victoria to the King of the Belgians

Osborne, 29th August 1848

MY DEAREST UNCLE,—Most warmly do I thank you for your very kind and dear letter of the 26th, with so many good wishes for that *dearest* of days. It is indeed to me one of eternal thankfulness, for a purer, more perfect being than my beloved Albert the Creator could *not* have sent into this troubled world. I feel that I could *not* exist without him, and that I should sink under the troubles and annoyances and *dégoûts* of my *very* difficult position, were it not for *his* assistance, protection, guidance, and comfort. Truly do I thank you for your *great* share in bringing about our marriage.

Stockmar I do not quite understand, and I cannot believe that he *really wishes to ruin* all the smaller States, though his principal object is that unity which I fear he will *not* obtain.

I do not either at all agree in his wish that Prussia should take the lead; his love for Prussia is to me incomprehensible, for it is the country of all others which the *rest* of Germany dislikes. Stockmar cannot be my good old friend if he has such notions of injustice as I hear attributed to him. But whatever they may be, I do *not* believe the *Ausführung* to be possible....

Memorandum by Queen Victoria

Balmoral, 19th September 1848

I said to Lord John Russell, that I must mention to him a subject, which was a serious one, one which I had delayed mentioning for some time, but which I felt I must speak quite openly to him upon now, namely about Lord Palmerston; that I felt really I could hardly go on with him, that I had no confidence in him, and that it made me seriously anxious and uneasy for the welfare of the country and for the peace of Europe in general, and that I felt very uneasy from one day to another as to what might happen. Lord John replied that he was aware of it; that he had considered the matter already, having heard from his brother (the Duke of Bedford) how strongly I felt about it; that he felt the truth of all that I had said, but that, on the other hand, Lord Palmerston was a very able man, entirely master of his office and affairs, and a very good colleague, never making any difficulties about other questions, but (certainly *unreasonably*) complaining of other people mixing with and interfering in the affairs of his office. I said that ... I fully believed that the Spanish marriage question, which had been the original cause of so many present misfortunes, would never have become so *embrouillé* had it not been for Lord Palmerston. This led Lord John to say, that though he disapproved the length of Lord Palmerston's correspondence, still that we could not have done otherwise than object to the marriage. This is true enough. I repeated that all that had been done in Italy last winter had also done harm, as it was done by *Lord Palmerston*, who was distrusted everywhere abroad, which Lord John regretted. I said that I thought that he often endangered the honour of England by taking a very prejudiced and one-sided view of a question; ... that his writings were always as bitter as gall and did a great harm, which Lord John entirely assented to, and that I often felt quite ill from anxiety; that I wished Lord Clarendon (who, I had heard, was tired of Ireland) could come over and be Secretary of State for Foreign Affairs, and Lord Palmerston go to Ireland as Lord-Lieutenant. Lord John said nothing would be better, for that he was sure that Lord Palmerston would make an admirable Lord-Lieutenant, but that another thing to be considered was the danger of making Lord Palmerston an enemy by displacing him, that Lord Minto (who was formerly a great friend and admirer of Lord Palmerston's) had told Lady John when she spoke to him on the subject of placing Lord Palmerston in another office, that *he* (Lord Palmerston) would certainly turn against the Government if displaced. I said that might be, but that sometimes there were great interests at stake which exceeded the danger of offending one man, and that this was here the case; Lord John said it was very true, but that at moments like these one of course was anxious not to do anything which could cause internal trouble. I admitted this, but repeated my anxiety, which Lord John quite understood, though he thought I a little overrated it, and said I was afraid that some day I should have to tell Lord John that I could not put up with Lord Palmerston any longer, which might be very disagreeable and awkward.

It ended by Lord John's promising to bear the subject in mind, and I must say that he took it all just as I could wish.

VICTORIA R.

Queen Victoria to Lord John Russell

Osborne 7th October 1848

The Queen sends Lord Palmerston's answer to her last letter, of which the Queen has sent a copy to Lord John Russell, and encloses likewise a copy of her present answer. The partiality of Lord Palmerston in this Italian question really *surpasses all conception*, and makes the Queen *very uneasy* on account of the character and honour of England, and on account of the danger to which the peace of Europe will be exposed. It is now clearly proved by Baron Wessenberg that upon the conclusion of the Armistice with Sardinia, negotiations for peace would have speedily been entered into, had our *mediation* not been offered to the King, to whom the offer of Lombardy was too tempting not to accept, and now that promise is by fair or unfair means to be made good. The Queen cannot see any principle in this, as the principle upon which Lord Palmerston goes is *Italian Nationality and Independence from a foreign Yoke and Tyranny*. How can the Venetian territory then be secured to Austria and if this is done, on what ground can Lombardy be wrung from her? It is really not safe to settle such important matters without principle and by personal *passion* alone. When the *French* Government say they cannot control public feeling, Lord Palmerston takes this as an unalterable fact, and as a sufficient reason to make the Austrians give up Lombardy; when, however, the *Austrian* Government say they cannot give up Lombardy on account of the feeling of the Army which had just reconquered it with their blood and under severe privations and sufferings, Lord Palmerston flippantly tells the Austrian Government, 'if that were so, the Emperor had better abdicate and make General Radetzky Emperor.' When Charles Albert burned the whole of the suburbs of Milan to keep up the delusion that he meant to defend the town, Lord Palmerston said nothing; and now that the Austrian Governor has prohibited revolutionary placards on the walls, and prolonged the period at which arms are to be surrendered, at the end of which persons concealing arms are to be tried by court-martial, he writes to Vienna: 'that this savage proclamation, which savours more of the barbarous usages of centuries long gone by than of the spirit of the present times, must strike everybody as a proof of the fear by which the Austrian Commander is inspired,' etc., etc., etc.

Venice was to have been made over to Austria by the Armistice, and now that this has not been done, Austria is not even to retake it, in order (as Lord Normanby says) to keep something in hand against which Austria is to make further concessions. Is all this fair? In the meantime, from the account of our Consul at Venice, the French agents are actively employed in intrigues against Austria in that town, and have asked him to assist, which he refused. Lord Palmerston merely approved his conduct, and did not write a line to Paris about it. Now the question at issue is not even to be submitted to a Conference of European powers, but to be settled by the French Republic and Lord Palmerston alone, Lord Normanby being the instrument who has pledged himself over and over again for Italian *independence* (so called). If Austria makes peace with Sardinia, and gives her Italian provinces separate National Institutions with a liberal constitutional Government, *who can force* upon her another arrangement?

Queen Victoria to Viscount Palmerston

Osborne, 8th October 1848

The Queen cannot refrain from telling Lord Palmerston what a painful impression the perusal of a draft of his to Lord Normanby referring to the affairs of Greece has made upon her, being so little in accordance with the calm dignity which she likes to see in all the proceedings of the British Government; she was particularly struck by the language in which Lord Palmerston speaks of King Otho, a Sovereign with whom she stands in friendly relations, and the asperity against the Government of the King of the French, who is really sufficiently lowered and suffering for the mistakes he may have committed, and that of all this a copy is to be placed in the hands of the Foreign Minister of the French *Republic,* the Queen can only see with much regret.

Queen Victoria to Earl Grey

Windsor Castle, 26th October 1848

The Queen has received Lord Grey's letter, and is glad to hear that Sir H. Smith's wound was not of a serious nature. The loss of so many officers, the Queen is certain, proceeds from their wearing a blue coat whilst the men are in scarlet; the Austrians lost a great proportion of officers in Italy from a similar difference of dress.

As to the Medal for Major Edwardes, the Queen did not approve but disapprove the step, and wished the Bath to be given instead, which has been done. The medals for troops in general (given by the East India Company) are a new and doubtful thing, and now it is proposed to reward even a special case of personal distinction by the *Company's* conferring a mark of honour. Lord Grey will agree with the Queen that it will be better not to establish two fountains of honour in the Realm. If the East India Company wish to mark the approbation, perhaps they might send Major Edwardes a fine sword or something of that kind.

Queen Victoria to the King of the Belgians

Windsor Castle, 21st November 1848

MY DEAREST UNCLE,— ... You will grieve to hear that our good, dear, old friend Melbourne is dying; there is *no* hope, and I enclose a pretty letter of Lady Beauvale's, which I think will interest you, and which I beg you to return. One cannot forget how good and kind and amiable he was, and it brings back so many recollections to my mind, though, God knows! I never wish that time back again. ...

Viscount Palmerston to Queen Victoria

Brocket Hall, 25th November 1848

Viscount Palmerston presents his humble duty to your Majesty, and has to state that Viscount Melbourne was released from further suffering at about six o'clock yesterday afternoon. His bodily strength had been rapidly declining during the last few days, and it was only at intervals that he retained any degree of apparent consciousness. The last transition took place quietly and with almost imperceptible gradation.

Pope Pius IX to Queen Victoria

To the Most Serene and Potent Sovereign Victoria, the Illustrious Queen of England, Pius Papa Nonus.

Most Serene and Most Potent Queen, Greeting! Your Royal Majesty has already learned what a subversion of public affairs has taken place at Rome, and what utterly unheard-of-violence was, on the 16th of the late month of November, offered to us in our very Palace of the Quirinal, in consequence of a nefarious conspiracy of abandoned and most turbulent men. Hence, in order to avoid more violent commotions and more serious dangers, as likewise for the purpose of freely performing the functions of our apostolic Ministry, we, not without the deepest and most heartfelt sorrow, have been constrained to depart for a time from our Holy City, and from the whole state of our pontifical dominions; and in the meanwhile we come as far as Gaëta, where, as soon as we had arrived, our first care was to declare to our subjects the sentiments of our mind and will, by a public edict, a copy of which we transmit to your Royal Majesty, together with these our letters. Without doubt, through your own wisdom, you will perfectly understand, Most Serene and Potent Sovereign, that amongst the other most cruel difficulties by which we are pressed, we must be chiefly solicitous concerning those subject to our temporal rule and the rights and possessions of the Roman Church, which, moreover, your august Uncle and the other Princes of Europe protected with so much zeal. But we do not in the least doubt that, in conformity with your exalted magnanimity, your justice, and your known desire to maintain order in public affairs, you will by no means suffer this same to be wanting to us at this most lamentable time. Trusting indeed in this hope, we do not cease, in the humility and affliction of our heart, from earnestly beseeching God, the All Good and All Great, that He may heap upon your Royal Majesty and your whole House all true and solid prosperity, and that He may unite you with us in perfect charity.

Given at Gaëta, the 4th day of December 1848, in the third year of our Pontificate.   Pius PP. IX*

Queen Victoria to the King of the Belgians

Osborne, 19th December 1848

My DEAREST, KINDEST UNCLE,—Your dear letter, full of interesting topics, which I received yesterday, gave me great pleasure, and I thank you much for it. The success of Louis Napoleon† is an extraordinary event, but valuable as a universal condemnation of the Republic since February.

It will, however, perhaps be more difficult to get rid of him again than one at *first* may imagine. Nemours thinks it better that none of themselves should be *called* into action for some time to come. I fear that *he feels* now that they *ought* to have *foreseen* the dangers in February, and *ought not* to have yielded; when I said to him that the Pope had declared that he would *never* quit Rome, and *did so do* the *very next day*, he said: 'Ah! mon Dieu, on se laisse entraîner dans ces moments.' Louise said to me that *her Father* had *so often declared he would never quit Paris alive*, so that when she heard of his flight she always believed it was untrue and he must be dead. . . .

1849

Draft]   *Queen Victoria to Pope Pius IX*

MOST EMINENT SIR,—I have received the letter which your Holiness addressed to me from Gaëta on the 4th of December last, and in which you acquaint me that in consequence of the violent proceedings

---

* This letter was suitably acknowledged in general terms.
† He was elected President on 10th December, by an immense majority.

of certain of your subjects, you had felt yourself obliged to depart from Rome, and for a time to quit your dominions. I assure your Holiness that I have been deeply pained at the intelligence of the events to which your letter refers, and that I do the fullest justice to the motives which induced your Holiness to withdraw for a time from your capital. Your Holiness has given so many proofs of being animated by a sincere desire to improve the condition of the people whom, under Divine Providence, you have been chosen to govern, and the clemency of your heart and the rectitude of your intentions are so well known and so truly appreciated, that I cannot but hope that the trials which you have experienced in consequence of popular commotion will speedily come to an end, and will be succeeded by a cordial, good understanding between your Holiness and the Roman people. I request your Holiness to believe that it would afford me real pleasure to be able in any degree to contribute to a result so much to be desired; and I am happy in having this opportunity of assuring you of my sincere friendship, and of the unfeigned respect and esteem which I entertain for your person and character.

Given at Windsor Castle the [   ] day of January 1849.

Queen Victoria to Lord John Russell

Windsor Castle, 22nd January 1849

The Queen has just received Lord John Russell's letter and enclosures, the contents of which have deeply grieved her, as the honour of her Government has always been nearest to her heart.* She feels deeply the humiliation to have to make an apology to the Government of Naples, which stands so very low in public estimation, and she naturally dreads the effect this disclosure about the guns will have

---

* Hostilities were in progress between the Sicilian insurgents and their Sovereign. An agent for the former came to England to purchase arms, but was informed by the contractor to whom he applied that the whole of his stock had been pledged to the Ordnance Office. Lord Palmerston, without consulting the Cabinet, allowed this stock to be transferred to the insurgents. The matter became public property, and the Premier brought it before the Cabinet on 23rd January, when, somewhat unexpectedly, the Foreign Secretary consented to make an apology to the Neapolitan Government; so that the crisis terminated for the time.

in the world, when she considers how many accusations have been brought against the good faith of this country latterly by many different Governments. Of course they will all consider their suspicions and accusations, however absurd they may have been, as justified and proved.

The Queen supposes that the proposition Lord John makes to her about moving Lord Palmerston to Ireland is the result of his conviction that after this disclosure it will be no longer to the advantage of the public service to leave the direction of the Foreign Affairs in these critical times in Lord Palmerston's hands. The Queen will be anxious to see Lord John upon this subject. All she wishes for is, that matters may be so managed as to reflect the least possible discredit upon the Government and Lord Palmerston himself.

Queen Victoria to the Marquis of Lansdowne

Osborne, 3rd March 1849

The Queen sends Lord Lansdowne the book* she mentioned to him. It is an extraordinary production for people of the working classes, and there are a great many sound and good observations in it on education; the observations on the deficiency in the religious instruction and in the *preaching* the Queen thinks are particularly true. It likewise shows a lofty and enlarged *view* of education which is often overlooked.

The Queen takes this occasion of repeating her hope that *Gaelic* will be taught in future in the Highland schools, as well as English, as it is really a great mistake that the people should be constantly *talking* a language which they often cannot read and generally not write. Being very partial to her loyal and good Highlanders, the Queen takes much interest in what she thinks will tend more than anything to keep up their simplicity of character, which she considers a great merit in these days.

The Queen thinks equally that Welsh should be taught in Wales as well as English.

* This book was probably *Popular Education, as regards Juvenile Delinquency,* by Thos. Bullock, 1849.

Lord John Russell to Queen Victoria

Chesham Place, 16th March 1849

Lord John Russell presents his humble duty to your Majesty, and has the honour to state that the debate last night was brought to a close.

Mr Cobden and Mr Disraeli made very able speeches at the end of the debate.

The debate has been a remarkable one, and the division shows tolerably well the strength of parties. The Protectionists, animated by the cry of agricultural distress, are disposed to use their power to the utmost. Mr Disraeli shows himself a much abler and less passionate leader than Lord George Bentinck.

On the other hand, the friends of Sir Robert Peel and the party of Mr Cobden unite with the Government in resisting the Protectionist party. The House of Commons thus gives a majority, which, though not compact, is decided at once against the extreme Tory and the extreme Radical party. With such a House of Commons the great interests of the Throne and the Constitution are safe. An abrupt dissolution would put everything to hazard.

Queen Victoria to the King of the Belgians

Windsor Castle, 10th April 1849

MY DEAREST UNCLE,— . . . The victory of Novara* seems to have been one of the hardest fought and most brilliant battles known for years and years, and old Radetzky says that he must name every individual if he was to do justice to officers and men. But the loss was very severe. The regiment of Kinsky lost *twenty-four* officers! The Archduke Albert distinguished himself exceedingly, which is worthy of his noble father. I could work myself up to a great excitement about these exploits, for there is nothing I admire more than great military exploits and daring.

* In which Marshal Radetzky defeated the Piedmontese.

Queen Victoria to the King of the Belgians

Buckingham Palace, 22nd May 1849

MY DEAREST UNCLE,— ... I hope that you will not have been alarmed by the account of the occurrence which took place on Saturday, and which I can assure you did *not* alarm *me* at all.* *This* time it is quite clear that it was a wanton and wicked wish merely to *frighten,* which is very wrong, and will be tried and punished as a *misdemeanour.* The account in the *Times* is quite correct. The indignation, loyalty, and affection this act has called forth is very gratifying and touching.

Alice gives a very good account of it, and Lenchen even says, 'Man shot, tried to shoot dear Mamma, must be punished.' They, Affie, and Miss Macdonald were with me. Albert was riding, and had just returned before me. Augustus and Clém had left us just two hours before. ...

Queen Victoria to the King of the Belgians

Lodge, Phœnix Park, 6th August 1849

MY DEAREST UNCLE,—Though this letter will only go to-morrow, I will begin it to-day and tell you that everything has gone off beautifully since we arrived in Ireland, and that our entrance into Dublin was really a magnificent thing. By my letter to Louise you will have heard of our arrival in the Cove of Cork. Our visit to Cork was very successful; the Mayor was knighted *on deck* (on board the *Fairy*), like in times of old. Cork is about seventeen miles up the River Lee, which is beautifully wooded and reminds us of Devonshire scenery. We had previously stepped on shore at *Cove*, a small place, to enable them to call it *Queen's Town*; the enthusiasm is immense, and at Cork there was more firing than I remember since the Rhine. ...

7th ... The entrance at seven o'clock into Kingston Harbour was splendid; we came in with ten steamers, and the whole harbour, wharf, and every surrounding place was *covered* with *thousands* and thousands of people, who received us with the greatest enthusiasm. We disembarked yesterday morning at ten o'clock, and took two

* The Queen, while driving down Constitution Hill, was fired at by one William Hamilton, the pistol being charged only with powder. He was tried under the Act of 1842, and sentenced to seven years' transportation.

hours to come here. The most perfect order was maintained in spite of the immense mass of people assembled, and a more good-humoured crowd I never saw, but noisy and excitable beyond belief, talking, jumping, and shrieking instead of cheering. There were numbers of troops out, and it really was a wonderful scene. This is a very pretty place, and the house reminds me of dear Claremont. The view of the Wicklow Mountains from the windows is very beautiful, and the whole park is very extensive and full of very fine trees.

We drove out yesterday afternoon and were followed by jaunting-cars and riders and people running and screaming which would have amused you. In the evening we had a dinner party, and so we have to-night. This morning we visited the Bank, the Model School (where the Protestant and Catholic Archbishops received us), and the College, and this afternoon we went to the Military Hospital. To-morrow we have a Levée, where 1,700 are to be presented, and the next day a Review, and in the evening the Drawing-Room, when 900 ladies are to be presented. . . .

You see more ragged and wretched people here than I ever saw anywhere else. *En revanche*, the women are really very handsome—quite in the lowest class—as well at Cork as here; such beautiful black eyes and hair and such fine colours and teeth.

I must now take my leave. Ever your most affectionate Niece,

VICTORIA R.

The Earl of Clarendon to Sir George Grey

Vice-Regal Lodge, 14th August 1849

MY DEAR GREY,—If I had known where to direct I should have thanked you sooner for your two welcome letters from Belfast, where everything seems to have gone off to our hearts' desire, and the Queen's presence, as the Stipendiary Magistrate writes word, has united all classes and parties in a manner incredible to those who know the distance at which they have hitherto been kept asunder.

The enthusiasm here has not abated, and there is not an individual in Dublin that does not take as a personal compliment to himself the Queen's having gone upon the paddle-box and having ordered the Royal Standard to be lowered three times.

Even the ex-Clubbists,* who threatened broken heads and windows before the Queen came, are now among the most loyal of her subjects, and are ready, according to the police reports, to fight any one who dare say a disrespectful word of Her Majesty.

In short, the people are not only enchanted with the Queen and the gracious kindness of her manner and the confidence she has shown in them, but they are pleased with themselves for their own good feelings and behaviour, which they consider have removed the barrier that hitherto existed between the Sovereign and themselves, and that they now occupy a higher position in the eyes of the world. Friend Bright was with me to-day, and said he would not for the world have missed seeing the embarkation at Kingston, for he had felt just the same enthusiasm as the rest of the crowd. 'Indeed,' he added, 'I'll defy any man to have felt otherwise when he saw the Queen come upon the platform and bow to the people in a manner that showed her heart was with them.' He didn't disguise either that the Monarchical principle had made great way with him since Friday. Ever yours truly,   CLARENDON

Queen Victoria to the King of the Belgians

Osborne, 11th December 1849

MY DEAREST UNCLE,—Thank you much for your kind letter of the 6th; you will have received mine of the 4th shortly after you wrote. I know *how* you would mourn with us over the death of our beloved Queen Adelaide. *We* have lost the kindest and dearest of friends, and the *universal* feeling of sorrow, of regret, and of *real* appreciation of her character is very touching and gratifying. *All* parties, *all* classes, join in doing her justice. Much was done to set Mamma against her, but the dear Queen ever forgave this, ever showed love and affection, and for the last eight years their friendship was as great as ever. Ever yours affectionately,   VICTORIA R.

* Seditious clubs had been an important factor in the Irish disturbances of 1848.

1850

Queen Victoria to Viscount Palmerston

Buckingham Palace, 17th February 1850

The Queen sent the day before yesterday the proposed draft to Mr Wyse back to Lord Palmerston, enclosing a Memorandum from Lord John Russell, and telling Lord Palmerston 'that she entirely concurred with Lord John, and wished the draft to be altered accordingly.' She has not yet received an answer from Lord Palmerston, but just hears from Lord John, in answer to her enquiry about it, that Lord Palmerston has *sent* the draft off *unaltered*. The Queen must remark upon this sort of proceeding, of which this is not the first instance, and plainly tell Lord Palmerston that this must not happen again. Lord Palmerston has a perfect right to state to the Queen his reasons for disagreeing with her views, and will always have found her ready to listen to his reasons; but she cannot allow a servant of the Crown and her Minister to act contrary to her orders, and this without her knowledge.

Memorandum by the Prince Albert

Windsor Castle, 3rd March 1850

Before leaving Town yesterday we saw Lord John Russell, who came to state what had passed with reference to Lord Palmerston. He premised that Lord Palmerston had at all times been a most agreeable and accommodating colleague; that he had acted with Lord John ever since 1831, and had not only never made any difficulty, but acted most boldly and in the most spirited manner on all political questions; besides, he was very popular with the Radical part of the House of Commons as well as the Protectionist, so that both would be ready to receive him as their Leader; he (Lord John) was therefore most anxious to do nothing which could hurt Lord Palmerston's feelings, nor to bring about a disruption of the Whig Party, which at this moment of Party confusion was the only one which still held together. On the other hand, the fact that the Queen distrusted Lord Palmerston was a serious impediment to the carrying on of the Government. Lord John was therefore anxious to adopt a plan by which Lord Palmerston's services could be retained with his own goodwill, and the Foreign Affairs entrusted to other hands. The only plan he could think of was to give Lord Palmerston the lead in the House of Commons—the highest position a statesman could aspire to—and to go himself to the House of Lords. He had communicated his views to Lord Lansdowne, who agreed in them, and thought he could do nothing better than speak to Lord Palmerston at once. Lord Palmerston said that he could not have helped to have become aware that he had forfeited the Queen's confidence, but he thought this had not been on *personal* grounds, but merely on account of his line of policy, with which the Queen disagreed. (The Queen interrupted Lord John by remarking that she distrusted him on *personal* grounds also, but I remarked that Lord Palmerston had so far at least seen rightly; that he had become disagreeable to the Queen, not on account of his person, but of his political doings, to which the Queen assented.) Lord Palmerston appeared to Lord John willing to enter into this agreement.

On the question how the Foreign Office should be filled, Lord John said that he thought his father-in-law, Lord Minto, ought to take the Foreign Office.... As the Queen was somewhat startled by this announcement, I said I thought that would not go down with the public. After Lord Palmerston's removal (who was considered one of the ablest men in the country) he ought not to be replaced but by an equally able statesman; the Office was of *enormous* importance, and ought not to be entrusted to any one but Lord John himself or Lord Clarendon. On the Queen's enquiry why Lord Clarendon had not been proposed for it, Lord John said he was most anxious that the change of the Minister should not produce a change in the general line of policy which he considered to have been quite right, and that Lord Clarendon did not approve of it; somehow or other he never could agree with Lord Clarendon on Foreign Affairs; he thought Lord Clarendon very anti-French and for an alliance with Austria and Russia. The Queen replied she knew Lord Clarendon's bad opinion of the mode in which the Foreign Affairs had been conducted, and thought that a merit in him, but did not think him Austrian or Russian, but merely disapproving of Lord Palmerston's behaviour. I urged Lord John to take the Foreign Affairs himself, which he said would have to be done if the Queen did not wish Lord Minto to take them; he himself would be able to do the business when in the House of Lords, although he would undertake it unwillingly; with the business in the House of Commons it would have been impossible for him. The Queen insisted on his trying it with a seat in the House of Lords, adding that, if he found it too much for him, he could at a later period perhaps make the Department over to Lord Clarendon.

I could not help remarking that it was serious risk to entrust Lord Palmerston with the lead in the House of Commons, that it might be that the Government were defeated and, if once in opposition, Lord Palmerston might take a different line as leader of the Opposition from that which Lord John would like, and might so easily force himself back into office as Prime Minister. Lord John, however, although admitting that danger, thought Lord Palmerston too old to do much in the future (having passed his sixty-fifth year); he admitted that Sir George Grey was the natural leader of the Commons, but expected that a little later the lead would still fall into his hands.

The arrangements of the Offices as proposed would be that Lord Palmerston would take the Home Office, and Sir George Grey the Colonial Office, and Lord Grey vacate this office for the Privy Seal. If Lord Minto, however, was not to have the Foreign Office, the arrangement must be recast. Lord Clarendon would become Secretary of State for Ireland, after the abolition of the Lord Lieutenancy. Possibly also Sir George Grey might take the office, and Lord Clarendon take the Colonies, which Lord Grey would be glad to be rid of. On my observing that I had thought the Colonies would have done best for Lord Palmerston, leaving Sir George Grey at the Home Office. Lord John acknowledged that he would likewise prefer this arrangement, but considered it rendered impossible from its having been the very thing Lord Grey had proposed in 1845, and upon which the attempt to form a Whig Government at that time had broken down, Lord Palmerston having refused to enter the Cabinet on those terms. Lord John ended by saying that Lord Palmerston having agreed to the change, it was intended that nothing should be done about it till after the close of the Session, in order to avoid debates and questions on the subject; moreover, Lord Lansdowne had agreed to continue still this Session his labours as Leader in the House of Lords, and begged for the *utmost secrecy* at present.   ALBERT

Memorandum by Baron Stockmar

12th March 1850

The least the Queen has a right to require of her Minister is:

1. That he will distinctly state what he proposes in a given case, in order that the Queen may know as distinctly to what she has to give her royal sanction.

2. Having given once her sanction to a measure, the Minister who, in the execution of such measure alters or modifies it arbitrarily, commits an act of dishonesty towards the Crown, which the Queen has an undoubted constitutional right to visit with the dismissal of that Minister.   STOCKMAR

Queen Victoria to the King of the Belgians

Windsor Castle, 26th March 1850

MY DEAREST UNCLE,—Albert made a really beautiful speech the other day, and it has given the greatest satisfaction and done great good. He is indeed *looked up to and beloved*, as *I* could *wish* he should be; and the *more* his *rare qualities* of mind and heart are *known*, the *more* he will be understood and appreciated. People are much struck at his great powers and energy; his great self-denial, and constant wish to work for others, is so striking in his character; but it is the *happiest* life; pining for what one cannot have, and trying to run after what is pleasantest, *invariably* ends in disappointment.

I must now conclude. Ever your devoted Niece,   VICTORIA R.

Queen Victoria to the King of the Belgians

Windsor Castle, 29th March 1850

MY DEAREST UNCLE,— . . . I shall duly answer your dear letter of the 25th on Tuesday, but am anxious to correct the impression that

Albert read his fine speech. He *never* has done so with any of his fine speeches, but speaks them, having first prepared them and written them down,—and does so *so well*, that no one believes that he is ever nervous, which *he is*. This last he is said to have spoken in so particularly English a way.

We have still sadly cold winds. Ever your devoted Niece,

VICTORIA R.

Queen Victoria to Lord John Russell

Buckingham Palace, 14th April 1850

The Queen has received Lord John Russell's letter with the drafts, which he mentioned last night to her, and she has sent his letter with them to Lord Palmerston.

Lord Palmerston's conduct in this Spanish question in not communicating her letter to Lord John, as she had directed, is really too bad, and most disrespectful to the Queen; she can really hardly communicate with him any more; indeed it would be better she should not.

Lord John Russell to Queen Victoria

Pembroke Lodge, 28th April 1850

...Lord John Russell cannot but assent to your Majesty's right to claim every consideration on the part of your Majesty's Ministers. He will take care to attend to this subject, and is much concerned to find that your Majesty has so frequently occasion to complain of Lord Palmerston's want of attention.

The Marquis of Dalhousie to Queen Victoria

Simla, 15th May 1850

...When the Governor-General had the honour of addressing your Majesty from Bombay, the arrangements for the transmission of the Koh-i-noor were incomplete. He therefore did not then report to your Majesty, as he now humbly begs leave to do, that he conveyed the jewel himself from Lahore in his own charge, and deposited it in the Treasury at Bombay. One of your Majesty's ships had been ordered to Bombay to receive it, but had not then arrived, and did not arrive till two months afterwards, thus causing delay. The *Medea*, however, sailed on 6th April, and will, it is hoped, have a safe and speedy passage to England.

By this mail the Governor-General transmits officially a record of all that he has been able to trace of the vicissitudes through which the Koh-i-noor has passed. The papers are accurate and curious.

In one of them it is narrated, on the authority of Fugueer-ood-deen, who is now at Lahore, and who was himself the messenger, that Runjeet Singh sent a message to Wufa Begum, the wife of Shah Sooja, from whom he had taken the gem, to ask her its value. She replied, 'If a strong man were to throw four stones, one north, one south, one east, one west, and a fifth stone up into the air, and if the space between them were to be filled with gold, all would not equal the value of the Koh-i-noor.' The Fugueer, thinking probably that this appraisement was somewhat imaginative, subsequently asked Shah Sooja the same question. The Shah replied that its value was 'good fortune; for whoever possessed it had conquered their enemies.'

The Governor-General very respectfully and earnestly trusts that your Majesty, in your possession of the Koh-i-noor, may ever continue to realise its value as estimated by Shah Sooja.

He has the honour to subscribe himself, with deep respect, your Majesty's most obedient, most humble, and most faithful Subject and Servant,   DALHOUSIE

Queen Victoria to Lord John Russell

Osborne, 9th June 1850

The Queen has received Lord John Russell's two letters. If the Cabinet *think* it impossible to do otherwise, of course the Queen consents—though *most reluctantly*—to a compliance with the vote respecting the Post Office.* The Queen thinks it a very *false* notion of obeying God's will, to do what will be the cause of much annoyance and possibly of great distress to private families. At any rate, she

* Lord Ashley carried a resolution forbidding the Sunday delivery of letters; a Committee of Inquiry was appointed, and reported against the proposed change, which was abandoned.

thinks decidedly that great caution should be used with respect to any alteration in the transmission of the mails, so that at least *some means* of communication may still be possible.

Queen Victoria to Lord John Russell

Buckingham Palace, 21st June 1850

The Queen has received Lord John Russell's letter and read his speech in the House of Commons. She regrets exceedingly the position in which the Government has been placed by the Motion of Lord Stanley in the House of Lords. Whichever way the Debate in the House of Commons may terminate, the Queen foresees great troubles. A defeat of the Government would be *most inconvenient*. The Queen has always approved the *general* tendency of the policy of the Government to let despotism and democracy fight out their battles abroad, but must remind Lord John that in the execution of this policy Lord Palmerston has *gone a long way* in taking up the side of democracy in the fight, and this is the 'detail of negotiations' which Lord John is afraid may be confounded with the general principle of our Foreign Policy. Indeed it is already confounded by the whole of the foreign and the great majority of the British public, and it is to be feared that the discussion will place despotic and democratic principles in array against each other in this country, whilst the original question turns only upon the justice of Don Pacifico's claims.

Lord John Russell to Queen Victoria

Chesham Place, 26th June 1850

Lord John Russell presents his humble duty to your Majesty, and has the honour to report that in the debate of last night Viscount Palmerston defended the whole Foreign Policy of the Government in a speech of four hours and three quarters.* This speech was one

---

* It lasted from dusk till dawn, and the Minister asked for a verdict on the question whether, as the Roman in days of old held himself free from indignity when he could say, *Civis Romanus sum,* so also a British subject, in whatever land he may be, shall feel confident that the watchful eye and the strong arm of England will protect him against injustice and wrong. Peel, who made his last appearance in the House, voted against Palmerston.

of the most masterly ever delivered, going through the details of transactions in the various parts of the world, and appealing from time to time to great principles of justice and of freedom.

The cheering was frequent and enthusiastic. The debate was adjourned till Thursday, when it will probably close.

The expectation is that Ministers will have a majority, but on the amount of that majority must depend their future course.

Queen Victoria to the King of the Belgians

Buckingham Palace, 2nd July 1850

MY DEAREST UNCLE,— . . . By my letter to Louise you will have learnt all the details of this certainly very disgraceful and very inconceivable attack.* I have not suffered except from my head, which is still very tender, the blow having been extremely violent, and the brass *end* of the stick fell on my head so as to make a considerable noise. I own it makes me nervous out driving, and I start at any person coming near the carriage, which I am afraid is natural. We have, alas! now another cause of much greater anxiety in the person of our excellent Sir Robert Peel,† who, as you will see, has had a most serious fall, and though going on well at first, was very ill last night; thank God! he is better again this morning, but I fear still in great danger. I cannot bear even to think of losing him; it would be the greatest loss for the whole country, and irreparable for us, for he is so trustworthy, and so entirely to be depended on. *All* parties are in great anxiety about him. I will leave my letter open to give you the latest news. . . .

---

* The Queen, as she was leaving Cambridge House, where she had called to inquire after the Duke of Cambridge's health, was struck with a cane by one Robert Pate, an ex-officer, and a severe bruise was inflicted on her forehead. The outrage was apparently committed without motive, but an attempt to prove Pate insane failed, and he was sentenced to seven years' transportation.

† On the day following the Don Pacifico debate, Sir Robert Peel, after attending a meeting of the Exhibition Commissioners, had gone out riding. On his return, while passing up Constitution Hill, he was thrown from his horse, and, after lingering three days in intense pain, died on the 5th of July.

The King of the Belgians to Queen Victoria

Laeken, 5th July 1850

MY DEAREST VICTORIA,—It gave me the greatest pain to learn of the death of our true and kind friend, Sir Robert Peel. That he should have met with his end—he so valuable to the whole earth—from an accident so easily to be avoided with some care, is the more to be lamented. You and Albert lose in him a friend whose moderation, correct judgment, great knowledge of everything connected with the country, can never be found again. Europe had in him a benevolent and a truly wise statesman. . . .

Give my best thanks to Albert for his kind letter. I mean to send a messenger probably on Sunday or Monday to write to him. I pity him about the great Exhibition. I fear he will be much plagued, and I was glad to see that the matter is to be treated in Parliament. Alas! in all human affairs one is sure to meet with violent passions, and Peel knew that so well; great care even for the most useful objects is necessary. . . .

Queen Victoria to Viscount Palmerston

Osborne, 19th July 1850

Before this draft to Lord Bloomfield about Greece is sent, it would be well to consider whether Lord Palmerston is justified in calling the Minister of the Interior of Greece 'a notorious defaulter to the amount of 200,000 drachms,' and should he be so, whether it is a proper thing for the Queen's Foreign Secretary to say in a public despatch!

Queen Victoria to Lord John Russell

Osborne, 28th July 1850

The Queen will have much pleasure in seeing the Duke and Duchess of Bedford here next Saturday, and we have invited them. She will be quite ready to hear the Duke's opinions on the Foreign Office. Lord John may be sure that she fully admits the great difficulties in the way of the projected alteration, but she, on the other hand, feels the duty she owes to the country and to herself, not to allow a man in whom she can have no confidence, who has conducted himself in *anything but* a straightforward and proper manner to herself, to remain in the Foreign Office, and thereby to expose herself to insults from other nations, and the country to the constant risk of serious and alarming complications. The Queen considers these reasons as much graver than the other difficulties. Each time that we were in a difficulty, the Government seemed to be determined to move Lord Palmerston, and as soon as these difficulties were got over, those which present themselves in the carrying out of this removal appeared of so great a magnitude as to cause its relinquishment. There is no chance of Lord Palmerston reforming himself in his sixty-seventh year, and after having considered his last escape as a triumph. ... The Queen is personally convinced that Lord Palmerston at this moment is secretly planning an armed Russian intervention in Schleswig, which may produce a renewal of revolutions in Germany, and possibly a general war.

The Queen only adduces this as an instance that there is no question of delicacy and danger in which Lord Palmerston will not arbitrarily and without reference to his colleagues or Sovereign engage this country.

Memorandum by the Prince Albert

Osborne, 8th August 1850

Lord John Russell came down here yesterday in order to report to the Queen what had passed between him and Lord Palmerston the day before, on whom he had called in order to have an explanation on the Foreign Affairs.

Lord John reminded him of former communications, but admitted that circumstances were much changed by the recent debates in both Houses of Parliament; still, it was necessary to come to an understanding of the position. The *policy* pursued with regard to the Foreign Affairs had been right and such as had the approval of Lord John himself, the Cabinet generally, and he believed the greater part of the country. But the manner in which it had been executed had been unfortunate, led to irritation and hostility; although peace had actually been preserved, and England stood in a position requiring

no territorial aggrandisement or advantage of any kind, yet all
Governments and Powers, not only Russia and Austria, but also
France and the liberal states, had become decidedly hostile to us,
and our intercourse was not such as was desirable. Lord John could
instance many cases in which they had been unnecessarily slighted
and provoked by Lord Palmerston, like M. Drouyn de Lhuys in
the Greek affair. Lord Palmerston's conduct towards the Queen
had been disrespectful and wanting in due attention and deference
to her, and had been much complained of. . . .

Lord Palmerston was much pleased to hear of Lord John's intention to stay in the House of Commons, said all was changed
now; there had been a great conspiracy against him, he had been
accused in Parliament, put on his trial and acquitted. The acquittal
had produced the greatest enthusiasm for him in the country, and
he was now supported by a strong party; he owned, however, that
his success had been chiefly owing to the handsome manner in which
Lord John and his colleagues had supported him in the debate.
That he should incur the momentary enmity of those states whose
interests and plans he might have to cross was quite natural; he
had never intended any disrespect to the Queen, and if he had
been guilty of any he was quite unconscious of it and sorry for it.

Lord John reminded him that although the Government had got
a majority in the House of Commons in the Foreign debate, it was
not to be forgotten that the fate of the Government had been staked
upon it, and that many people voted on that account who would
not have supported the Foreign policy; that it was remarkable that
all those who had the strongest reason to be anxious for the continuance of the Government, but who could not avoid *speaking,*
were obliged to speak and vote against the Government. Sir R. Peel's
speech was a most remarkable instance of this.

Lord Palmerston saw in Sir Robert's speech nothing but a reluctant
effort to defend Lord Aberdeen, whom he was bound to defend.
If he (Lord Palmerston) were to leave the Foreign Office, there
must be a ground for it, such as his having to take the lead in the
House of Commons, which was evidently impossible with the conduct of Foreign Department at the same time. (It had killed Mr
Canning, and after that failure nobody ought to attempt it.) But

without such a ground it would be loss of character to him, which he could not be expected to submit to. There was not even the excuse of wishing to avoid a difficulty with a foreign country, as all was smooth now. Those who had wished to injure him had been beat, and now it would be giving them a triumph after all. If the Queen or the Cabinet were dissatisfied with his management of the Foreign Affairs, they had a right to demand his resignation, and he would give it, but they could not ask him to lower himself in public estimation. Lord John answered that his resignation would lead to a further split of parties: there were parties already enough in the House, and it was essential that at least the Whig party should be kept together, to which Lord Palmerston assented. He (Lord Palmerston) then repeated his complaints against that plot which had been got up in this country against him, and urged on by foreigners, complained particularly of Lord Clarendon, Mr Greville of the Privy Council, Mr Reeve, ditto, and their attack upon him in the *Times,* and of Mr Delane, the Editor of the *Times,* of Guizot, Princess Lieven, etc., etc., etc. However, they had been convinced that they could not upset him, and Mr Reeve had declared to him that he had been making open and honourable (? ! !) war upon him; now he would make a lasting peace. With Russia and France he (Lord Palmerston) had just been signing the Danish Protocol, showing that they were on the best terms together.

Lord John felt he could not press the matter further under these circumstances, but he seemed much provoked at the result of his conversation. We expressed our surprise that he had not made Lord Palmerston any offer of any kind. Lord John replied he had not been sure what he could have offered him. . . .   ALBERT

Queen Victoria to Lord John Russell

Osborne, 12th August 1850

With reference to the conversation about Lord Palmerston which the Queen had with Lord John Russell the other day, and Lord Palmerston's disavowal that he ever intended any disrespect to her by the various neglects of which she has had so long and so often to complain, she thinks it right, in order *to prevent any mistake* for the *future,* shortly to explain *what it is she expects from her Foreign Secretary.* She requires: (1) That he will distinctly state what he proposes in a given case, in order that the Queen may know as distinctly to *what* she has given her Royal sanction; (2) Having *once given* her sanction to a measure, that it be not arbitrarily altered or modified by the Minister; such an act she must consider as failing in sincerity towards the Crown, and justly to be visited by the exercise of her Constitutional right of dismissing that Minister. She expects to be kept informed of what passes between him and the Foreign Ministers before important decisions are taken, based upon that intercourse; to receive the Foreign Despatches in good time, and to have the drafts for her approval sent to her in sufficient time to make herself acquainted with their contents before they must be sent off. The Queen thinks it best that Lord Russell should show this letter to Lord Palmerston.

Queen Victoria to Viscount Palmerston

Osborne, 26th August 1850

The Queen wishes Lord Palmerston to give directions for a Court mourning according to those which are usual for an abdicated King. She likewise wishes that every assistance should be given, and every attention shown to the afflicted Royal Family, who have been so severely tried during the last two years, on the melancholy occasion of the poor King of the French's death.

The Queen starts for Scotland to-morrow.

Lord John Russell to Queen Victoria

Dunkeld, 7th September 1850

...Lord John Russell has had the honour of receiving at Taymouth a letter from the Prince. He agrees that the office of Poet Laureate ought to be filled up. There are three or four authors of nearly equal merit, such as Henry Taylor, Sheridan Knowles, Professor Wilson, and Mr Tennyson, who are qualified for the office.

Viscount Palmerston to Queen Victoria

Broadlands, 8th October 1850

Viscount Palmerston presents his humble duty to your Majesty, and has had the honour to receive your Majesty's communication of the 4th instant, expressing your Majesty's wish that an alteration should be made in his answer to Baron Koller's note of the 5th of September, on the subject of the attack made upon General Haynau; but Viscount Palmerston begs to state that when Baron Koller was at this place about ten days ago, he expressed so much annoyance at the delay which had already taken place in regard to the answer to his note of the 5th September, and he requested so earnestly that he might immediately have the reply, that Viscount Palmerston could do no otherwise than send him the answer at once, and Baron Koller despatched it the next day to Vienna.

Viscount Palmerston had put the last paragraph into the answer, because he could scarcely have reconciled it to his own feelings and to his sense of public responsibility to have put his name to a note which might be liable to be called for by Parliament, without expressing in it, at least as his own personal opinion, a sense of the want of propriety evinced by General Haynau in coming to England at the present moment.

The state of public feeling in this country about General Haynau and his proceedings in Italy and Hungary was perfectly well known; and his coming here so soon after those events, without necessity or obligation to do so, was liable to be looked upon as a bravado, and as a challenge to an expression of public opinion.

Baron Koller indeed told Viscount Palmerston that Prince Metternich and Baron Neumann had at Brussels strongly dissuaded General Haynau from coming on to England; and that he (Baron Koller) had after his arrival earnestly entreated him to cut off those long moustachios which rendered him so liable to be identified.

With regard to the transaction itself, there is no justifying a breach of the law, nor an attack by a large number of people upon one or two individuals who cannot resist such superior force; and though in the present case, according to Baron Koller's account, the chief injury sustained by General Haynau consisted in the tearing of his coat, the loss of a cane, and some severe bruises on his left arm, and though four or five policemen proved to be sufficient protection, yet a mob who begin by insult lead each other on to outrage; and there is no saying to what extremes they might have proceeded if they had not been checked.

Such occurrences, however, have taken place before; and to go no further back than the last summer, the attacks on Lord Talbot at the Stafford meeting, and on Mr Bankes, Mr Sturt, and others at the Dorchester meeting, when a man was killed, were still more violent outrages, and originated simply in differences of political opinion; whereas in this case the brewers' men were expressing their feeling at what they considered inhuman conduct on the part of General Haynau.

The people of this country are remarkable for their hospitable reception of foreigners, and for their forgetfulness of past animosities. Napoleon Bonaparte, the greatest enemy that England ever had, was treated while at Plymouth with respect, and with commiseration while at St Helena. Marshal Soult, who had fought in many battles against the English, was received with generous acclamation when he came here as Special Ambassador. The King of the French, Mons. Guizot, and Prince Metternich, though all of them great antagonists of English policy and English interests, were treated in this country with courtesy and kindness. But General Haynau was looked upon as a great moral criminal; and the feeling in regard to him was of the same nature as that which was manifested towards Tawell* and the Mannings,† with this only difference, that General Haynau's bad deeds were committed upon a far larger scale, and upon a far larger number of victims. But Viscount Palmerston can assure your Majesty that those feelings of just and honourable indignation have not been confined to England, for he had good reason to know that General Haynau's ferocious and unmanly treatment of the unfortunate inhabitants of Brescia and of other towns and places in Italy, his savage proclamations to the people of Pesth, and his

---

* Executed for the Salt Hill murder.

† Marie Manning (an ex-lady's maid, whose career is said to have suggested Hortense in *Bleak House* to Dickens) was executed with her husband, in 1849, for the murder of a guest. She wore black satin on the scaffold, a material which consequently became unpopular for some time.

barbarous acts in Hungary excited almost as much disgust in Austria as in England, and that the nickname of 'General Hyæna' was given to him at Vienna long before it was applied to him in London.

Queen Victoria to Lord John Russell

Buckingham Palace, 11th October 1850

The Queen having written to Lord Palmerston in conformity with Lord John Russell's suggestion respecting the draft to Baron Koller, now encloses Lord Palmerston's answer, which she received at Edinburgh yesterday evening. Lord John will see that Lord Palmerston has not only *sent* the draft, but passes over in silence her injunction to have a corrected copy given to Baron Koller, and adds a vituperation against General Haynau, which clearly shows that he is not sorry for what has happened, and makes a merit of sympathising with the draymen at the brewery and the Chartist Demonstrations. . . .

The Queen encloses likewise a copy of her letter to Lord Palmerston, and hopes Lord John will write to him.*

Queen Victoria to Viscount Palmerston

Buckingham Palace, 12th October 1850

The Queen has received Lord Palmerston's letter respecting the draft to Baron Koller. She cannot suppose that Baron Koller addressed his note to Lord Palmerston in order to receive in answer an expression of his *own personal opinion*; and if Lord Palmerston could not reconcile it to his own feelings to express the regret of the Queen's Government at the brutal attack and wanton outrage committed by a ferocious mob on a distinguished foreigner of past seventy years of age, who was quietly visiting a private establishment in this metropolis, without

* Lord John insisted on the note being withdrawn, and another substituted with the offensive passage omitted. After threatening resignation, Lord Palmerston somewhat tamely consented.

Lord John Russell wrote to the Prince Albert that he would be 'somewhat amused, if not surprised, at the sudden and amicable termination of the dispute regarding the letter to Baron Koller. The same course may be adopted with advantage if a despatch is ever again sent which has been objected to, and to which the Queen's sanction has not been given.'

adding *his censure of the want of propriety* evinced by General Haynau in coming to England—he might have done so in a private letter, where his personal feelings could not be mistaken for the opinion of the Queen and her Government. She must repeat her request that Lord Palmerston will rectify this.

The Queen can as little approve of the introduction of Lynch Law in this country as of the *violent* vituperations with which Lord Palmerston accuses and condemns public men in other countries, acting in most difficult circumstances and under heavy responsibility, without having the means of obtaining correct information or of sifting evidence.

Lord John Russell to Queen Victoria

Bishopthorpe, 25th October 1850

Lord John Russell presents his humble duty to your Majesty; he has read with attention the letter of the Duchess of Norfolk.* He has also read the Pope's Bull. It strikes him that the division into twelve territorial dioceses of eight ecclesiastical vicariats is not a matter to be alarmed at. The persons to be affected by this change must be already Roman Catholics before it can touch them.

The matter to create rational alarm is, as your Majesty says, the growth of Roman Catholic doctrines and practices within the bosom of the Church. Dr Arnold said very truly, 'I look upon a Roman Catholic as an enemy in his uniform; I look upon a Tractarian as an enemy disguised as a spy.'

It would be very wrong to do as the Bishop of Oxford proposed,

---

* Two important events in the history of the English Church had just occurred. The Bishop of Exeter had refused to institute Mr Gorham to a Crown living in his diocese, on the ground that his teaching on baptism was at variance with the formularies of the Church. This decision, though upheld in the Court of Arches, was reversed (though not unanimously) by the Privy Council. High Church feeling was much aroused by the judgment.

In September, Pius IX (now re-established in the Vatican) promulgated a papal brief, restoring the Roman Catholic hierarchy in England, and dividing it territorially into twelve sees, and in October Cardinal Wiseman, as Archbishop of Westminster, issued his Pastoral, claiming that Catholic England had been restored to its orbit in the ecclesiastical firmament. The Duchess of Norfolk, writing from Arundel, had criticised the proselytising action of certain Roman Catholic clergy.

and confer the patronage of the Crown on any of these Tractarians. But, on the other hand, to treat them with severity would give the whole party vigour and union.

The Dean of Bristol is of opinion that the Tractarians are falling to pieces by dissension. It appears clear that Mr Denison and Mr Palmer have broken off from Dr Pusey.

Sir George Grey will ask the Law Officers whether there is anything illegal in Dr Wiseman's assuming the title of Archbishop of Westminster. An English Cardinal is not a novelty.*

Lord John Russell to Queen Victoria

Downing Street, 11th December 1850

Lord John Russell presents his humble duty to your Majesty, and has the honour to state that the Cabinet to-day considered at great length the question of the steps to be taken in respect to the Papal Aggression.

The inclination of the majority was not to prosecute, but to bring a Bill into Parliament to make the assumption of any titles of archbishop, etc., of any place in the United Kingdom illegal, and to make any gift of property conveyed under such title null and void.

Queen Victoria to the Duchess of Gloucester

Windsor Castle, 12th December 1850

MY DEAR AUNT,—Many thanks for your kind letter; you are quite right not to distress the Duchess of Cambridge by mentioning to

* Lord John wrote on 4th November to Dr. Maltby, Bishop of Durham, denouncing the assumption of spiritual superiority over England, in the documents issued from Rome. But what alarmed him more (he said) was the action of clergymen within the Church leading their flocks dangerously near the brink, and recommending for adoption the honour paid to saints, the claim of infallibility for the Church, the superstitious use of the sign of the cross, the muttering of the liturgy so as to disguise the language in which it was said, with the recommendation of auricular confession and the administration of penance and absolution.

Lord John was pictorially satirised in *Punch* as the boy who chalked up 'No popery' on the door and ran away.

her what I wrote to you about the Bishop of London. I am glad that you are pleased with my answers to the Addresses; I thought them very proper.

I would never have consented to say anything which breathed a spirit of intolerance. Sincerely Protestant as I always have been and always shall be, and indignant as I am at those who *call themselves Protestants,* while they in fact *are* quite the *contrary,* I much regret the unchristian and intolerant spirit exhibited by many people at the public meetings. I cannot bear to hear the violent abuse of the Catholic religion, which is so painful and cruel towards the many good and innocent Roman Catholics. However, we must hope and trust this excitement will soon cease, and that the wholesome effect of it on our own *Church* will be the lasting result of it. Ever yours. . . .

VICTORIA R.

1851

Queen Victoria to Lord John Russell

Windsor Castle, 25th January 1851

The Queen approves of the elevation of Mr Pemberton Leigh to the Peerage, which she considers a very useful measure, and not likely to lead to any permanent increase of the Peerage, as he is not likely to marry at his present age, and considering that he has only a life interest in his large property.

With regard to the creation of Dr Lushington as a Peer, without remainder, the Queen has again thoroughly considered the question, and is of opinion that the establishment of the principle of creation for life—in cases where public advantage may be derived from the grant of a Peerage, but where there may be no fortune to support the dignity in the family—is most desirable. The mode in which the public will take the introduction of it will however chiefly depend upon the merits of the first case brought forward. Dr Lushington appears to the Queen so unobjectionable in this respect that she cannot but approve of the experiment being tried with him.

It would be well, however, that it should be done quietly; that it should not be talked about beforehand or get into the papers, which so frequently happens on occasions of this kind, and generally does harm.

Lord John Russell to Queen Victoria

Chesham Place, 21st February 1851

Lord John Russell presents his humble duty to your Majesty, and has the honour to report that on a motion of Mr Locke King's yesterday the Government was defeated by a hundred to fifty-two.

This is another circumstance which makes it probable the Ministry cannot endure long. The Tories purposely stayed away.

Memorandum by the Queen

Buckingham Palace, 5th March 1851

The Queen would give every facility to the selection of a good site for a new National Gallery, and would therefore not object to its being built on to Kensington Palace or anywhere in Kensington Gardens; but does not see why it should exactly be placed upon the site of the present Palace, if not for the purpose of taking from the Crown the last available set of apartments. She is not disposed to trust in the disposition of Parliament or the public to give her an equivalent for these apartments from time to time when emergencies arise. The surrender of Kensington Palace will most likely not be thanked for at the moment, and any new demand in consequence of such surrender would be met with lavish abuse. As to economy in the construction, it will most likely be best consulted by building on a spot perfectly free and unencumbered.

Queen Victoria to Sir George Grey

Buckingham Palace, 30th March 1851

The Queen approves of the draft of a letter to the Archbishop of Canterbury. With respect to the Archbishop's letter and the address, the Queen will receive it in the Closet. It seems strange to propose as a remedy for the present evils in the Church, and for its evident great disunion, 600 more churches to be built! There ought clearly to be some security given to those who are to encourage such a scheme against the extension of those evils.

Lord John Russell to the Prince Albert

Pembroke Lodge, 19th April 1851

SIR,—Lord Granville came here yesterday to speak to me upon the order for opening the Exhibition at one o'clock on the 1st of May. He is anxious to have the order changed, and the season-ticket bearers admitted at eleven o'clock.

I did not give him any positive opinion on the subject. But the account he gave me of the route which the Queen will follow in going to the Exhibition takes away the main objection which I felt to the admission of visitors before one o'clock. It appears there cannot well be any interruption to Her Majesty's progress to and from the Crystal Palace on the 1st of May.

I conclude that Her Majesty will not go in the State Coach, but in the same manner that Her Majesty goes in state to the theatres....

I feel assured there will be no undue and inconvenient pressure of the crowd in the part of the building in which Her Majesty may be. Colonel Wemyss and Colonel Bouverie might easily be in attendance to request the visitors not to crowd where the Queen is. At the same time, I am ready to abide by the existing order, if Her Majesty wishes it to be enforced....

Queen Victoria to the King of the Belgians

Buckingham Palace, 3rd May 1851

MY DEAREST UNCLE,— ... I wish you *could* have witnessed the *1st May 1851,* the *greatest* day in our history, the *most beautiful* and *imposing* and *touching* spectacle ever seen, and the triumph of my beloved Albert. Truly it was astonishing, a fairy scene. Many cried, and all felt touched and impressed with devotional feelings. It was the *happiest, proudest* day in my life, and I can think of nothing else. Albert's dearest name is immortalised with this *great* conception, *his* own, and my *own* dear country *showed* she was *worthy* of it. The triumph is *immense*, for up to the *last hour* the difficulties, the opposition, and the ill-natured attempts to annoy and frighten, of a certain set of fashionables and Protectionists, were immense; but Albert's temper, patience, firmness, and energy surmounted all, and the feeling is universal. *You* will be astounded at this great work when you see it!—the beauty of the building and the vastness of it all. I can never thank God enough. I feel *so* happy, so proud. Our dear guests were much pleased and impressed. You are right to like the dear Princess, for she is a noble-minded, warm-hearted, distinguished person, much attached to you, and who revered dearest Louise. Oh!*how* I thought of *her* on that great day, how kindly she would have rejoiced in our success! Now good-bye, dearest Uncle. Ever your devoted Niece,

VICTORIA R.

Queen Victoria to Lord John Russell

Buckingham Palace, 18th June 1851

... The Queen, at the risk of not appearing sufficiently modest (and yet, why should a wife ever be modest about her husband's merits?), must say that she thinks Lord John Russell will admit now that the Prince is possessed of very extraordinary powers of mind and heart. She feels so proud at being his wife that she cannot refrain from herself paying a tribute to his noble character.

Queen Victoria to the King of the Belgians

Balmoral Castle, 16th September 1851

MY DEAREST UNCLE,— ... My letter is terribly *décousu*, for it has been twice interrupted. I was out the whole day with Albert, in the forest in a perfectly tropical heat. Since we went to Allt-na-Giuthasach, our little bothy near Loch Muich on the 12th, the heat of the sun has been daily increasing, and has reached a pitch which makes it almost sickening to be out in it, though it is beautiful to behold. The sky these last two evenings has been like an Italian one, and for the last few days—at least the last four—without the slightest particle of cloud, and the sun blazing. With this, not a breath of air. The mountains look quite crimson and lilac, and everything glows with the setting sun. The evenings are quite a *relief*. Really one cannot undertake expeditions, the heat is so great. We thought of you, and wished you could be here; you would fancy yourself in Italy.

Albert got a splendid stag to-day. I must hastily conclude, hoping to hear from you that you *will come*. Our moonlights have been magnificent also. Ever your devoted Niece,   VICTORIA R.

Queen Victoria to Lord Palmerston

Windsor Castle, 13th October 1851

The Queen returns Lord Howden's letter, and thinks that the best answer to the Queen of Spain's request will be that the Statutes do not allow the Garter to be bestowed upon a lady; that the Queen herself possesses no order of knighthood from any country.

With reference to the claim for the King arising out of the Prince having received the Fleece, it may be well to say that the offer of the Fleece had in the first instance been declined for fear of establishing a ground for the necessity of giving the Garter in return, and was at its second offer accepted by the Prince, together with the first orders of almost every country, on the understanding that no return would be expected. It would have been impossible to give the Garter to every Sovereign, and very difficult to make a selection. The Queen of Spain ought to be made aware of the fact that among the reigning Sovereigns, the Emperors of Austria and Brazil, and the Kings of Sweden, Denmark, Bavaria, Holland, Sardinia, Naples, Greece, etc., etc., have not got the Garter, although many of them have expressed a wish for it, and that amongst the Kings Consort, the King of Portugal, the Queen's first cousin, has not received it yet, although the Queen has long been anxious to give it to him.

Anything short of these explanations might offend, or leave the claim open to be repeated from time to time.

Lord John Russell to Queen Victoria

Pembroke Lodge, 31st October 1851

Lord John Russell presents his humble duty to your Majesty; he has the honour to submit to your Majesty a correspondence* which has taken place between Lord Palmerston and himself.

After Lord Palmerston's answer, Lord John Russell can have but little hope that Lord Palmerston will not see M. Kossuth. Lord John Russell cannot separate the private from the public man in this instance; the reception of Kossuth, if it takes place, will be a reception by your Majesty's Secretary of State for Foreign Affairs. Whether that reception is to take place in Downing Street or Carlton Terrace does not appear to him material.

Lord John Russell would, as a last resource, humbly advise your Majesty to command Lord Palmerston not to receive M. Kossuth.

It appears to him that your Majesty owes this mark of respect to your Majesty's ally, and generally to all States at peace with this country.

Lord John Russell has no other copy of this letter to Lord Palmerston.

Lord John Russell to Queen Victoria

Pembroke Lodge, 21st November 1851

Lord John Russell presents his humble duty to your Majesty. He had the honour of receiving last night your Majesty's communication respecting Lord Palmerston.

Lord John Russell presumes that it is the substance of this communication which your Majesty wishes to be laid before the Cabinet.

But before doing so he cannot refrain from mentioning some circumstances which appear to him to weigh materially in the consideration of Lord Palmerston's conduct.

---

* Lord Palmerston wished to receive Kossuth at the Foreign Office. In the correspondence here referred to, which will be found in Russell's *Life*, the Premier 'positively requested' Lord Palmerston to decline to receive Kossuth. The rejoinder, written while the messenger waited, was: 'There are limits to all things. I do not choose to be dictated to as to who I may or may not receive in my own house. ... I shall use my own discretion. ... You will, of course, use yours as to the composition of your Government.'

In many instances Lord Palmerston has yielded to the remonstrances of Lord John Russell, supported as they have been by your Majesty.

He did so on the question of furnishing guns to the Sicilians.

He did so in respect to the letter to Baron Koller on the affair of Count Haynau.

He gave way likewise in this last instance, when, after assuring Lord Dudley Stuart that he would see Kossuth whenever he chose to call upon him, he consented to intimate privately to Lord Dudley that he requested him not to call.

This last concession must have been mortifying to Lord Palmerston, and he has consoled himself in a manner not very dignified by giving importance to the inflated addresses from some meetings in the suburbs of London.

But it appears to Lord John Russell that every Minister must have a certain latitude allow him which he may use, perhaps with indiscretion, perhaps with bad taste, but with no consequence of sufficient importance to deserve notice.

Lord John Russell must, however, call your Majesty's attention to an article in the *Morning Post*, which denies the accuracy of the report of Lord Palmerston's answer to what is there called 'the froth and folly of an address to Downing Street.'

Lord John Russell, in admitting that he has more than once represented to your Majesty that the expulsion of Lord Palmerston would break up the Government, begs to explain that he has always done so upon one of two grounds:

First, if Lord Palmerston should be called upon by your Majesty to resign on account of a line of Foreign Policy of which his colleagues had approved, and for which they were, with him, responsible.

Second, in case no difference of opinion had arisen, and the transaction should bear the character of an intrigue, to get rid of an inconvenient colleague.

It must be remembered that Lord Palmerston was recommended to the late King by Lord Grey as Foreign Secretary, and remained in that Office from 1830 to 1834; that he was afterwards replaced in the same Office by Lord Melbourne, and remained from 1835 to 1841.

He has thus represented the Foreign Policy of the Whig Party fifteen years, and has been approved not only by them but by a large portion of the country. In the advice which Lord John Russell has humbly tendered to your Majesty, he has always had in view the importance of maintaining the popular confidence which your Majesty's name everywhere inspires. Somewhat of the good opinion of the Emperor of Russia and other foreign Sovereigns may be lost, but the good will and affection of the people of England are retained, a great security in these times.

Lord John Russell has made out a note of his address to the Cabinet for your Majesty's information. He prays to have it returned.

Queen Victoria to Lord John Russell

Osborne, 4th December 1851

The Queen has learnt with surprise and concern the events which have taken place at Paris.* She thinks it is of great importance that Lord Normanby should be instructed to remain entirely passive, and to take no part whatever in what is passing. Any word from him might be misconstrued at such a moment.

Queen Victoria to Lord John Russell

Osborne, 13th December 1851

The Queen sends the enclosed despatch from Lord Normanby to Lord John Russell, from which it appears that the French Govern-

---

* On 2nd December, Louis Napoleon seized the Government of France, arrested his chief opponents, put an end to the National Assembly and Council of State, and declared Paris in a state of siege. On the 3rd the tidings of the *coup d'état* reached London. Count Walewski announced it to Lord Palmerston, who expressed his approval of it, and wrote to Lord Normanby disavowing surprise that the President had struck the blow when he did, 'for it is now well known here that the Duchess of Orleans was preparing to be called to Paris this week with her younger son to commence a new period of Orleans dynasty'. Lord Normanby, having applied for instructions as to his future conduct, was desired to make no change in his relations with the French Government, and to abstain from even the appearance of interference in her internal affairs. Having made a communication to this effect M. Turgot, the latter replied that M. Walewski had notified to him that Lord Palmerston had already expressed to him his 'entire approbation of the act of the President', and his 'conviction that he could not have acted otherwise'.

ment *pretend to have received* the entire approval of the late *coup d'état* by the British Government, as conveyed by Lord Palmerston to Count Walewski. The Queen cannot believe in the truth of the assertion, as such an approval given by Lord Palmerston would have been in complete *contradiction* to the line of strict neutrality and passiveness which the Queen had expressed her desire to see followed with regard to the late convulsion at Paris, and which was approved by the Cabinet, as stated in Lord John Russell's letter of the 6th inst. Does Lord John know anything about the alleged approval, which, if true, would *again* expose the honesty and dignity of the Queen's Government in the eyes of the world?

Lord John Russell to Queen Victoria

Woburn Abbey, 19th December 1851

Lord John Russell presents his humble duty to your Majesty, and has the honour to submit to your Majesty a correspondence with Viscount Palmerston, which terminates with a letter of this day's date.

Lord John Russell has now to advise your Majesty that Lord Palmerston should be informed that your Majesty is ready to accept the Seals of Office, and to place them in other hands.

Lord John Russell has summoned a Cabinet for Monday.

They may be of opinion that they cannot continue a Government.

But that is not Lord John Russell's opinion; and should they agree with him, he will proceed without delay to recommend a successor to your Majesty.

The Earl Granville appears to him the person best calculated for that post, but the Cabinet may be of opinion that more experience is required.

Queen Victoria to the King of the Belgians

Windsor Castle, 23rd December 1851

MY DEAREST UNCLE,—I have the greatest pleasure in announcing to you a piece of news which I know will give you as much satisfaction and relief as it does to us, and will do to the *whole* of the world. *Lord Palmerston* is *no longer Foreign Secretary*—and Lord Granville is already named his successor! ! He had become of late really quite reckless. ... Lord John wrote to him that *he could no longer remain Foreign Secretary*, for that perpetual misunderstanding and breaches of decorum were taking place which endangered the country. Lord Palmerston answered instantly that he would give up the Seals the moment his successor was named! Certain as we all felt that he could not have continued long in his place, we were quite taken by surprise when we learnt of the *dénouement*. ...

1852

Queen Victoria to the King of the Belgians

Buckingham Palace, 3rd February 1852

MY DEAREST UNCLE,— ... Albert grows daily fonder and fonder of politics and business, and is so wonderfully *fit* for both—such perspicacity and such *courage*—and I grow daily to dislike them both more and more. We women are not *made* for governing—and if we are good women, we must *dislike* these masculine occupations; but there are times which force one to take *interest* in them *mal gré bon gré*, and *I* do, of course, *intensely*.

I must now conclude, to dress for the opening of Parliament. ... Ever your devoted Niece, VICTORIA R.

Lord John Russell to the Prince Albert

Chesham Place, 16th February 1852

SIR,—I have seen the Duke of Wellington this morning, and have given him the Depôt plan.

It may be useful if your Royal Highness will see him from time to time in relation to the Army. On the one hand, your Royal Highness's authority may overcome the indisposition to change which he naturally entertains; and on the other, his vast experience may be of great use to your Royal Highness in regard to the future. I have the honour to be, Sir, your Royal Highness's most dutiful Servant,

JOHN RUSSELL

Queen Victoria to the King of the Belgians

Buckingham Palace, 17th February 1852

MY DEAREST UNCLE,— ... Albert becomes really a *terrible* man of business; I think it takes a little off from the gentleness of his character, and makes him so preoccupied. I grieve over all this, as I *cannot* enjoy these things, *much* as I interest myself in *general* European politics; but I am every day more convinced that *we women*, *if* we *are* to be *good* women, *feminine* and *amiable* and *domestic*, are *not fitted to reign*; at least it is *contre gré* that they drive themselves to the *work* which it entails.

However, this cannot now be helped, and it is the duty of every one to fulfil all that they are called upon to do, in whatever situation they may be! . . .

Memorandum by the Prince Albert

Buckingham Palace, 21st February 1852

Lord John Russell came this morning at twelve o'clock to explain that after the vote of yesterday it was impossible for him to go on any longer with the Government. He considered it a vote of censure, and an entirely unprecedented case not to allow a Minister of the Crown even to lay his measure on the Table of the House; that he had expected to the last that the respectable part of the House would see all this, but there seemed to have been a pre-arranged determination between Lord Palmerston and the Protectionists to defeat the Government; that the Peelites also had agreed to vote against them. Sir James Graham and Mr Cardwell had stayed away, but Mr Gladstone and Mr S. Herbert had voted against them, the latter even misrepresenting what Lord John had said. . . .

At a quarter past four Lord John came back from the Cabinet, and formally tendered the resignations of himself and colleagues. The Cabinet had been unanimous that there was no other course to pursue, and that it would not be advisable to make use of the Queen's permission to advise a Dissolution. Lord Granville had ascertained through Dr Quin from Lord Lyndhurst that Lord Derby was prepared with an Administration, having obtained Mr Thomas Baring's consent to act as Leader of the House of Commons. . . .

Memorandum by the Prince Albert

Buckingham Palace, 23rd February 1852

... After he had kissed hands upon his entering upon his office, Lord Derby had a further conversation with me on Household appointments. I told him he must now, as Prime Minister, consider himself to a certain degree in the position of the Confessor; that formerly the Lord Chancellor was Keeper of the King's Conscience, the office might be considered to have descended on the Prime Minister. The Queen must then be able to confer with him on personal matters, or I, on her behalf, with the most entire confidence, and that she must be sure that nothing was divulged which passed between them on these matters, and he might repose the same confidence in us. As to the formation of the Household, the Queen made two conditions, viz. that the persons to compose her Court should not be on the verge of bankruptcy, and that their moral character should bear investigation. On the Queen's accession Lord Melbourne had been very careless in his appointments, and great harm had resulted to the Court therefrom. Since her marriage I had insisted upon a closer line being drawn, and though Lord Melbourne had declared 'that that damned morality would undo us all,' we had found great advantage in it and were determined to adhere to it. . . .   ALBERT

Colonel Phipps to Queen Victoria

Buckingham Palace, 10th March 1852

Colonel Phipps' humble duty to your Majesty.

He has this day visited the Marionette Theatre, and feels quite certain not only that it would not be a suitable theatre for your Majesty to visit, but that your Majesty would derive no amusement from it.

The mechanism of the puppets is only passable, and the matter of the entertainment stupid and tiresome, consisting in a great part of worn-out old English songs, such as 'The death of Nelson'! Colonel Phipps considers 'Punch' a much more amusing performance. Lady Mount Edgecumbe, who was in a box there, would probably give your Majesty an account of it. . . .

Queen Victoria to the King of the Belgians

Buckingham Palace, 30th March 1852

MY DEAREST UNCLE,—Many thanks for your dear letter of the 26th, which I received on Saturday. Here we shall have some trouble with our Militia Bill, which all of a sudden seems to have caused dissatisfaction and alarm. Lord Derby is quite prepared to drop Protection, as he knows that the Elections will bring a Free Trade, though a Conservative majority. Mr Disraeli (*alias* Dizzy) writes very curious reports to me of the House of Commons proceedings—much in the style of his books. . . .

The King of the Belgians to Queen Victoria

Laeken, 10th September 1852

MY DEAREST VICTORIA,— . . . That Mr Neild* should have left that great fortune to you delighted me; it gives the possibility of forming a private fortune for the Royal Family, the necessity of which nobody can deny. Such things only still happen in England, where there exists loyalty and strong affection for Royalty, a feeling unfortunately much diminished on the Continent of Europe, though it did exist there also. . . .

Memorandum by the Prince Albert

Balmoral, 17th September 1852

The death of the Duke of Wellington has deprived the Country of her greatest man, the Crown of its most valuable servant and adviser, the Army of its main strength and support. We received the sad news on an expedition from Allt-na-Giuthasach to the Dhu Loch (one of the wildest and loneliest spots of the Highlands) at four

* John Camden Neild, an eccentric and miserly bachelor, nominally a barrister, died on 30th August, bequeathing substantially the whole of his fortune (amounting to half a million) to the Queen. As there were no known relatives, the Queen felt able to accept this legacy; but she first increased the legacies to the executors from £100 to £1000 each, made provision for Mr Neild's servants and others who had claims on him, restored the chancel of North Marston Church, Bucks, where he was buried, and inserted a window there to his memory.

o'clock yesterday afternoon. We hurried home to Allt-na-Giuthasach, and to-day here, where it became important to settle with Lord Derby the mode of providing for the command of the Army, and the filling up of the many posts and places which the Duke had held.

I had privately prepared a list of the mode in which this should be done, and discussed it with Victoria, and found, to both Lord Derby's and our astonishment, that it tallied in *every* point with the recommendations which he had thought of making.

I explained to Lord Derby the grounds upon which I thought it better not to assume the Command myself, and told him of the old Duke's proposal, two years ago, to prepare the way to my assuming the Command by the appointment of a Chief of the Staff, on Sir Willoughby Gordon's death, and the reasons on which I then declined the offer. Lord Derby entirely concurred in my views, and seemed relieved by my explanation; we then agreed that for the loss of *authority* which we had lost with the Duke, we could only make up by increase in *efficiency* in the appointments to the different offices. That Lord Hardinge was the only man fit to command the Army. . . .

Victoria wishes the Army to mourn for the Duke as long as for a member of the Royal Family. . . .

Queen Victoria to the King of the Belgians

Balmoral, 17th September 1852

MY DEAREST UNCLE,— . . . For *him* it is a blessing that he should have been taken away in the possession of his great and powerful mind and without a lingering illness. But for this country, and for us, his loss—though it could not have been long delayed—is irreparable! He was the pride and the *bon génie*, as it were, of this country! He was the GREATEST man this country ever produced, and the most *devoted* and *loyal* subject, and the staunchest supporter the Crown ever had. He was to us a true, kind friend and most valuable adviser. To think that all this is gone; that this great and immortal man belongs now to History and no longer to the present, is a truth which we cannot realise. We shall soon stand sadly alone; Aberdeen is almost the only personal friend of that kind we have left. Melbourne, Peel, Liverpool—and now the Duke—*all* gone! . . .

The Earl of Derby to Queen Victoria

St James's Square, 3rd December 1852
(Friday night, twelve o'clock p.m.)

Lord Derby, with his humble duty, ventures to hope that your Majesty may feel some interest in hearing, so far as he is able to give it, his impression of the effect of Mr Disraeli's announcement of the Budget this evening. Lord Derby was not able to hear quite the commencement of the Speech, having been obliged to attend the House of Lords, which, however, was up at a quarter past five, Mr Disraeli having then been speaking about half an hour. From that time till ten, when he sat down, Lord Derby was in the House of Commons, and anxiously watching the effect produced, which he ventures to assure your Majesty was most favourable, according to his own judgment after some considerable experience in Parliament, and also from what he heard from others. Mr Disraeli spoke for about five hours, with no apparent effort, with perfect self-possession, and with hardly an exception to the fixed attention with which the House listened to the exposition of the views of your Majesty's servants. It was altogether a most masterly performance, and he kept alive the attention of the House with the greatest ability, introducing the most important statements, and the broadest principles of legislature, just at the moments when he had excited the greatest anxiety to learn the precise measures which the Government intended to introduce. The Irish part of the question was dealt with with remarkable dexterity, though probably a great part of the point will be lost in the newspaper reports. It is difficult to foresee the ultimate result, but Lord Derby has no hesitation in saying that the general first impression was very favourable, and that, as a whole, the Budget seemed to meet with the approval of the House.

Memorandum by the Prince Albert

Osborne, 18th December 1852

Yesterday evening Lord Derby arrived from Town formally to tender his resignation. We retired to the Queen's room after dinner with him to hear what he had to say on the crisis. . . . He had heard lately from good authority that the Whigs and Peelites had come to an agreement, and were ready to form an Administration on Conservative principles, to the exclusion of the Radicals, under the lead of Lord Aberdeen. Although only 150 strong, they thought, that with all the talent they had at their command, they would be able to obtain the confidence of the country, and hold the balance between the two extreme Parties in the House. . . .

He then gave it rather jokingly as his opinion that he thought less than 32 could hardly be the number of the new Cabinet, so many former Ministers would expect to be taken in; the Whigs said 36. Lord John Russell was designated for the Home Office, Lord Canning for the Foreign, Mr Gladstone for the Colonial Department, Lord Clanricarde for the Post Office, Lord Granville for Ireland. These were the reports.   ALBERT

Memorandum by Queen Victoria

Windsor Castle, 25th December 1852

Lord Aberdeen came this afternoon to announce the completion of his Cabinet.

From many of them answers have not yet been received.

The day before it looked very bad. Lord John Russell had sent in such a list of persons whom he required in the Cabinet (Sir Francis Baring, Sir George Grey, etc., etc.), that, having been very yielding hitherto, Lord Aberdeen was obliged to be peremptory in his refusal. Now that the Cabinet was formed on a due proportion, he was inclined to let Lord John have his own way pretty much with regard to the minor Offices, considering that he brought 250 followers, and he (Lord Aberdeen) only 50.

It was to Lord Clarendon that the persuasion of Lady John was finally due, but Lord Aberdeen had to add his own promise to that of Lord Clarendon, that the latter would take the Foreign Office whenever she thought Lord John ought to be relieved from it.

Lady Palmerston had been most anxious to bring her husband into office again; Lord Aberdeen had seen the first symptom of their joint wish in the earnestness with which Lord Palmerston's friends declared in all places that, had he been well enough, he would certainly have voted against the Government. . . .

Memorandum by the Prince Albert

Windsor Castle, 28th December 1852

The delivery of the Seals of Office of the outgoing Ministers into the Queen's hands, and her bestowal of them upon the new Ministers, took place to-day.

Of the former, Mr Disraeli seemed to feel most the loss of office. . . .

1853

The Prince Albert to Mr Gladstone

Buckingham Palace, 19th April 1853

MY DEAR MR GLADSTONE,—I must write to you a line in order to congratulate you on your success of last night. I have just completed a close and careful perusal of your speech, which I admire extremely, and I have heard from all sides that the effect it has produced is very good. Trusting that your Christian humility will not allow you to become dangerously elated, I cannot resist sending you the report which Lord John Russell made to the Queen for your perusal; knowing that it will give you pleasure, and that these are the best rewards which a public man can look for. Ever yours truly,   ALBERT

1854

The Earl of Aberdeen to Queen Victoria

London, 6th January 1854

LORD ABERDEEN presents his humble duty to your Majesty. He cannot wonder at the indignation expressed by your Majesty at the base and infamous attack made upon the Prince during the last two or three weeks in some of the daily papers.* They are chiefly to be found in those papers which represent ultra-Tory or extreme Radical opinions; but they are not sanctioned by the most respectable portion of the Press. Lord Aberdeen has received some information respecting the origin of these attacks; but it is vague and uncertain. At all events he believes that your Majesty may safely make yourself at ease upon the subject, as he is satisfied that these hostile feelings are shared by few. It is much to be desired that some notice of the subject may be taken in Parliament, when, by being treated in a proper manner, it may be effectually stopped. Lord Aberdeen has spoken to Lord John Russell, who will be quite prepared to moot it in the House of Commons.

It cannot be denied that the position of the Prince is somewhat anomalous, and has not been specially provided for by the Constitution; but the ties of Nature, and the dictates of common sense are more powerful than Constitutional fictions; and Lord Aberdeen can only say that he has always considered it an inestimable blessing that your Majesty should possess so able, so zealous, and so disinterested an adviser. It is true that your Ministers are alone responsible for the conduct of public affairs, and although there is no man in England whose opinion Lord Aberdeen would more highly respect and value, still if he had the misfortune of differing from His Royal Highness, he would not hesitate to act according to his own convictions, and a sense of what was due to your Majesty's service.

The Prince has now been so long before the eyes of the whole country, his conduct so invariably devoted to the public good, and his life so perfectly inattackable, that Lord Aberdeen has not the slightest apprehension of any serious consequences arising from these contemptible exhibitions of malevolence and faction.

* A section of the Press, favourable to Lord Palmerston, had insinuated that his resignation was due to 'an influence behind the throne'. Similar attacks were made by other journals, and not abandoned upon Lord Palmerston's re-admission to the Cabinet: the most extravagant charges of improper interference in State affairs were made against the Prince, and it was even rumoured that he had been impeached for high treason and committed to the Tower! The cartoons in *Punch* usually present a faithful reflection of current popular opinion, and in one of them the Prince was depicted as skating, in defiance of warning, over dangerous ice.

Your Majesty will graciously pardon Lord Aberdeen for writing thus plainly; but there are occasions on which he almost forgets your Majesty's station, and only remembers those feelings which are common to all ranks of mankind.

Queen Victoria to Mr Gladstone

Windsor Castle, 7th February 1854

The Queen must apologise for having kept the enclosed papers so long, and in now sending them back she does so without feeling sure in her mind that she could with safety sanction Mr Gladstone's new and important proposal.* The change it implies will be very great in principle and irretrievable, and the Queen must say that Lord John Russell's apprehensions as to the spirit it is likely to engender amongst the future civil servants of the Crown have excited a similar feeling in her mind. Where is moreover the application of the principle of public competition to stop, if once established? and must not those offices which are to be exempted from it necessarily degrade the persons appointed to them in public estimation?

Mr Gladstone to Queen Victoria

Downing Street, 17th February 1854

The Chancellor of the Exchequer presents his humble duty to your Majesty, and has the honour to acknowledge your Majesty's gracious letter.

He takes blame to himself for having caused your Majesty trouble by omitting to include in his short memorandum an explanation of the phrase 'qualified persons.'

Experience at the universities and public schools of this country has shown that in a large majority of cases the test of open examination is also an effectual test of character; as, except in very remarkable cases, the previous industry and self-denial, which proficiency evinces, are rarely separated from general habits of virtue.

* Mr Gladstone had written on 26th January on the subject of competitive examinations for the Civil Service; in reply to the Queen's letter, he referred to the discontent existing in the Service with the system of appointment by favour, and of promotion by seniority alone.

But he humbly assures your Majesty that the utmost pains will be taken to provide not only for the majority but for all cases, by the strictest enquiries of which the case will admit; and he has the most confident belief that the securities for character under the system, although they cannot be unerring, will be stronger and more trustworthy than any of which the present method of appointment is susceptible.

Queen Victoria to the King of the Belgians

Buckingham Palace, 21st February 1854

MY DEAREST UNCLE,— ... War is, I fear, *quite* inevitable. You will have seen that the Emperor Nicholas has not given a favourable answer to *our Brother* Napoleon (which I hear has disappointed him extremely, as he expected very great results from it); and the last proposals or attempts made by Buol it is to be hoped will not be accepted by Russia, for France and England could *not* accept them; but if Austria and Prussia go with us—as we hope they will—the War will only be a local one. Our beautiful Guards sail to-morrow. Albert inspected them yesterday. George is quite delighted to have a division. . . .

Queen Victoria to the King of the Belgians

Buckingham Palace, 28th February 1854

MY DEAREST UNCLE,— ... The last battalion of the Guards (Scots Fusiliers) embarked to-day. They passed through the courtyard here at seven o'clock this morning. We stood on the balcony to see them —the morning fine, the sun rising over the towers of old Westminster Abbey—and an immense crowd collected to see these fine men, and cheering them immensely as they with difficulty marched along. They formed line, presented arms, and then cheered us *very heartily,* and went off cheering. It was a *touching and beautiful* sight; many sorrowing friends were there, and one saw the shake of many a hand. My best wishes and prayers will be with them all. . . .

Queen Victoria to the Earl of Aberdeen

[Undated]

The Queen was rather annoyed at the manner in which Lord Clarendon pressed the Duke of Cambridge's going to the Tuileries last night. She thought it an immense boon upon her part to allow the Duke of Cambridge *to go to Paris*—and instead of its being considered as such by Lord Clarendon and Count Walewski, the Queen was told it would offend the Emperor if the Duke did not go to the Tuileries also. The Queen observed that it was unnecessary and unusual for the Duke, or any Prince almost, to live at the *Palace* of the Sovereign, unless he was a very particular friend or near relation. The Duke of Genoa had refused going there, though he had received other civilities here; in the same manner *no Prince* comes to this *Palace* unless he is a very *near relation* or particular friend. To this Lord Clarendon replied that it was 'because the *Emperor wished* it,' which rather shocked the Queen, and she spoke *strongly* to him upon the subject. The result was that the Queen said she would speak to the Duke of Cambridge about it, and see, as the Emperor made *so great a point of it*, and Lord Clarendon considered that the *Alliance depended upon it*, what he would do. . . .

The Queen must and *will* protest, for she cannot mix up personal friendship with a political Alliance. The former is the *result* of the *experience* of years of mutual friendship, and cannot be *carried by storm*. . . .

There would be nothing unusual in apartments being offered to the Duke of Cambridge, and declined by him. This was done by the King of the Belgians only last summer at Berlin and Vienna, without anybody's construing it into an affront. The Queen adds a list of the Royal personages who have been in England and never resided at the Palace. Lord Aberdeen may show this letter to Lord Clarendon.

Queen Victoria to the King of the Belgians

Osborne, 14th March 1854

MY DEAREST UNCLE,—Your kind letter of the 9th arrived here on Saturday just when we returned from a splendid and never-to-be-forgotten sight—the sailing of our noble Fleet for the Baltic; the Navy and Nation were particularly pleased at *my leading them out,* as they call it, which in fact was the case, as, in our little *Fairy* we went on and lay to, to see them all come out, which (the wind being fair) they did, with sails set, each passing us close by, and giving us three hearty cheers, as I think none but British tars *can* give. Gloriously they bore along, followed by the prayers and good wishes of all. You should read the account in yesterday's *Times.* Another sailing squadron goes to-morrow. The Captains and Admirals all took leave on board, and seemed much impressed with the solemnity of the moment. . . . Ever your truly devoted Niece,

VICTORIA R.

Queen Victoria to the Earl of Aberdeen

1st April 1854

The Queen rejoices to see the Debate was favourable in the House of Lords, and that it was concluded in the House of Commons.*. . .

Lord John Russell to Queen Victoria

Pembroke Lodge, 9th April 1854

Lord John Russell presents his humble duty to your Majesty; he cannot think it consistent with fairness to conceal from your Majesty the deep feelings of mortification which affect him on reviewing the proceedings of the Cabinet yesterday. . . .†

* On 27th March the Queen announced to Parliament that the negotiations with the Czar had terminated, and that she felt bound 'to afford active assistance to her ally, the Sultan'. Next day the Declaration of War was issued, containing a narrative of the events which finally led to the rupture. The debates on the Address in answer to the message took place on 31st March, Mr Bright, in the Commons, censuring the declaration, and being replied to by Lord Palmerston. The addresses were presented to the Queen on 3rd April.

† Lord John Russell's actions at this period of his career seem often incomprehensible; but his private domestic anxieties seem to have weighed him down. Having made the great sacrifice, for an ex-Premier, of taking office under an old opponent, he was now engaged in trying to regain the first place for himself. Lord Aberdeen had always contemplated retiring in his favour, but would not give up the Premiership in the face of the dangers threatening the country. Moreover, he had believed his continuance in office

Queen Victoria to the Earl of Aberdeen

Buckingham Palace, 26th June 1854

The Queen has not yet acknowledged Lord Aberdeen's letter of the 24th. She is very glad to hear that he will take an opportunity to-day of dispelling misapprehensions which have arisen in the public mind in consequence of his last speech in the House of Lords, and the effect of which has given the Queen very great uneasiness.* She knows Lord Aberdeen so well that she can fully enter into his feelings and understand what he means, but the public, particularly under strong excitement of patriotic feeling, is impatient and annoyed to hear at this moment the first Minister of the Crown enter into an *impartial* examination of the Emperor of Russia's character and conduct. The qualities in Lord Aberdeen's character which the Queen values most highly, his candour and his courage in expressing opinions even if opposed to general feelings of the moment, are in this instance dangerous to him, and the Queen hopes that in the vindication of his own conduct to-day, which ought to be triumphant, as it wants in fact *no* vindication, he will not undertake the ungrateful and injurious task of vindicating the Emperor of Russia from any of the exaggerated charges brought against him and his policy at a time when there is enough in it to make us fight with all might against it.

to be a guarantee for peace. Lord John Russell, after accepting the Foreign Office, had then insisted on being a Minister without office; later still, by displacing Mr Strutt and transferring Lord Granville to the Duchy, he himself became Lord President of the Council, an office which no commoner had held since the reign of Henry VIII. By such action, coupled with perpetual threats of resignation, he marred his prospects of succeeding Lord Aberdeen, and, as will be seen, failed in his attempt to construct an Administration when the opportunity was offered him.

* The speech of Lord Aberdeen, to which the Queen here refers, had created a very unsatisfactory impression. On 19th June the venerable Lord Lyndhurst had denounced the aggressive policy and the perfidy of Russia; in the debate which followed, Lord Aberdeen spoke coldly, in a strain of semi-apology for Russia, and with an unlucky reference to the Treaty of Adrianople. Popular feeling against Russia being then at a white heat, the speech was considered indicative of apathy on behalf of the Government in the prosecution of the war. Accordingly, by moving on a later day for a copy of his own despatch of 1829, relative to the Treaty, the Premier obtained an opportunity of dispelling some of the apprehensions which his speech had excited.

Queen Victoria to the Earl of Clarendon

Buckingham Palace, 27th June 1854

The Queen observes in Lord Cowley's letter a suggestion of M. Drouyn de Lhuys to stop, if possible, the Russian Loan. She thinks this of the highest importance as *cutting* the *sinews* of war of the enemy. The Queen does not know whether we have by law the power to forbid the quotation of this stock in our market, but a short Act of Parliament might be obtained for the purpose. The London and Paris markets rejecting such paper would have the greatest influence upon its issue.

Queen Victoria to the Duke of Newcastle

Buckingham Palace, 3rd July 1854

In consequence of the departure of these additional 5,000 men for the East, the Queen feels very uneasy at the very defenceless state in which the country will be left, not from any want of confidence arising from the present conjuncture of affairs, but from a strong sense of the impolicy and danger of leaving this great country in such a helpless state under any circumstances, for we never can foresee what events may not suddenly spring up at any moment (like Greece, for instance) which may require a force to be in readiness for any particular purpose.

The Queen therefore wishes the Duke of Newcastle to give her detailed answers upon the various points stated in the accompanying paper; but the Queen wishes to have the *'effective* state' and not 'the state upon paper only.' The Duke will be able to obtain these reports from the different departments.

What store of muskets are there *here?*

When will the new ones be ready?

What is the force of Artillery left in the country in men and horses?

What amount of troops are there in the country of Infantry (deducting the 5,000 men under orders for the East), and of Cavalry, and where are they stationed?

How much Militia has been and will be embodied?

What is the Naval Force at home?

How much serviceable ammunition is there both of Artillery and small arms in the country?

The Earl of Aberdeen to Queen Victoria

London, 1st September 1854

Lord Aberdeen, with his humble duty, begs to lay before your Majesty the pensions proposed to be granted on the Civil List at this time. The only case requiring any special remark is that of the children of Lord Nelson's adopted daughter. There seems little doubt that the person referred to was really Lord Nelson's daughter, according to evidence recently produced, and was recommended by him to the care of the country, just before the battle of Trafalgar.*

A numerous party in the House of Commons wished that your Majesty's Government should propose a special vote for this person and her family; but the Cabinet thought that it would give rise to much scandal and disagreeable debate, and finally recommended Lord Aberdeen to place the three daughters on the Pension List. The circumstances of the case are, no doubt, very peculiar; and although Lord Aberdeen does not feel perfectly satisfied with the course pursued, he thinks it very desirable to avoid the sort of Parliamentary debates to which the discussion of such a subject would necessarily give rise.

Queen Victoria to the Earl of Clarendon

Balmoral, 30th September 1854

The Queen returns the enclosed letters. The French show their usual vivacity in pressing so hard for decision upon what is to be done with Sebastopol when taken. Surely we ought to have taken it first before we can dispose of it, and everything as to the decision about it must depend upon the state in which we receive it, and the opinion of the Military and Naval Commanders after they find themselves in possession of it. The Queen hopes, therefore, that Lord Clarendon will succeed in restraining French impatience as he has often done before.

---

* Horatia, daughter of Nelson and Lady Hamilton, was born on 29th January 1801, and married in 1822 the Rev. Philip Ward of Tenterden. She died in 1881.

The Earl of Aberdeen to Queen Victoria

Haddo House, 1st October 1854

... Lord Aberdeen humbly presumes to offer his most cordial congratulations to your Majesty on the great intelligence received by telegraph this morning. The account sent by Lord Stratford of the victory
on the Alma must be correct; the report mentioned by Mr Colquhoun
may possibly be so too. At all events, we may fairly hope that the
fall of Sebastopol cannot long be delayed. . . .

... The fall of Sebastopol would in fact be the conquest of the
Crimea, and the Allies might winter there with perfect security, as,
by occupying the lines of Perekop, any access to the Crimea would
effectively be prevented by land. Lord Aberdeen thought that with
a view to peace, and the restitution of the Crimea to Russia, it would
be more easy for the Emperor to accept the destruction of the forti-
fications when accomplished, than to agree to any stipulation having
such an object.

Queen Victoria to the King of the Belgians

Hull, 13th October 1854

MY DEAREST UNCLE,— ... We are, and indeed the whole country is, *entirely* engrossed with one idea, one *anxious* thought—the *Crimea*. We
have received all the *most* interesting and *gratifying* details of the
splendid and decisive victory of the Alma; alas! it was a bloody one.
Our loss was a heavy one—many have fallen and many are wounded,
but my noble Troops behaved with a *courage* and *desperation* which
was beautiful to behold. The Russians expected their position would
hold out three weeks; their loss was immense—the whole garrison
of Sebastopol was out. Since that, the Army has performed a wonderful
march to Balaklava, and the bombardment of Sebastopol has begun.
Lord Raglan's behaviour was worthy of the old Duke's—such cool-
ness in the midst of the hottest fire. We have had all the details from
young Burghersh (a remarkably nice young man), one of Lord Raglan's Aides-de-camp whom he sent home with the Despatches, who
was in the midst of it all. I feel so *proud* of my dear noble Troops,
who, they say, bear their privations, and the sad disease which still
haunts them, with such courage and good humour.

Queen Victoria to Lord Raglan

Windsor Castle, 18th November 1854

The Queen has received with pride and joy the telegraphic news of the glorious, but alas! bloody victory of the 5th.* These feelings of pride and satisfaction are, however, painfully alloyed by the grievous news of the loss of so many Generals, and in particular Sir George Cathcart—who was so distinguished and excellent an officer. . . .

The Queen cannot sufficiently express her high sense of the great services he has rendered and is rendering to her and the country, by the very able manner in which he has led the bravest troops that ever fought, and which it is a pride to her to be able to call her own. To mark the Queen's feelings of approbation she wishes to confer on Lord Raglan the Baton of Field-Marshal. It affords her the sincerest gratification to confer it on one who has so nobly earned the highest rank in the Army, which he so long served in under the immortal hero, who she laments could not witness the success of a friend he so greatly esteemed. . . .

The Duke of Newcastle to Queen Victoria

War Department, 22nd December 1854

. . . The Duke of Newcastle assures your Majesty that the condition of the Hospital at Scutari, and the entire want of all method and arrangement in everything which concerns the comfort of the Army, are subjects of constant and most painful anxiety to him, and he wishes most earnestly that he could see his way clearly to an early and complete remedy. . . .†

---

* The English loss at the battle of Inkerman was over 2,500 killed and wounded; the French lost 1,800. The loss of the enemy was doubtful, but the Russian estimate (much smaller than our own) was about 12,000 killed, wounded, and prisoners. The Grand Dukes Nicholas and Michael both fought in the battle.

† Early in November, a band of capable and devoted nurses, under the superintendence of Miss Florence Nightingale, had arrived at Scutari, the experiment having been devised and projected by Mr Sidney Herbert, who was a personal friend of Miss Nightingale. The party was accompanied by Mr and Mrs Bracebridge, whose letters describing the condition of the hospitals had been sent by the Queen to the Duke of Newcastle.

1855

Lord John Russell to the Earl of Aberdeen

Chesham Place, 23rd January 1855

MY DEAR LORD ABERDEEN,—Mr Roebuck has given notice of a Motion to enquire into the conduct of the war. I do not see how this Motion is to be resisted. But as it involves a censure of the War Departments with which some of my colleagues are connected, my only course is to tender my resignation.

I therefore have to request you will lay my humble resignation of the office, which I have the honour to hold, before the Queen, with the expression of my gratitude for Her Majesty's kindness for many years. I remain, my dear Lord Aberdeen, yours very truly,

J. RUSSELL

Queen Victoria to Lord John Russell

Windsor Castle, 24th January 1855

The Queen has this moment received Lord John Russell's letter and enclosure, and must express to him her surprise and concern at hearing so abruptly of his intention to desert her Government on the Motion of Mr Roebuck.

Viscount Palmerston to Queen Victoria

144 Piccadilly, 26th January 1855

Viscount Palmerston presents his humble duty to your Majesty, and begs to state that Lord John Russell having made his statement, concluding with an announcement that he did not mean to vote on Mr Roebuck's Motion, and Viscount Palmerston having made a few remarks on that statement, Mr Roebuck rose to make his Motion; but the paralytic affection under which he has for some time laboured soon overpowered him, and before he had proceeded far in his speech he became so unwell that he was obliged to finish abruptly, make his Motion, and sit down....

Viscount Palmerston regrets to say that the general aspect of the House was not very encouraging.

Memorandum by Queen Victoria

Windsor Castle, 31st January 1855

We went up to Buckingham Palace and saw Lord Derby at half-past eleven. The Queen informed him of the resignation of the Government, and of her desire that he should try to form a new one. She addressed herself to him as the head of the largest Party in the House of Commons, and which had by its vote chiefly contributed to the overthrow of the Government.... He owned that his Party was the most compact—mustering about two hundred and eighty men—but he had no men capable of governing the House of Commons, and he should not be able to present an Administration that would be accepted by the country unless it was strengthened by other combinations; he knew that the whole country cried out for Lord Palmerston as the only man fit for carrying on the war with success, and he owned the necessity of having him in the Government, were it even only to satisfy the French Government, the confidence of which was at this moment of the greatest importance; but he must say, speaking without reserve, that whatever the ignorant public might think, Lord Palmerston was totally unfit for the task. He had become very deaf as well as very blind, was seventy-one years old, and ... in fact, though he still kept up his sprightly manners of youth, it was evident that his day had gone by....*

Queen Victoria to Viscount Palmerston

Windsor Castle, 4th February 1855

Lord John Russell having just informed the Queen that he was obliged to resign the task which the Queen confided to him, she

---

*Lord Derby's judgment was not borne out by subsequent events. Lord Palmerston was Prime Minister when he died on 18th October 1865, ten years later. 'The half-opened cabinet-box on his table, and the unfinished letter on his desk, testified that he was at his post to the last.'

addresses herself to Lord Palmerston to ask him whether he can undertake to form an Administration which will command the confidence of Parliament and efficiently conduct public affairs in this momentous crisis? Should he think that he is able to do so, the Queen commissions him to undertake the task. She does not send for him, having fully discussed with him yesterday the state of public affairs, and in order to save time. The Queen hopes to receive an answer from Lord Palmerston as soon as possible, as upon this her own movements will depend.

Queen Victoria to the King of the Belgians

Buckingham Palace, 6th February 1855

MY DEAREST UNCLE,— ... *Six o'clock p.m.*—One word to say that *Lord Palmerston* has just *kissed* hands as *Prime* Minister. ALL the *Peelites* except poor dear Aberdeen (whom I am deeply grieved to lose) and the Duke of Newcastle, remain. It is *entirely* Aberdeen's *doing,* and very patriotic and handsome of him. In haste, ever your devoted Niece,   VICTORIA R.

Queen Victoria to the King of the Belgians

Buckingham Palace, 27th February 1855

MY DEAREST UNCLE,— ... On Thursday we saw twenty-six of the wounded Coldstream Guards, and on Friday thirty-four of the Scotch Fusileers. A most interesting and touching sight—*such* fine men, and so brave and patient! *so ready* to go back and '*be at them again.*' A great many of them, I am glad to say, will be able to remain in the Service. Those who have lost their limbs cannot, of course. There were two poor boys of nineteen and twenty—the one had lost his leg, quite high up, by the bursting of a shell in the trenches, and the other his poor arm so shot that it is perfectly useless. Both had smooth girls' faces; these were in the Coldstream, who certainly look the worst. In the Scotch Fusileers, there were also two very young men—the one shot through the cheek, the other through the *skull*—but both recovered! Among the Grenadiers there is one very sad object, shot *dreadfully,* a ball having gone in through the cheek and behind the nose and eye and out through the other side! He is shockingly disfigured, but is recovered. I feel so much for them, and am *so fond* of my dear soldiers—so *proud* of them! We could not have avoided sending the Guards; it would have been their ruin if they had not gone. . . .

From Sir Ralph Abercromby

The Hague, 2nd March 1855
(Received 3.45 p.m.)

The Emperor Nicholas died this morning at 1 a.m. of Pulmonic Apoplexy, after an attack of Influenza.*

Queen Victoria to Lord Panmure

Buckingham Palace, 5th March 1855

The Queen is very anxious to bring before Lord Panmure the subject which she mentioned to him the other night, viz. that of Hospitals for our sick and wounded soldiers. This is absolutely necessary, and *now* is the moment to have them built, for no doubt there would be no difficulty in obtaining the money requisite for this purpose, from the strong feeling now existing in the public mind for improvements of all kinds connected with the Army and the well-being and comfort of the soldier.

Nothing can exceed the attention paid to these poor men in the Barracks at Chatham (or rather more Fort Pitt and Brompton), and they are in that respect very comfortable; but the buildings are bad— the wards more like prisons than hospitals, with the windows so high that no one can look out of them; and the generality of the

---

* Nothing had been known publicly of the Czar's illness, and the startling news of his death caused a sensation in England of tragedy rather than of joy. Mr Kinglake has vividly depicted the feelings of agony and mortification which the news of the earlier Russian reverses had been received by Nicholas. On 1st March, he received the full account of the disaster at Eupatoria, after which he became delirious, and died on the following day. He had stated, in referring to the horrors of that Crimean winter, that Russia had still two Generals on whom she could rely: Generals Janvier and Février; and Leech, now made his famous cartoon—'General Février turned traitor', depicting Death, in the uniform of a Russian officer, laying his bony hand on the Emperor's heart.

wards are small rooms, with hardly space for you to walk between the beds. There is no dining-room or hall, so that the poor men must have their dinners in the same room in which they sleep, and in which some may be dying, and at any rate many suffering, while others are at their meals. The proposition of having hulks prepared for their reception will do very well at first, but it would not, the Queen thinks, do for any length of time. A hulk is a very gloomy place, and these poor men require their spirits to be cheered as much as their physical sufferings to be attended to. The Queen is particularly anxious on this subject, which is, she may truly say, constantly in her thoughts, as is everything connected with her beloved troops, who have fought so bravely and borne so heroically all their sufferings and privations.

The Queen hopes before long to visit all the Hospitals at Portsmouth, and to see in what state they are.

When will the medals be ready for distribution?

Memorandum by Queen Victoria

Buckingham Palace, 2nd May 1855

The recent visit of the Emperor Napoleon III to this country is a curious page of history, and gives rise to many reflections. A remarkable combination of circumstances has brought about the very intimate alliance which now unites England and France, for so many centuries the bitterest enemies and rivals, and this, under the reign of the present Emperor, the nephew of our greatest foe, and bearing his name, and brought about by the policy of the late Emperor of Russia, who considered himself as the head of the European Alliance against France!

In reflecting on the character of the present Emperor Napoleon, and the impression I have conceived of it, the following thoughts present themselves to my mind:

That he *is* a very *extraordinary* man, with great qualities there can be *no* doubt—I might almost say a mysterious man. He is evidently possessed of *indomitable courage, unflinching firmness of purpose, self-reliance, perseverance,* and *great secrecy*; to this should be added, a great reliance on what he calls his *Star,* and a belief in omens and incidents as connected with his future destiny, which is almost romantic —and at the same time he is endowed with wonderful *self-control,* great *calmness,* even *gentleness,* and with a *power* of *fascination,* the effect of which upon all those who become more intimately acquainted with him is *most sensibly* felt.

How far he is actuated by a strong *moral* sense of *right* and *wrong* is difficult to say. On the one hand, his attempts at Strasbourg and Boulogne, and this last after having given a solemn promise never to return or make a similar attempt—in which he openly called on the subjects of the then King of the French to follow him as the successor of Napoleon, the *Coup d'État* of December 1851, followed by great . . . severity and the confiscation of the property of the unfortunate Orleans family, would lead one to believe that he is not. On the other hand, his kindness and gratitude towards all those, whether high or low, who have befriended him or stood by him through life, and his straightforward and steady conduct towards us throughout the very difficult and anxious contest in which we have been engaged for a year and a half, show that he is possessed of noble and right feelings.

My impression is, that in all these apparently inexcusable acts, he has invariably been guided by the belief that he is *fulfilling a destiny* which God has *imposed* upon him, and that, though cruel or harsh in themselves, they were *necessary* to obtain the result which he considered *himself* as *chosen* to carry out, and *not* acts of *wanton* cruelty or injustice; for it is impossible to know him and not to see there is much that is truly amiable, kind, and honest in his character. Another remarkable and important feature in his composition is, that everything he says or expresses is the *result* of deep reflection and of settled purpose, and not merely *des phrases de politesse,* consequently when we read words used in his speech made in the City, we may feel sure that he *means* what he says; and therefore I would rely with confidence on his behaving honestly and faithfully towards us. I am not able to say whether he is deeply versed in History—I should rather think not, as regards it *generally,* though he may be, and probably is, well informed in the history of his own country, certainly fully so in that of the *Empire,* he having made it his special study to contemplate and reflect upon all the acts and designs of his great uncle. He is very well read in German literature, to which he seems to be very partial. It is said, and I am inclined to think with truth, that he reads but little, even as regards despatches from his own foreign Ministers, he having expressed his surprise at my reading them daily. He seems to be singularly ignorant in matters not connected with the branch of his *special* studies, and to be ill informed upon them by those who surround him.

If we compare him with poor King Louis Philippe, I should say that the latter (Louis Philippe) was possessed of vast knowledge upon all and every subject, of immense experience in public affairs, and of great activity of mind; whereas the Emperor possesses greater judgment and much greater firmness of purpose, but no experience of public affairs, nor mental application; he is endowed, as was the late King, with much fertility of imagination.

Another great difference between King Louis Philippe and the Emperor is, that the poor King was *thoroughly French* in character, possessing all the liveliness and talkativeness of that people, whereas the Emperor is as *unlike* a *Frenchman* as possible, being much more *German* than French in character.... How could it be expected that the Emperor *should* have any *experience* in *public affairs*, considering that till six years ago he lived as a poor exile, for some years even in prison, and never having taken the slightest part in the *public* affairs of *any* country?

It is therefore the more astounding, indeed almost incomprehensible, that he should show all those powers of Government, and all that wonderful tact in his conduct and manners which he evinces, and which many a King's son, nurtured in palaces and educated in the midst of affairs, never succeeds in attaining. I likewise believe that he would be incapable of such tricks and over-reachings as practised by poor King Louis Philippe (for whose memory, as the old and kind friend of my father, and of whose kindness and amiable qualities I shall ever retain a lively sense), who in great as well as in small things took a pleasure in being cleverer and more cunning than others, often when there was no advantage to be gained by it, and which was, unfortunately, strikingly displayed in the transactions connected with the Spanish marriages, which led to the King's downfall and ruined him in the eyes of all Europe. On the other hand, I believe that the Emperor Napoleon would not hesitate to do a thing by main force, even if in itself unjust and tyrannical, should he consider that the *accomplishment of his destiny* demanded it.

The *great advantage* to be derived for the permanent alliance of England and France, which is of such vital importance to both countries, by the Emperor's recent visit, I take to be this: that, with his peculiar character and views, which are very personal, a kind, un-affected, and hearty reception by *us personally* in our own family will make a lasting impression upon his mind; he will see that he can rely upon our friendship and honesty towards him and his country so long as he remains faithful towards us; naturally frank, he will see the advantage to be derived from continuing so; and if he reflects on the downfall of the former dynasty, he will see that it arose *chiefly* from a *breach* of pledges, . . . and will be sure, if I be not very much mistaken in his character, to *avoid* such a course. It must likewise not be overlooked that this kindly feeling towards us, and con-sequently towards England (the interests of which are *inseparable* from us), must be increased when it is remembered that we are almost the only people in *his* own position with whom he has been able to be on any terms of intimacy, consequently almost the only ones to whom he could talk easily and unreservedly, which he cannot do naturally with his inferiors. He and the Empress are in a most isolated position, unable to trust the only relations who are near them in France, and surrounded by courtiers and servants, who from fear or interest do not tell them the truth. It is, therefore, natural to believe that he will not willingly separate from those who, like us, do not scruple to put him in possession of the real facts, and whose conduct is guided by justice and honesty, and this the more readily as he is supposed to have always been a searcher after truth. I would go still further, and think that it is in our power to *keep* him in the right course, and to protect him against the extreme flightiness, changeable-ness, and to a certain extent want of honesty of his own servants and nation. We should never lose the opportunity of checking in the bud any attempt on the part of his agents or ministers to play us false, frankly informing him of the facts, and encouraging him to bring forward in an equally frank manner whatever he has to complain of. This is the course which we have hitherto pursued, and as he is France in his own sole person, it becomes of the utmost importance to encourage by every means in our power that very open intercourse which I must say has existed between him and Lord Cowley for the last year and a half, and now our personal acquaintance, between ourselves.

As I said before, the words which fall from his lips are the result of deep reflection, and part of the deep plan which he has staked out for himself, and which he intends to carry out. I would therefore lay stress on the following words which he pronounced to me immediately after the investiture of the Order of the Garter: *'C'est un lien de plus entre nous, j'ai prêté serment de fidélité à votre Majesté et je le garderai soigneusement. C'est un grand événement pour moi, et j'espère pouvoir prouver ma reconnaissance envers votre Majesté et son Pays.'* In a letter said to be written by him to Mr F. Campbell, the translator of M. Thiers's *History of the Consulate and Empire,* when returning the proof-sheets in 1847, he says: 'Let us hope the day may yet come when I shall carry out the intentions of my Uncle by uniting the policy and interests of England and France in an indissoluble alliance. That hope cheers and encourages me. It forbids my repining at the altered fortunes of my family.'

If these be truly his words, he certainly has acted up to them, since he has swayed with an iron hand the destinies of that most versatile nation, the French. That he should have written this at a moment when Louis Philippe had succeeded in all his wishes and seemed securer than ever in the possession of his Throne, shows a calm reliance in his destiny and in the realisation of hopes entertained from his very childhood which borders on the supernatural.

These are a few of the many reflections caused by the observation and acquaintance with the character of this most extraordinary man, in whose fate not only the interests of this country, but the whole of Europe are intimately bound up. I shall be curious to see if, after the lapse of time, my opinion and estimate of it has been the right one.

VICTORIA R.

Queen Victoria to the King of the Belgians

Balmoral Castle, 11th September 1855

MY DEAREST UNCLE,—The great event has at length taken place— *Sebastopol has fallen!* We received the news here last night when we were sitting quietly round our table after dinner. We did what we could to celebrate it; but that was but little, for to my grief we have not *one* soldier, no band, nothing here to make any sort of demonstration. What we did do was in Highland fashion to light a *bonfire* on the top of a hill opposite the house, which had been built last year when the premature news of the fall of Sebastopol deceived every one, and which we had to leave *unlit*, and found here on our return!...

Queen Victoria to the King of the Belgians

Balmoral, 22nd September 1855

My dearest Uncle,—I profit by your own messenger to confide to *you*, and to *you alone*, begging you not to mention it to your children, that *our* wishes on the subject of a future marriage for Vicky *have* been realised in the *most gratifying* and *satisfactory* manner.

On Thursday (20th) after breakfast, Fritz Wilhelm said he was anxious to speak of a subject which *he* knew his parents had never broached to us—which *was to belong to our* Family; that this had long been his wish, that he had the entire concurrence and *approval* not only of his parents but of the King—and that finding Vicky *so allerliebst*, he could delay *no* longer in making this proposal. I need *not* tell you with *what* joy *we* accepted him *for* our part; but the child herself is to know nothing till *after* her confirmation, which is to take place next Easter, when he probably will come over, and, as he wishes himself, make her the proposal, which, however, I have little—indeed no—doubt she will gladly *accept*. He is a dear, excellent, charming young man, whom we shall give our dear child to with perfect confidence. What pleases us greatly is to see that he is really delighted with Vicky.

Now, with Albert's affectionate love, and with the prayer that *you* will give *your* blessing to this alliance, as you have done to ours, ever your devoted Niece and Child,   Victoria R.

Viscount Palmerston to Queen Victoria

Piccadilly, 22nd September 1855

... Viscount Palmerston begs to state that the Professorship of Greek at the University of Oxford, which was held by the late Dean of

Christchurch, is still vacant, Viscount Palmerston having doubts as to the best person to be appointed. The present Dean of Christchurch admitted that the Professorship ought to be separated from the Deanery; he has now recommended for the Professorship the Rev. B. Jowett, Fellow and Tutor of Balliol College, who is an eminent Greek scholar and won the Hertford Scholarship; and Viscount Palmerston submits, for your Majesty's gracious approval, that Mr Jowett may be appointed.

1856

Queen Victoria to Lord Panmure

Windsor Castle, 5th January 1856

The Queen returns the drawings for the 'Victoria Cross.' She has marked the one she approves with an X; she thinks, however, that it might be a trifle smaller. The motto would be better 'For Valour' than 'For the Brave,' as this would lead to the inference that only those are deemed brave who have got the Victoria Cross.

Queen Victoria to the King of the Belgians

Windsor Castle, 29th January 1856

MY DEAREST UNCLE,— ... The *peace negotiations* occupy every one; *if* Russia is *sincere*, they will end most probably in peace; but *if* she is *not*, the war will be *carried* on with *renewed vigour*. The recollection of last year makes one *very distrustful*.

England's policy throughout has been the *same, singularly unselfish,* and *solely* actuated by the *desire* of *seeing Europe saved* from the *arrogant* and *dangerous pretensions* of that *barbarous power* Russia— and of having *such safeguards* established for the *future*, which may ensure us against a *repetition* of similar *untoward events*.

I repeat now, what we have said from the beginning, and what I have *repeated* a *hundred* times, *if Prussia* and *Austria* had held *strong and decided* language to *Russia in '53*, we should *never* have had *this war!* ...

Queen Victoria to Miss Florence Nightingale

Windsor Castle, [January] 1856

DEAR MISS NIGHTINGALE,—You are, I know, well aware of the high sense I entertain of the Christian devotion which you have displayed during this great and bloody war, and I need hardly repeat to you how warm my admiration is for your services, which are fully equal to those of my dear and brave soldiers, whose sufferings you have had the *privilege* of alleviating in so merciful a manner. I am, however, anxious of marking my feelings in a manner which I trust will be agreeable to you, and therefore send you with this letter a brooch, the form and emblems of which commemorate your great and blessed work, and which, I hope, you will wear as a mark of the high approbation of your Sovereign!

It will be a very great satisfaction to me, when you return at last to these shores, to make the acquaintance of one who has set so bright an example to our sex. And with every prayer for the preservation of your valuable health, believe me, always, yours sincerely,

VICTORIA R.

Queen Victoria to Viscount Palmerston

Buckingham Palace, 6th March 1856

With reference to Lord Clarendon's letter, the Queen must say that she, though *very reluctantly*, shares his opinion, that we have no choice *now* but to accept the peace, even if it is not all we could desire, and if another campaign might have got us better terms. She feels certain that the bad accounts of the French Army in the Crimea, which appears to suffer *now* all the misery which ours suffered last year at the worst time of the siege, will more than ever indispose the Emperor from risking a renewal of hostilities. It is affirmed that the French have beyond 20,000 men in hospital!

If we are to have this peace, however, the Queen must again agree with Lord Clarendon that we ought not *ourselves* to depreciate it, as our Press has done the deeds of our Army. . . .

Queen Victoria to the King of the Belgians

Windsor Castle, 1st April 1856

MY DEAREST UNCLE,— ... *Peace is signed!* But till the ratifications have taken place its terms cannot be known. That so *good* a Peace *has* been obtained, and that this country stands in the high position she now does by *having* made peace, but *not* yielding to *unworthy* and dishonourable terms, is *all* owing to Lord Clarendon, whose difficulties were immense, and who cannot be too highly praised. ...

Queen Victoria to Viscount Palmerston

Buckingham Palace, 11th April 1856

Now that the moment for the ratification of the Treaty of Peace is near at hand, the Queen wishes to delay no longer the expression of her satisfaction as to the manner in which both the War has been brought to a conclusion, and the honour and interests of this country have been maintained by the Treaty of Peace, under the zealous and able guidance of Lord Palmerston. She wishes as a public token of her approval to bestow the Order of the Garter upon him. Should the two vacant Ribbons already have been promised to the Peers whose names Lord Palmerston has on a former occasion submitted to the Queen, there could be no difficulty in his being named an extra Knight, not filling up the next vacancy which may occur; this course was followed when Lord Grey received the Garter from the hands of King William.

Memorandum by Queen Victoria

Windsor Castle, May 1856

It is a strange omission in our Constitution that while *the wife* of a *King* has the highest rank and dignity in the realm after her husband assigned to her by law, the *husband* of a *Queen regnant* is entirely ignored by the law. This is the more extraordinary, as a husband has in this country such particular rights and such great power over his wife, and as the Queen is married just as any other woman is, and swears to obey her lord and master, as such, while by law he has no rank or defined position. This is a strange anomaly. No doubt, as is the case *now*—the Queen *can* give her husband the highest *place* by *placing* him *always near her person,* and the Nation would give it him as a *matter of course.* Still, when I first married, we had much difficulty on this subject; much bad feeling was shown, and several members of the Royal Family showed bad grace in giving precedence to the Prince, and the late King of Hanover positively resisted doing so. I gave the Prince precedence by issuing Letters Patent, but these give no rank in Parliament—or at the Council Board—and it would be far better to put this question beyond all doubt, and to secure its settlement for *all future Consorts of Queens,* and thus have this omission in the Constitution rectified. Naturally my own feeling would be to give the Prince the same title and rank as I have, but a Titular King is a complete novelty in this country, and might be productive of more inconveniences than advantages to the individual who bears it. Therefore, upon mature reflection, and after considering the question for nearly *sixteen years,* I have come to the conclusion that the title which is now by universal consent given him of 'Prince Consort,' with the highest rank in and out of Parliament immediately after the Queen, and before every other Prince of the Royal Family, should be the one assigned to the husband of the Queen regnant *once and for all.* This ought to be done before our children grow up, and it seems peculiarly easy to do so *now* that none of the old branches of the Royal Family are still alive.

The present position is this: that while every British subject, down to the Knight, Bachelor, Doctor, and Esquire, has a rank and position by *Law,* the Queen's husband alone has one by *favour*—and by his wife's favour, who may grant it or not! When granted as in the present case, it does not extend to Parliament and the Council, and the children may deny the position which their mother has given to their father as a usurpation over them, having the law on their side; or if they waive their rights in his favour, he will hold a position granted by the forbearance of his children. In both cases this is a position most derogatory to the Queen as well as to her husband, and most dangerous to the peace and well-being of her family. If the children resist, the Queen will have her husband pushed away from her side by her children, and they will take precedence over the man whom she is bound to obey; if they are dutiful, she will owe her peace of mind to their continued generosity.

With relation to Foreign Courts, the Queen's position is equally humiliating in this respect. *Some* Sovereigns (crowned heads) address her husband as 'Brother,' some as 'Brother and Cousin,' some merely as 'Cousin.' When the Queen has been abroad, her husband's position has always been a subject of negotiation and vexation; the position which has been accorded to him the Queen has always had to acknowledge as a grace and favour bestowed on her by the Sovereign whom she visited. While last year the Emperor of the French treated the Prince as a Royal personage, his uncle declined to come to Paris avowedly because he would not give precedence to the Prince; and on the Rhine in 1845 the King of Prussia could not give the place to the Queen's husband which common civility required, because of the presence of an Archduke, the third son of an uncle of the then reigning Emperor of Austria, who would not give the *pas,* and whom the King would not offend.

The only legal position in Europe, according to international law, which the husband of the Queen of England enjoys, is that of a younger brother of the Duke of Saxe-Coburg, and this merely because the English law does not know of him. This is derogatory to the dignity of the Crown of England.

But *nationally* also it is an injury to the position of the Crown that the Queen's husband should have no other title than that of Prince of Saxe-Coburg, and thus be perpetually represented to the country as a foreigner. 'The Queen and her foreign husband, the Prince Albert of Saxe-Coburg and Gotha!'

The Queen has a right to claim that her husband should be an Englishman, bearing an English title, and enjoying a legal position which she has not to defend with a wife's anxiety as a usurpation against her own children, her subjects, and Foreign Courts.

The question has often been discussed by me with different Prime Ministers and Lord Chancellors, who have invariably entirely agreed with me; but the wish to wait for a good moment to bring the matter before Parliament has caused one year after another to elapse without anything being done. If I become *now* more anxious to have it settled, it is in order that it should be so before our children are grown up, that it might not appear to be done in order to guard their father's position against them personally, which could not fail to produce a painful impression upon their minds.

If properly explained to Parliament and the country, I cannot foresee the slightest difficulty in getting such a necessary measure passed, particularly if it be made quite clear to the House of Commons that it is in no way connected with a desire to obtain an increased grant for the Prince.   VICTORIA R.

1857

Viscount Palmerston to Queen Victoria

Broadlands, 13th January 1857

Viscount Palmerston presents his humble duty to your Majesty, and he and Lady Palmerston will have the honour of waiting upon your Majesty as soon as he is able to move. He is, however, at present on crutches, and can hardly expect to be in marching order for some few days to come. With regard to the matters that are likely to be discussed when Parliament meets, Viscount Palmerston would beg to submit that the one which has for some months past occupied the attention of all Europe, namely, the execution of the Treaty of Paris, has been settled in a manner satisfactory to all parties; and this is not only a great relief to the Government, but is also a security for the continuance of the Anglo-French Alliance, which would have been greatly endangered by the discussions and explanations that might otherwise have been forced on. . . .

Viscount Palmerston hears from persons likely to know, that the Conservative Party are not more united than they were last Session. That Mr Disraeli and the great bulk of his nominal followers are far from being on good terms together, and that there is no immediate junction to be expected between Mr Disraeli and Mr Gladstone.

Mr Cobden has given it to be understood that he wishes at the next General Election to retire from the West Riding of Yorkshire. The real fact being that the line he took about the late war has made him so unpopular with his constituents that he would probably not be returned again.

Viscount Palmerston has heard privately and confidentially that Lord John Russell wrote some little time ago to the Duke of Bedford to say that it had been intimated to him that an offer would be made to him if he were disposed to accept it, to go to the House of Lords and to become there the Leader of the Government. In case your Majesty may have heard this report, Viscount Palmerston thinks it right to say that no such communication to Lord John Russell was ever authorised by him, nor has been, so far as he is aware, ever made, and in truth Viscount Palmerston must candidly say that in the present state of public opinion about the course which Lord John has on several occasions pursued, he is not inclined to think that his accession to the Government would give the Government any additional strength.

Viscount Palmerston to Queen Victoria

Piccadilly, 26th June 1857

... Viscount Palmerston is sorry to have received the accompanying account of the extension of the Mutiny among the native troops in India, but he has no fear of its results.* The bulk of the European force is stationed on the North-West Frontier, and is, therefore, within comparatively easy reach of Delhi, and about six thousand European troops will have returned to Bombay from Persia. It will, however, seem to be advisable to send off at once the force amounting to nearly eight thousand men, now under orders for embarkation for India; and when the despatches arrive, which will be about the middle of next week, it will be seen whether any further reinforcements will be required.

The extent of the Mutiny appears to indicate some deeper cause than that which was ascribed to the first insubordination. That cause may be, as some allege, the apprehension of the Hindoo priests that

* Alarming accounts of disturbances in India had been received for some weeks past, but Lord Palmerston failed to grasp the gravity of the situation. Even after the intelligence reached England of the mutiny of the native regiments at Meerut, on 10th May, and of the horrible massacres of women and children, the Ministry did not fully realise the peril threatening our Indian possessions.

their religion is in danger by the progress of civilisation in India, or it may be some hostile foreign agency.

Queen Victoria to Lord Panmure

Buckingham Palace, 3rd July 1857

The Queen has received Lord Panmure's letter of yesterday. She has sanctioned the going of four Regiments to the East Indies. With regard to the reduction of the garrison of Malta to four Regiments, she hopes the Government will well consider whether this will not reduce this valuable and exposed spot to a state of insecurity.

The Queen is sorry to find Lord Panmure still objecting to a proper Brigade system, without which no army in the world can be efficient. We want General Officers, and cannot train them unless we employ them on military duty, not on clerks' duty in district or colony, but in the command of troops. The detachment of Regiments is no reason for having no system, and the country will not pay for General Officers whose employment is not part of a system; our Army is then deprived of its efficiency by the refusal to adopt a system on the part of the Government.

Viscount Palmerston to Queen Victoria

Piccadilly, 27th July 1857

Viscount Palmerston presents his humble duty to your Majesty, and begs to state that Mr Disraeli this afternoon, in a speech of three hours, made his Motion on the state of India. His Motion was ostensibly for two papers, one of which does not exist, at least in the possession of the Government, and the other of which ought not to be made public, as it relates to the arrangements for defending India against external attack. He represented the disturbances in India as a national revolt, and not as a mere military mutiny; and he enumerated various causes which in his opinion accounted for and justified this general revolt. Some of these causes were various measures of improved civilisation which from time to time during the last ten years the Indian Government had been urged by Parliament to take. Mr Vernon Smith followed, and in a very able speech answered in great detail Mr Disraeli's allegations. Sir Erskine Perry, who evidently had furnished Mr Disraeli with much of his mistaken assertions, supported his views. Mr Campbell, Member for Weymouth, who had been many years in India, showed the fallacy of Mr Disraeli's arguments, and the groundlessness of many of his assertions. Mr Whiteside supported the Motion. Lord John Russell, who had after Mr Disraeli's speech communicated with the Government, expressed his disapprobation of Mr Disraeli's speech, and moved as an Amendment an Address to your Majesty expressing the assurance of the support of the House for measures to suppress the present disturbances, and their co-operation with your Majesty in measures for the permanent establishment of tranquillity and contentment in India. Mr Mangles, the Chairman of the Directors, replied at much length, and very conclusively to Mr Disraeli's speech. Mr Liddell, with much simplicity, asked the Speaker to tell him how he should vote, but approved entirely of Lord John Russell's address. Mr Ayrton moved an adjournment to the Debate, which was negatived by 203 to 79. Mr Hadfield then shortly stated in his provincial dialect that 'we can never keep our 'old upon Hindia by the Force of Harms.' Mr Disraeli then made an animated reply to the speeches against him, but in a manner almost too animated for the occasion. Mr Thomas Baring set Mr Disraeli right, but in rather strong terms, about some proceedings of the Committee on Indian Affairs in 1853, with regard to which Mr Disraeli's memory had proved untrustworthy. Viscount Palmerston shortly made some observations on the Motion and the speech which had introduced it; and the Motion was then negatived without a division, and the Address was unanimously carried.

Queen Victoria to Viscount Palmerston

Osborne, 22nd August 1857

The Queen is afraid from the telegram of this morning that affairs in India have not yet taken a favourable turn. Delhi seems still to hold out, and the death of Sir H. Lawrence is a great loss. The Queen must repeat to Lord Palmerston that the measures hitherto taken by the Government are not commensurate with the magnitude of the crisis.

We have given nearly all we have in reinforcements, and if new efforts should become necessary, by the joining of the Madras and Bombay Armies in the Revolt, for instance, it will take months to prepare Reserves which ought now to be ready. Ten Battalions of Militia to be called out is quite inadequate; forty, at least, ought to be the number, for these also exist only on paper. The augmentation of the Cavalry and the Guards has not yet been ordered.

Financial difficulties don't exist; the 14,000 men sent to India are taken over by the Indian Government, and their expense saved to us; and this appears hardly the moment to make savings on the Army estimates.

Queen Victoria to the King of the Belgians

Balmoral Castle, 2nd September 1857

DEAREST UNCLE,— ... We are in sad anxiety about India, which engrosses all our attention. Troops cannot be raised fast or largely enough. And the horrors committed on the poor ladies—women and children—are unknown in these ages, and make one's blood run cold. Altogether, the whole is so much more distressing than the Crimea—where there was *glory* and honourable warfare, and where the poor women and children were safe. Then the distance and the difficulty of communication is such an additional suffering to us all. I know you will feel much for us all. There is not a family hardly who is not in sorrow and anxiety about their children, and in all ranks—India being *the* place where every one was anxious to place a son! ...

Viscount Palmerston to Queen Victoria

Brocket, 10th September 1857

Viscount Palmerston presents his humble duty to your Majesty and begs to submit that an impression is beginning to prevail that it would be a proper thing that a day should be set apart for National Prayer and Humiliation with reference to the present calamitous state of affairs in India, upon the same principle on which a similar step was taken during the Crimean War; and if your Majesty should approve, Viscount Palmerston would communicate on the subject with the Archbishop of Canterbury. . . . It is usual on such occasions that the Archbishop of Canterbury should attend, but in consideration of the distance his attendance might well be dispensed with on the present occasion.

Queen Victoria to Viscount Palmerston

Balmoral, 11th September 1857

Lord Palmerston knows what the Queen's feelings are with regard to Fast-days, which she thinks do not produce the desired effect—from the manner in which they are appointed, and the selections made for the Service—but she will not oppose the natural feeling which any one must partake in, of a desire to pray for our fellow-countrymen and women who are exposed to such imminent danger, and therefore sanctions his consulting the Archbishop on the subject. She would, however, suggest its being more appropriately called a day of prayer and intercession for our suffering countrymen, than of fast and humiliation, and of its being on a *Sunday*, and not on a week-day: on the last Fast-day the Queen heard it generally remarked, that it produced more harm than good, and that, if it were on a Sunday, it would be much more generally observed. However, she will sanction whatever is proper, but thinks it ought to be as soon as possible (in a fortnight or three weeks) if it is to be done at all. She will hold a Council whenever it is wished.*

1858

Memorandum by the Prince Albert

Buckingham Palace, 21st February 1858

Lord Palmerston came at five o'clock from the Cabinet, and tendered his resignation in his own name, and that of his Colleagues. The

* Shortly after the date of this letter came the intelligence from India that Delhi had not fallen, and that the Lucknow garrison was not yet relieved. This news, coupled with the tiding of fresh outbreaks, and the details of the horrors of Cawnpore, generated deep feelings of resentment in the country.

Cabinet had well considered their position and found that, as the vote passed by the House, although the result of an accidental combination of parties, was virtually a vote of censure upon their conduct, they could not with honour or with any advantage to the public service carry on the Government.

The combination was the whole of the Conservative Party (Lord Derby's followers), Lord John Russell, the Peelites, with Mr Gladstone and the whole of the Radicals; but the Liberal Party generally is just now very angry with Lord Palmerston personally chiefly on account of his apparent submission to French dictation, and the late appointment of Lord Clanricarde as Privy Seal, who is looked upon as a reprobate.* Lord Clanricarde's presence in the House of Commons during the Debate, and in a conspicuous place, enraged many supporters of Lord Palmerston to that degree that they voted at once with the Opposition.

The Queen wrote to Lord Derby the letter here following; he came a little after six o'clock. He stated that nobody was more surprised in his life than he had been at the result of the Debate, after the Government had only a few days before had a majority of more than 100 on the introduction of their Bill. He did not know how it came about, but thought it was the work of Lord John Russell and Sir James Graham in the interest of the Radicals; Mr Gladstone's junction must have been accidental. As to his own people, they had, owing to his own personal exertions, as the Queen was aware, though many very unwillingly, supported the Bill; but the amendment of Mr Milner Gibson was so skilfully worded, that it was difficult for them not to vote for it; he had to admit this when they came to him to ask what they should do, merely warning them to save the Measure itself, which the Amendment did. He then blamed the Government very much for leaving Count Walewski's despatch un-

---

* Since his triumph at the polls in 1857, Lord Palmerston had been somewhat arbitrary in his demeanour, and had defied public opinion by taking Lord Clanricarde into the Government, after some unpleasant disclosures in the Irish Courts. While walking home on the 18th, after obtaining an immense majority on the India Bill, he was told by Sir Joseph Bethell that he ought, like the Roman Consuls in a triumph, to have some one to remind him that he was, as a minister, not immortal. Next day he was defeated.

answered before coming before Parliament, which he could hardly understand.

On the Queen telling him that the Government had resigned, and that she commissioned him to form a new Administration, he begged that this offer might not be made to him without further consideration, and would state clearly his own position. After what had happened in 1851 and 1855, if the Queen made the offer he *must* accept it, for if he refused, the Conservative Party would be broken up for ever. Yet he would find a majority of two to one against him in the House of Commons, would have difficulty in well filling the important offices, found the external and internal relations of the country in a most delicate and complicated position, war in India and in China, difficulties with France, the Indian Bill introduced and a Reform Bill promised; nothing but the forbearance and support of some of his opponents would make it possible for him to carry on any Government. The person who was asked first by the Sovereign had always a great disadvantage; perhaps other combinations were possible, which, if found not to answer, would make him more readily accepted by the country. The position of Lord Palmerston was a most curious one, the House of Commons had been returned chiefly for the purpose of supporting him *personally*, and he had obtained a working majority of 100 (unheard of since the Reform Bill), yet his supporters had no principles in common and they generally suspected him; the question of the Reform Bill had made him and Lord John run a race for popularity which might lead to disastrous consequences. Lord Derby did not at all know what support he would be able to obtain in Parliament.

The Queen agreed to deferring her offer, and to take further time for consideration on the understanding that if she made it it would at once be accepted. Lord Derby expressed, however, his fear that the resignation of the Palmerston Cabinet might only be for the purpose of going through a crisis in order to come back again with new strength, for there existed different kinds of resignations, some for this purpose, others really for abandoning office.

A conversation which I had with Lord Clarendon after dinner, convinced me that the Cabinet had sent in their resignations from the real conviction of the impossibility to go on with honour and success; all offers of the friends of the Government to pass a vote of confidence, etc., etc., had been rejected. Lord Derby was the only man who could form a Government; Mr Gladstone would probably join him. The whole move had been planned, and most dexterously, by Sir James Graham.

ALBERT

The Ministry as it stood on the 1st of January 1858.		The Ministry as formed by the Earl of Derby in February 1858.
VISCOUNT PALMERSTON	*First Lord of the Treasury*	EARL OF DERBY.
MARQUIS OF LANSDOWNE	*(Without Office).*	
LORD CRANWORTH	*Lord Chancellor*	LORD CHELMSFORD.
EARL GRANVILLE	*President of the Council*	MARQUIS OF SALISBURY.
MARQUIS OF CLANRICARDE	*Lord Privy Seal*	EARL OF HARDWICKE.
SIR GEORGE GREY	*Home Secretary*	Mr WALPOLE.
EARL OF CLARENDON	*Foreign Secretary*	EARL OF MALMESBURY.
Mr LABOUCHERE (afterwards LORD TAUNTON)	*Colonial Secretary*	LORD STANLEY (afterwards EARL OF DERBY).
LORD PANMURE (afterwards EARL OF DALHOUSIE)	*War Secretary*	General PEEL.
SIR G. C. LEWIS	*Chancellor of the Exchequer*	Mr DISRAELI (afterwards EARL OF BEACONSFIELD)
SIR CHARLES WOOD (afterwards VISCOUNT HALIFAX)	*First Lord of the Admiralty*	Sir JOHN PAKINGTON (afterwards LORD HAMPTON).
Mr VERNON SMITH (afterwards LORD LYVEDEN)	*President of the Board of Control*	EARL OF ELLENBOROUGH.
LORD STANLEY OF ALDERLEY	*President of the Board of Trade*	Mr HENLEY.
Mr M. T. BAINES	*Chancellor of the Duchy of Lancaster*	*(Not in the Cabinet.)*
DUKE OF ARGYLL	*Postmaster-General*	*(Not in the Cabinet.)*
(Not in the Cabinet)	*First Commissioner of Works and Public Buildings*	LORD JOHN MANNERS (afterwards DUKE OF RUTLAND).

Mr Disraeli to Queen Victoria

House of Commons, 12th March 1858
(Friday)

The Chancellor of the Exchequer with his humble duty to your Majesty.

The Opposition benches very full; the temper not kind.

The French announcement, which was quite unexpected, elicited cheers, but only from the Ministerial side, which, he confesses, for a moment almost daunted him.

Then came a question about the *Cagliari* affair,* on which the Government had agreed to take a temperate course, in deference to their predecessors—but it was not successful. The ill-humour of the House, diverted for a moment by the French news, vented itself on this head.

What struck the Chancellor of the Exchequer in the course of the evening most was the absence of all those symptoms of 'fair trial,' etc., which have abounded of late in journals and in Society.

Lord John said something; Mr Gladstone said something; but it was not encouraging.

Nevertheless, in 1852 'fair trial' observations abounded, and the result was not satisfactory; now it may be the reverse.

The House is wild and capricious at this moment.

Your Majesty once deigned to say that your Majesty wished in these remarks to have the temper of the House placed before your Majesty, and to find what your Majesty could not meet in newspapers. This is the Chancellor of the Exchequer's excuse for these rough notes, written on the field of battle, which he humbly offers to your Majesty.

* Two English engineers, Watt and Park, had been on the Sardinian steamer *Cagliari* when she was seized by the Neapolitan Government, and her crew, including the engineers, imprisoned at Naples. At the instance of the Conservative Government, who acted more vigorously than their predecessors had done, the engineers were released, and £3,000 paid to them as compensation.

Mr Disraeli to Queen Victoria

House of Commons, 22nd March 1858
(Monday, half-past eight o'clock)

The Chancellor of the Exchequer with his humble duty to your Majesty.

This evening was a great contrast to Friday. House very full on both sides. . . .

Mr B. Osborne commenced the general attack, of which he had given notice; but, after five years' silence, his weapons were not as bright as of yore. He was answered by the Government, and the House, which was very full, became much excited. The Ministerial benches were in high spirit.

The Debate that ensued, most interesting and sustained.

Mr Horsman, with considerable effect, expressed the opinions of that portion of the Liberal Party, which does not wish to disturb the Government.

Lord John Russell vindicated the Reform Bill of 1832 from the attacks of the Chancellor of the Exchequer, and with great dignity and earnestness.

He was followed by Mr Drummond on the same subject in a telling epigram. Then Lord Palmerston, in reply to the charges of Mr Horsman, mild and graceful, with a sarcastic touch. The general impression of the House was very favourable to the Ministry; all seemed changed; the Debate had cleared the political atmosphere, and, compared with our previous state, we felt as if the eclipse was over.

Mr Disraeli to Queen Victoria

House of Commons, 13th April
(Tuesday night)

The Chancellor of the Exchequer with his humble duty to your Majesty.

The night tranquil and interesting—Lord Bury, with much intelligence, introduced the subject of the Straits Settlements; the speech of Sir J. Elphinstone, master of the subject, and full of striking details, produced a great effect. His vindication of the convict population of Singapore, as the moral element of that strange society, might have been considered as the richest humour, had it not been for its unmistakable simplicity.

His inquiry of the Governor's lady, who never hired any servants but a convict, whether she employed in her nursery 'Thieves or Murderers?'—and the answer, 'Always murderers,' was very effective. . . .

The Secretary of State having sent down to the Chancellor of the Exchequer the telegram of the fall of Lucknow, the Chancellor of the Exchequer read it to the House, having previously in private shown it to Lord Palmerston and others of the late Government.

After this a spirited Debate on the conduct of Members of Parliament corruptly exercising their influence, in which the view recommended by the Government, through Mr Secretary Walpole, was adopted by the House.

Mr Disraeli to Queen Victoria

House of Commons, 24th June 1858

The Chancellor of the Exchequer with his humble duty to your Majesty.

The India Bill was read a second time without a division. Lord Stanley made a clear and vigorous exposition of its spirit and provisions; Mr Bright delivered a powerful oration on the condition of India—its past government and future prospects; the rest of the discussion weak and desultory. . . .

It will be a great thing to have carried the India Bill, which Mr Thomas Baring, to-night, spoke of in terms of eulogy, and as a great improvement on the project of the late Government. It is, the Chancellor of the Exchequer really thinks, a wise and well-digested measure, ripe with the experience of the last five months of discussion; but it is only the ante-chamber of an imperial palace; and your Majesty would do well to deign to consider the steps which are now necessary to influence the opinions and affect the imagination of the Indian populations. The name of your Majesty ought to be impressed upon their native life. Royal Proclamations, Courts of Appeal, in their own land, and other institutions, forms, and ceremonies, will tend to this great result.

Queen Victoria to the Earl of Derby

Babelsberg, 15th August 1858

The Queen has asked Lord Malmesbury to explain in detail to Lord Derby her objections to the draft of Proclamation for India. The Queen would be glad if Lord Derby would write it himself in his excellent language, bearing in mind that it is a female Sovereign who speaks to more than 100,000,000 of Eastern people on assuming the direct Government over them after a bloody civil war, giving them pledges which her future reign is to redeem, and explaining the principles of her Government. Such a document should breathe feelings of generosity, benevolence, and religious feeling, pointing out the privileges which the Indians will receive in being placed on an equality with the subjects of the British Crown, and the prosperity following in the train of civilisation.

Memorandum by Queen Victoria

Osborne, 4th September 1858

The Queen wishes the practice of the Office* with reference to submissions to her to be as nearly as possible assimilated to that of the Foreign Office.

All despatches, when received and perused by the Secretary of State, to be sent to the Queen. They may be merely forwarded in boxes from the Office without being accompanied by any letter from the Secretary of State, unless he should think an explanation necessary. No draft of instructions or orders to be sent out without having been previously submitted to the Queen. The label on the boxes of the Office containing such drafts to be marked 'For Approval.'

In cases of Civil appointments the Secretary of State will himself take the Queen's pleasure before communicating with the gentlemen to be appointed.

Copies or a *précis* of the Minutes of the Council to be regularly transmitted to the Queen.

* The India Office.

The Secretary of State to obtain the Queen's sanction to important measures previously to his bringing them before the Council for discussion.

Memorandum by the Prince Albert

Osborne, 4th September 1858

The most remarkable feature of the last Session of Parliament has been the extraordinary unpopularity of Lord Palmerston, for which nothing can account; the only direct reproach which is made to him, is to have appointed Lord Clanricarde Privy Seal, and to have been overbearing in his manner. Yet a House of Commons, having been elected solely for the object, and on the ground of supporting Lord Palmerston personally (an instance in our Parliamentary history without parallel), holds him suddenly in such abhorrence, that not satisfied with having upset his Government, which had been successful in all its policy, and thrown him out, it will hardly listen to him when he speaks. He is frequently received with hooting, and throughout the last Session it sufficed that [he] took up any cause for the whole House voting against it, even if contrary to the principles which they had themselves advocated, merely to have the satisfaction of putting him into a minority. How can this be accounted for? The man who was without rhyme or reason stamped the only *English* statesman, the champion of liberty, the man of the people, etc., etc., now, without his having changed in any one respect, having still the same virtues and the same faults that he always had, young and vigorous in his seventy-fifth year, and having succeeded in his policy, is now considered the head of a clique, the man of intrigue, past his work, etc., etc.—in fact hated! and this throughout the country. I cannot explain the enigma except by supposing that people had before joined in a cry which they thought was popular without themselves believing what they said and wrote, and that they now do the same; that the Radicals used his name to destroy other statesmen and politicians, and are destroying him now in his turn; that they hoped to govern through him, and that they see a better chance now of doing it through a weak and incapable Tory Government which has entered into a secret bargain for their support. Still the phenomenon remains most curious.*

Lord Palmerston himself remains, outwardly at least, quite cheerful, and seems to care very little about his reverses; he speaks on all subjects, bids for the Liberal support as before, even at the expense of his better conviction (as he used to do), and keeps as much as possible before the public; he made an official tour in Ireland, and is gone to visit the Emperor Napoleon at Paris; his Chinese policy upon which the general Dissolution had taken place in 1857 has just been crowned by the most complete success by the advantageous treaty signed at Pekin by Lord Elgin; and yet even for this the public will not allow him any credit. Lady Palmerston on the contrary, is said to be very unhappy and very much hurt.   ALBERT

Queen Victoria to Viscount Canning†

Windsor Castle, 2nd December 1858

The Queen acknowledges the receipt of Lord Canning's letter of the 19th October, which she received on the 29th November, which has given her great pleasure.

It is a source of great satisfaction and pride to her to feel herself in direct communication with that enormous Empire which is so bright a jewel of her Crown, and which she would wish to see happy, contented, and peaceful. May the publication of her Proclamation be the beginning of a new era, and may it draw a veil over the sad and bloody past!

The Queen rejoices to hear that her Viceroy approves this passage about Religion. She strongly insisted on it. She trusts also that the certainty of the Amnesty remaining open till the 1st January may not be productive of serious evil.

The Queen must express our admiration of Lord Canning's own Proclamation, the wording of which is beautiful. The telegram

---

* Charles Greville, in his Journal (16th June 1858), noted the same circumstance, and drew the inference that Palmerston's public career was drawing to a close.

† The Queen's Proclamation to her Indian subjects had been received by Lord Canning on 17th October, when he also learned that the title of Viceroy was in future to dignify the Governor-General's office.

received to-day brings continued good news, and announces her proclamation having been read, and having produced good effect....

The Earl of Malmesbury to Queen Victoria

London, 10th December 1858

The Earl of Malmesbury presents his humble duty to the Queen, and has already anticipated your Majesty's wishes respecting the Emperor Napoleon.* Lord Malmesbury has written to Lord Cowley a private letter, desiring him to show it to His Majesty. It is in the same sense as your Majesty's, and states that if he is anxious to improve the lot of the worst governed country, namely the Papal States, he should, instead of sulking with Austria, make an attempt with his Catholic brother to ameliorate the Papal Government. It is not for Protestant England to take the initiative, as her object would be misunderstood and attributed to sectarian motives; but England could give her moral support, and even her material aid *eventually*, if it were required to establish an improved Administration of the Roman States. Austria would gain by having a quiet frontier. The correspondence which took place in 1856 and 1857 between Lord Clarendon and Mr Lyons shows that this is the only effective way of ameliorating the condition of Italy without a war.

Lord Malmesbury thinks he can assure your Majesty that none is at present contemplated by the Emperor Napoleon (who has just contradicted the report officially), and Count Buol is of the same opinion. The latter is constantly hurting the vanity of the French Government by his irritable despatches, and neither party makes the slightest effort to command their temper; but it appears impossible that Napoleon can make a *casus belli* against Austria. Besides this, your Majesty may be assured that no warlike preparations are making in France, such as must precede such a plan as an Italian war.

* Viz. that the Emperor's mind should be diverted from his project of originating a war in Italy. On the previous day Lord Malmesbury had written to the Queen: 'Lord Clarendon may have told your Majesty that the Emperor Napoleon was so ignorant of the locality of Villafranca that he looked for it on the map in the Adriatic, and was confounded when Lord Clarendon showed His Majesty that it was the Port of Nice and ten miles from his frontier!'

Lord Malmesbury entirely agrees with your Majesty that it is desirable that His Royal Highness the Prince of Wales should visit and remain at Rome incognito. It is also indispensable that when there His Royal Highness should receive no foreigner or stranger *alone,* so that no reports of pretended conversations with such persons could be circulated without immediate refutation by Colonel Bruce. Lord Malmesbury will instruct Mr Odo Russell to inform His Holiness of your Majesty's intentions in respect of the Prince.

1859

Mr Odo Russell to Mr Corbett*
(Submitted to Queen Victoria)

Rome, 14th January 1859

Sir,—I had the honour of being received by the Pope at a private audience this morning at the Vatican. No one else was present.

His Holiness, whose manner towards me was most kind and benevolent, said: 'You are appointed to succeed a very good man, for whom I felt great affection, and I regret that he has left Rome. You may be as good as he was, and we shall become friends, but I do not know you yet, and Mr Lyons I had known for many years; he is going to America, I hear, and he will find the Americans far more difficult to deal with than with us.

'I am much gratified to hear that the Prince of Wales is likely to visit Rome, and Her Majesty, I feel sure, has done well to allow him to prosecute his studies here. It will be an honour to me to receive him at the Vatican, and I beg that you will confer with Cardinal Antonelli as to the best means of making the Prince's visit here useful and pleasant. We are anxious that all his wishes should be attended to, that he may preserve a pleasant recollection of Rome in the future. Alas! so many erroneous impressions exist about this country that I hope you will not judge of us too rashly. We are

---

* Secretary of Legation at Florence, resident in Rome, afterwards Lord Ampthill.

advised to make reforms, and it is not understood that those very reforms, which would consist in giving this country a Government of laymen, would make it cease to exist. It is called "States of the Church" (*États de l'Église*), and that is what it must remain. It is true I have lately appointed a layman to a post formerly held by an ecclesiastic, and I may do so occasionally; but, however small we may be, we cannot yield to outer pressure, and this country must be administered by men of the Church. For my part, I shall fulfil my duties according to my conscience, and should Governments and events turn against me they cannot make me yield. I shall go with the faithful to the Catacombs, as did the Christians of the early centuries, and there await the will of the Supreme Being, for I dread no human Power upon earth and fear nothing but God.'

'But, Holy Father,' I said, 'you speak as if some great danger threatened Rome—is there any [real?] cause for apprehension?'

'Have you not heard,' His Holiness answered, 'that great excitement prevails throughout Italy?—the state of Lombardy is deplorable; evil spirits are at work even in my dominions, and the late speech of the King of Sardinia is calculated to inflame the minds of all the revolutionary men of Italy. It is true he says he will observe existing Treaties, but that will scarcely counter-balance the effect produced by other portions of his speech. News has also reached me of an extensive amnesty granted by the King of Naples—he did not yield to outer pressure, and he was right—but now, on the occasion of the marriage of his son, an act of clemency on his part is well advised'.

'Is it true,' I said, 'that political prisoners are included in that Amnesty?'

'Yes,' His Holiness answered; 'I saw the name of Settembrini, and I think also of that other man in whom your Government took so much interest—his name begins with a "P" if I remember rightly——'

'Poerio,' I suggested.

'That is the name,' the Pope continued; 'and I fancy that all the other political prisoners will be released; they are to be sent to Cadiz at the expense of the King, they are to be clothed and receive some money, I believe, and after that arrangements have been made with the Minister of the United States to have them conveyed to that country; they are to be exiled for life. I hope this event may have the effect of making your Government and that of France renew diplomatic relations with Naples; I always regretted that rupture, but the King was right not to yield to outer pressure.

'It is lucky,' the Pope ended with a smile, 'that Lord Palmerston is not in office; he was too fond of interfering in the concerns of foreign countries, and the present crisis would just have suited him. *Addio, caro,*' the Pope then said, and dismissed me with his blessing.

I then, according to usage, called on Cardinal Antonelli, and recounted to him what had passed. He confirmed all the Pope had said, but denied that there was any very serious cause for immediate apprehension of any general disturbance of the Peace of Italy. I have, etc.,

ODO RUSSELL

The Earl of Derby to Queen Victoria

St James's Square, 3rd February 1859
(Thursday, 1 p.m.)

Lord Derby, with his humble duty, and in obedience to your Majesty's commands, received within this half hour through Lord Malmesbury, submits the accompanying very hastily drawn sketch of the language which, in his humble opinion, your Majesty might hold in a private and confidential letter to the Emperor of the French. Lord Derby is not sure that it is what your Majesty desired that he should submit; but he trusts that your Majesty will be pleased to receive it as an attempt to obey your Majesty's commands, and will excuse its many imperfections on account of the extreme haste in which it has unavoidably been written.

'I cannot refrain from taking this opportunity of expressing confidentially to your Imperial Majesty my deep anxiety for the preservation of the peace of Europe, nor can I conceal from myself how essentially that great object must depend upon the course which your Imperial Majesty may be advised to take. Your Majesty has now the opportunity, either by listening to the dictates of humanity and justice, and by demonstrating unmistakably your intention to adhere strictly to the faithful observance of Treaties, of calming the apprehensions of Europe, and restoring her confidence in your

Majesty's pacific policy; or, by permitting yourself to be influenced by the ambitious or interested designs of others, of involving Europe in a war, the extent and termination of which can hardly be foreseen, and which, whatever glory it may add to the arms of France, cannot but interfere materially with her internal prosperity and financial credit. I am sure that your Majesty will not doubt the sincerity of the friendship which alone induces me to write thus unreservedly to your Majesty, and if anything could add to the sorrow with which I should view the renewal of war in Europe, it would be to see your Majesty entering upon a course with which it would be impossible for England to associate herself.'

Queen Victoria to the King of the Belgians

Windsor Castle, 3rd May 1859

DEAREST UNCLE,—Many thanks for your dear, kind letter of the 30th. God knows we *are* in a sad mess. The rashness of the Austrians is indeed a *great* misfortune, for it has placed them in the wrong. Still there is *one* universal feeling of *anger* at the conduct of France, and of *great suspicion*. The Treaty with Russia is *denied*, but I am perfectly certain that there *are engagements*. . . .

Here the Elections are not as satisfactory as could be wished, but the Government still think they will have a clear gain of 25 to 30 seats, which will make a difference of 50 to 60 votes on a Division. It gives unfortunately no majority; still, it must be remembered that the Opposition are very much divided, and not at all a compact body, which the supporters of the Government are.

Lord John has been holding moderate and prudent language on Foreign Affairs, whereas Lord Palmerston has made bad and mischievous speeches, but *not* at all in accordance with the feelings of the country. The country wishes for strict neutrality, but strong defences, and we are making our Navy as strong as we can. . . .

The Earl of Malmesbury to Queen Victoria

15th May 1859

The Earl of Malmesbury presents his humble duty to the Queen, and has the honour to inform your Majesty that Count de Persigny called on him yesterday. He passed an hour in attempting to prove what it seems he really believes himself—that the Emperor has no plan or even intention to make war in Italy; that His Imperial Majesty was drawn into it step by step by M. de Cavour, who finally menaced to publish his most confidential correspondence, etc.; that his army was totally unprepared, and is now in a very imperfect state, and that he himself was overcome with surprise and fear when he learnt in the middle of last month that the Austrians had 120,000 men on the Ticino. The Emperor, however, now believes that he will easily gain a *couple* of victories, and that when he has *rejeté les Autrichiens dans leur tanière* (by which he means their great fortresses), he will return to govern at Paris, and leave a Marshal to carry on the sieges and the war. M. de Persigny's letters of appointment are not yet signed, and must go to Italy to be so. He stated that a week ago he was named Minister of Foreign Affairs, and that Fould, Walewski, and others were to be dismissed, but that two days before the Emperor's departure Madame Walewska and the Empress had on their knees obtained a reprieve, and that M. de Persigny was ordered to come here *sans raisonner.* . . .

The Earl of Derby to Queen Victoria

Downing Street, 2nd June 1859

Lord Derby, with his humble duty, submits to your Majesty that he has most anxiously, and with every desire to meet your Majesty's wishes, reflected upon the effect of the alterations suggested by your Majesty in the proposed Speech from the Throne. He has considered the consequences involved so serious that he has thought it right to confer upon the subject with the Chancellor of the Exchequer, as Leader of the House of Commons; and it is a duty which he owes to your Majesty not to withhold the expression of their clear and un-hesitating conviction. Lord Derby trusts that your Majesty will forgive the frankness with which, in the accompanying observations, he feels it necessary to submit to your Majesty the grounds for the view which they are compelled to take.

The first paragraph to which your Majesty takes exception is that which intimates your Majesty's 'intention' to maintain a strict and impartial neutrality, and 'hope' to be enabled to preserve peace. Your Majesty apprehends that this may be interpreted into a determination to preserve neutrality *à tout prix*; but Lord Derby would venture to observe that such an inference is negatived by the subsequent words, which only imply a 'hope' of preserving peace. With the cessation of that hope, neutrality would necessarily terminate. But as matters stand at present, Lord Derby is warranted in assuring your Majesty that if there is one subject on which more than another the mind of the country is unanimous, it is that of an entire abstinence from participation in the struggle now going on in Italy. He collects this from the language of politicians of almost every class, from all the public papers, from Addresses and Memorials which he receives every day—some urging, and some congratulating him upon the adoption of a perfectly neutral policy. The sympathies of the country are neither with France nor with Austria, but were it not for the intervention of France, they would be general in favour of Italy. The charge now made against your Majesty's servants, by the opposition Press, as the *Morning Post* and *Daily News,* is that their neutrality covers such wishes and designs in favour of Austria; and any word in your Majesty's Speech which should imply a doubt of the continuance of strict impartiality, would, undoubtedly, provoke a hostile Amendment, which might very possibly be carried in the Sardinian sense, and which, if so carried, would place your Majesty in the painful position of having to select an Administration, pledged against the interests of Austria and of Germany. Lord Derby says nothing of the personal results to your Majesty's present servants, because, in such cases, personal considerations ought not to be allowed to prevail; and it is in the interests of the country only, and even of the very cause which your Majesty desires to uphold, that he earnestly trusts that your Majesty will not require any alteration in this part of the Speech. There is, at this moment, in the country, a great jealousy and suspicion of France, and of her ulterior designs—as indicated by the demand of means of defence, the formation of Volunteer Corps, etc.—but it is neutralised partly by sympathy for Italy, partly by suspicions, industriously circulated, of the pro-Austrian tendencies of the present Government. It is very important that the language of the Speech should be so decided as to negative this impression, and Lord Derby cannot but feel that if neutrality be spoken of not as a thing decided upon, but which, it is hoped, may be maintained, such language will be taken to intimate the expectation of the Government that it may, at no distant time, be departed from. In Lord Derby's humble opinion Peace should be spoken of as subject to doubt, because, out of the present struggle, complications may arise which may necessarily involve us in war; but neutrality, as between the present belligerents, should be a matter open to no doubt or question. If there be no attempt made to run counter to public opinion, and Austria should sustain serious reverses, the jealousy of France will increase, and the feeling of the country will support your Majesty in a war, should such arise, against her aggression; but if the slightest pretext be afforded for doubting the *bonâ fide* character of British neutrality, or the firm determination to maintain it, an anti-German feeling will be excited, which will be fatal to the Administration, and seriously embarrassing to your Majesty.

The same observations apply, with hardly less force, to part of the Amendment suggested by your Majesty to the paragraph regarding the Navy. With submission to your Majesty, Lord Derby can hardly look upon it as humiliating to a great country, in announcing a large increase of its Naval Force, to disclaim any object of aggression. These words, however, might, if your Majesty were so pleased, be omitted, though Lord Derby cannot go so far as to say that in his humble judgment the omission would be an improvement; but he trusts that your Majesty will be satisfied with a general reference to the 'state of Europe' without speaking of the 'complications which a war carried on by some of the Great Powers may produce.' These words would infallibly lead to a demand for explanation, and for a statement of the nature of the 'complications' which the Government foresaw as likely to lead to war. In humbly tendering to your Majesty his most earnest advice that your Majesty will not insist on the proposed Amendments in his Draft Speech, he believes that he may assure your Majesty that he is expressing the unanimous opinion of his Colleagues. Of their sentiments your Majesty may judge by the fact that in the original draft he had spoken of your Majesty's 'intention' to preserve peace 'as long as it might be possible'; but by universal concurrence these latter words were struck out, and the 'hope' was, instead of them, substituted for the 'intention.' Should your Majesty, however, be pleased so to order, Lord Derby will immediately submit the question to the consideration of his Colleagues, in order that your Majesty may be put, in the most authentic form, in possession of their views. He assures your Majesty that nothing can be more repugnant to his feelings than to offer objections to any suggestions emanating from your Majesty; and he has only been induced to do so upon the present occasion by the deep conviction which he entertains of the danger attending the course proposed, and the serious embarrassments which it would cause your Majesty. He regrets more especially having been compelled to take this step at a moment when your Majesty's thoughts are very differently engaged, and when it may be doubly irksome to have matters of public business pressed upon your Majesty's consideration.

The above is humbly submitted by your Majesty's most dutiful Servant and Subject,   DERBY

Memorandum by Earl Granville

[Undated. 11th June 1859]

I waited at four o'clock this afternoon upon the Queen by Her Majesty's gracious commands. The Queen was pleased to remark upon the importance of the present crisis. Her Majesty informed me that Lord Derby had resigned, and that she had sent for me to desire that I should attempt to form another Administration, which Her Majesty wished should be strong and comprehensive. I respectfully assured the Queen that Her Majesty's commands came upon me by surprise; that at any time I felt my own insufficiency for such a post, and that at this time there were special difficulties; that I believed the only two persons who could form a strong Liberal Government were either Lord Palmerston or Lord John Russell; and that, although it had sometimes happened that two statesmen of equal pretensions preferred having a nominal chief to serving under one another, I said that I had reason to believe that Lords Palmerston and John Russell were ready to co-operate with one another, while I doubted whether either would consent to serve under a younger man of such small pretensions as myself.

The Queen in reply informed me that her first thoughts had been turned to Lord Palmerston and Lord John Russell, that they had both served her long and faithfully, and that Her Majesty felt it to be an invidious task to select one of the two. Her Majesty was also of opinion that as different sections of the Liberal Party were more or less represented by each, it might be more easy for the Party to act together under a third person. Her Majesty added that she had selected me as the Leader of the Liberal Party in the House of Lords, and a person in whom both Lord Palmerston and Lord John Russell had been in the habit of placing confidence, and she expressed her confident hope that their attachment to herself would induce them to yield that assistance without which it would be difficult to form a strong and comprehensive Government.

I proceeded to state some of the most salient difficulties of the task, and asked Her Majesty's permission to ascertain by negotiation what it would be possible to do.

Her Majesty informed me that Her Majesty's experience of former changes of administration had taught her that the construction of an administration had failed when the person entrusted with the task had acted merely as a negotiator, and that the success of other attempts had been owing to the acceptance of the charge by the person for whom she had sent. Her Majesty laid Her Majesty's commands upon me to make the attempt, and I had the honour of conveying two letters from Her Majesty to Lord Palmerston and Lord John Russell, stating that Her Majesty relied upon their assistance.

$$Queen\ Victoria\ to \begin{cases} Viscount\ Palmerston \\ Lord\ John\ Russell \end{cases}$$

Buckingham Palace, 11th June 1859

The Queen gives these lines to Lord Granville, whom she has entrusted with the task of forming an administration on the resignation of Lord Derby. She has selected him as the Leader of the Liberal Party in the House of Lords. She feels that it is of the greatest importance that both Lord Palmerston and Lord John Russell should lend their services to the Crown and country in the present anxious circumstances, and thought at the same time that they might do so most agreeably to their own feelings by acting under a third person. They having both served the Queen long and faithfully as her First Minister, she must not conceal from Lord Palmerston (John Russell) that it is a great relief to her feelings not to have to make the choice of one of them, and she trusts that they will feel no difficulty to co-operate with one in whom they have both been in the habit of placing confidence. From the long experience the Queen has had of Lord Palmerston's (John Russell's) loyal attachment to her and the service of the Crown, she feels confident she may rely on Lord Palmerston's (John Russell's) hearty assistance.

Earl Granville to Queen Victoria

Bruton Street, 12th June 1859
(2 a.m.)

Lord Granville presents his humble duty to your Majesty and begs to submit that he saw Lord Palmerston immediately after he had left Buckingham Palace. Lord Granville stated what had passed there, omitting any reference to your Majesty's objections to the effect likely to be produced on the Continent by Lord Palmerston's name, if he had the direction of the Foreign Affairs. Nothing could be more frank and cordial than Lord Palmerston's manner. He agreed to lead the House of Commons; he said that he had certainly anticipated that your Majesty would have sent for either Lord John or himself, but having taken a part in the defeat of the present Government, he felt bound to put aside any personal objects, and co-operate with me; and that there was no person whom he should prefer or even like as much as myself. He added that his co-operation must depend upon my being able to form a strong Government. Lord Granville then saw Lord John Russell, and had a very long conversation with him. Lord John had no objection to serving under Lord Granville, but thought that he could not give effect to his political views unless he was either Prime Minister or Leader of the House of Commons, and he doubted whether he had confidence in any one but Lord Palmerston for the Foreign Office. Lord Granville again saw Lord Palmerston, who informed him that if he had been sent for, he should have objected to go to the House of Lords, and that he could not now give up the lead of the House of Commons (which Lord

Granville had already proposed to him to retain) to Lord John. This answer rendered it unnecessary for Lord Granville to allude to the objections to his holding the Foreign Office. Lord Granville has seen Lord Clarendon, who acted up to the full spirit of your Majesty's letter, but deprecates strongly the attempt to form a Government without Lord John Russell. Sir George Grey is of the same opinion. Sir George Lewis, Mr Herbert, and Mr Gladstone think every effort should be made to secure Lord John, but that it would not be impossible to form a Government without him. Mr Milner Gibson, with whom Lord Granville had a more reserved conversation, considered it a *sine quâ non* condition of support from the Liberal Party below the gangway, that Lord John should be a member of the Government. Lord Granville thinks that in his third interview with Lord Palmerston he observed more dissatisfaction at not being sent for by your Majesty. Lord Palmerston suggested that Lord John's absence from the Government would make it more difficult for a Leader of the House, who was not Prime Minister, to hold his position.

Lord Granville has written to Lord John asking for a final answer before he informs your Majesty, whether he is able to attempt the task which your Majesty has with so much kindness and indulgence laid upon him.

Queen Victoria to the Earl of Derby

Buckingham Palace, 12th June 1859

The Queen writes to inform Lord Derby that after a fruitless attempt on the part of Lord Granville to form a Government comprising Lord Palmerston and Lord John Russell, she has now charged Lord Palmerston with the task, which she trusts may prove more successful....

Viscount Palmerston to Queen Victoria

94 Piccadilly, 1st July 1859

Viscount Palmerston presents his humble duty to your Majesty, and has been unable till within the last few minutes to make any Report about Mr Cobden, from whom he had received no communication till about an hour ago, when Mr Cobden came to him. The result of a long conversation between them has been that Mr Cobden, against the advice of all his friends and of his constituents, has decided to decline taking office. He grounds his decision upon feelings personal to himself. He thinks that after having so often and so strongly disapproved of the Foreign Policy of Viscount Palmerston as tending too much to involve this country in war, it would be inconsistent for him to join the present Cabinet, and he also said that, at his time of life and with his general habits, he does not consider himself fit for administrative office.

Viscount Palmerston used every [means] in his power to induce him to change his decision, and showed that, with respect to present and future action, there is no apparent difference between his views and those of Mr Cobden, since both would desire that this country should remain neutral in the war now raging in Italy. All his arguments, however, were useless, and though Mr Cobden discussed the matter in the most friendly and good-humoured manner, and promised to give out of office all support to the Government, and said that he thought he could do so more effectually out of office than in office, he could not be persuaded to make any change in the answer which he came to give.

Viscount Palmerston will consider what arrangement he may have to propose to your Majesty in consequence of Mr Cobden's answer.

The Ministry as formed by Viscount Palmerston, in the month of June 1859

First Lord of the Treasury	Viscount Palmerston
Lord Chancellor	Lord Campbell
President of the Council	Earl Granville
Lord Privy Seal	Duke of Argyll
Home Secretary	Sir G. C. Lewis.
Foreign Secretary	Lord John (afterwards Earl) Russell
Colonial Secretary	Duke of Newcastle
Secretary for War	Mr Sidney Herbert (afterwards Lord Herbert of Lea)
Secretary for India	Sir Charles Wood (afterwards Viscount Halifax)
Chancellor of the Exchequer	Mr Gladstone
First Lord of the Admiralty	Duke of Somerset
President of the Board of Trade	Mr. Milner Gibson (appointed in July)
Postmaster-General	Earl of Elgin
Chancellor of the Duchy of Lancaster	Sir George Grey
Chief Secretary for Ireland	Mr (afterwards Viscount) Cardwell

Viscount Palmerston to Queen Victoria

94 Piccadilly, 2nd July 1859

Viscount Palmerston presents his humble duty to your Majesty. . . .

Viscount Palmerston has heard from several persons that Mr Bright would be highly flattered by being made a Privy Councillor; would your Majesty object to his being so made if it should turn out that he wishes it? There have been instances of persons made Privy Councillors without office, and if Mr Bright could be led by such an honour to turn his thoughts and feelings into better channels such a change could not fail to be advantageous to your Majesty's service. . . .

Queen Victoria to Viscount Palmerston

Buckingham Palace, 2nd July 1859

The Queen has received Lord Palmerston's letter of to-day. She is sorry not to be able to give her assent to his proposal with regard to Mr Bright.* Privy Councillors have sometimes exceptionally been made without office, yet this has been as rewards, even in such cases, for services rendered to the State. It would be impossible to allege any service Mr Bright has rendered, and if the honour were looked upon as a reward for his systematic attacks upon the institutions of the country, a very erroneous impression might be produced as to the feeling which the Queen or her Government entertain towards these institutions. It is moreover very problematical whether such an honour conferred upon Mr Bright would, as suggested, wean him from his present line of policy, whilst, if he continued in it, he would only have obtained additional weight in the country by his propounding his views as one of the Queen's Privy Councillors.

* In 1859, Lord Palmerston, in offering Mr Cobden a seat in the Cabinet, rejected the idea of accepting Mr Bright as a colleague, on the ground that his public speeches made it impossible. Mr Bright, later in life, was a welcome guest at Windsor, and the Queen became warmly attached to him as one of her Ministers.

Earl Canning to Queen Victoria

Calcutta, 4th July 1859

Lord Canning presents his humble duty to your Majesty, and begs permission to offer to your Majesty his respectful thanks for your Majesty's most gracious letter of the 18th of May.

Lord Canning ventures to believe that he is well able to figure to himself the feelings with which your Majesty will have welcomed the termination of the Mutiny and Rebellion in India, and of the chief miseries which these have brought in their train. He hopes that your Majesty will not have thought that there has been remissness in not marking this happy event by an earlier public acknowledgment and thanksgiving in India, as has already been done in England. The truth is, that although this termination has long been steadily and surely approaching, it is but just now that it can be said to be complete in the eyes of those who are near to the scene of action. It is only within the last three weeks that the exertions of our Troops on the Oudh and Nepaulese frontier, and in some other parts, have been remitted, and almost every Gazette has recounted engagements with the rebels, which, although they have invariably had the same issue, would scarcely have consisted with a declaration that peace and tranquillity were restored. Now, however, military operations have fairly ceased, and the rains and the climate, which would make a continuance of those operations much to be regretted, will do their work amongst the rebels who are still in arms in the Nepaul jungles more terribly than any human avengers.

Lord Canning has used every exertion and device to bring these wretched men to submission; but many—it is difficult to say how many, but certainly some few thousands—still hold out. With some of them the reason no doubt is that they belong to the most guilty Regiments, and to those which murdered their officers; but this cannot apply to all; and it is to be feared that the prevailing cause is the bad influence of their leaders—the Nana, Bala Rao, and the Begum; or rather the Begum's infamous advisers. It is certain that all of these, believing their own position to be desperate, have spared no points to persuade their followers that the Government is seeking to entrap them, and that, if they submit, their lives will be taken. . . .

Lord John Russell to Queen Victoria

Pembroke Lodge, 10th July 1859
(7 p.m.)

Lord John Russell presents his humble duty to your Majesty. He has just received from Lord Palmerston, who is here, the paper, a copy of which is enclosed.*

Lord John Russell has to add that Lord Palmerston and he are humbly of opinion that your Majesty should give to the Emperor of the French the moral support which is asked. It is clearly understood that if the Emperor of Austria declines to accept the propositions, Great Britain will still maintain her neutral position.

But it is probable that her moral support will put an end to the war, and your Majesty's advisers cannot venture to make themselves responsible for its continuance by refusing to counsel your Majesty to accept the proposal of France.

Queen Victoria to Lord John Russell

Pavilion, Aldershot, 10th July 1859

The Queen has just received Lord John Russell's letter with the enclosure which she returns, and hastens to say in reply, that she does not consider the Emperor of the French or his Ambassador justified in asking the support of England to proposals he means to make to his antagonist to-morrow. He made war on Austria in order to wrest her two Italian kingdoms from her, which were assured to her by the treaties of 1815, to which England is a party; England declared her neutrality in the war. The Emperor succeeded in driving the Austrians out of one of these kingdoms after several bloody battles.

---

* At the seat of war, a series of decisive French victories had culminated in the battle of Solferino, on Midsummer Day. But the French Emperor was beginning to think these successes too dearly purchased, at the expense of so many French lives, and, actuated either by this, or some similar motive, he attempted, on 6th July, to negotiate through the British Government with Austria. The attempt was a failure, but an armistice was signed on the 8th, and again the Emperor sought the moral support of England. The paper which Lord John Russell submitted was a rough memorandum of M. de Persigny's, proposing as a basis of negotiation the cession of Lombardy to Piedmont, the independence of Venetia, and the erection of an Italian Confederation.

He means to drive her out of the second by diplomacy, and neutral England is to join him with her moral support in this endeavour.

The Queen having declared her neutrality, to which her Parliament and people have given their unanimous assent, feels bound to adhere to it. She conceives Lord John Russell and Lord Palmerston ought not to ask her to give her 'moral support' to one of the belligerents. As for herself, she sees no distinction between moral and general support; the moral support of England *is* her support, and she ought to be prepared to follow it up.

The Queen wishes this letter to be communicated to the Cabinet.

Queen Victoria to Lord John Russell

Osborne, 13th July 1859

The Queen has received the news of a concluded peace, which Lord John Russell has sent to her yesterday, with as much surprise as it must have caused Lord John. It was a joyous intelligence, as far as the stopping of the further effusion of innocent blood and the security against further diplomatic complications is concerned, but it gives cause for serious reflection. The Emperor Napoleon, by his military successes, and great apparent moderation or prudence immediately after them, has created for himself a most formidable position of strength in Europe. It is remarkable that he has acted towards Austria now just as he did towards Russia after the fall of Sebastopol; and if it was our lot then to be left alone to act the part of the extortioner whilst he acted that of the generous victor, the Queen is doubly glad that we should not now have fallen into the trap, to ask Austria (as friends and neutrals) concessions which he was ready to waive. He will now probably omit no occasion to cajole Austria as he has done to Russia, and turn her spirit of revenge upon Prussia and Germany— the Emperor's probable next victims. Should he thus have rendered himself the master of the entire Continent, the time may come for us either to obey or to fight him with terrible odds against us. This has been the Queen's view from the beginning of this complication, and events have hitherto wonderfully supported them. How Italy is to prosper under the Pope's presidency, whose misgovernment of his own small portion of it was the ostensible cause of the war, the Queen is at a loss to conceive. But the Emperor will be able to do just as he pleases, being in military command of the country, and having Sardinia, the Pope, and Australia as his debtors.

The Queen would like this letter to be communicated to the Cabinet.

Mr Odo Russell to Lord John Russell
(Submitted to the Queen)

Rome, 17th July 1859

MY LORD,—Some days since a letter from the 'Pontifical Antechamber,' directed to 'Signor Odoni Russell, Agente Officioso di Sua Maestà Britannica,' informed me that His Holiness the Pope desired to see me.

In consequence I proceeded to the Vatican, and was ushered into the presence of His Holiness by Monsignore Talbot, the 'Cameriere' in waiting, who immediately withdrew, and I remained alone with the Pope.

His Holiness welcomed me with his usual benevolence and good humour. He seemed very gay, and spoke with more than customary frankness, so much so indeed that I have felt some hesitation as to the propriety of submitting what passed between us to your Lordship. But after mature reflection, I think it best you should be in possession of an accurate and conscientious account of the sentiments of His Holiness in the present important juncture of affairs.

'Caro mio Russell,' the Pope said, 'you have been so long at Naples that I was already thinking of sending after you to bring you back; we do not like you to leave us, and the more so as I have heard you were attached to the Mission of Mr Elliot, who is a son of Lord Minto; and if he entertains the same political views as his father, he is a dangerous man to the peace of Italy. Now I knew Lord Minto here, and although he may be a very good man, I do not think him a man of any capacity, and his doctrines were calculated to bring on the ruin of Italy.'

I replied, 'I cannot agree with your Holiness, for I consider Lord Minto to be a very clever man, whose honest, sound, and liberal views, had they been listened to, might have prevented the crisis which is now convulsing Italy.'

The Pope said, 'Well, of course you belong to his party, but, Poveri

253

noi! what is to become of us with your uncle and Lord Palmerston at the head of affairs in England? They have always sympathised with the turbulent spirits of Italy, and their accession to power will greatly increase the hopes of the Piedmontese Party. Indeed, I well know what the English Government want: they want to see the Pope deprived of his temporal power.'

I replied, 'Again I regret to find your Holiness so entirely mistaken with respect to the policy of England. We derive great happiness from our free institutions, and we would be glad to see our neighbours in Europe as happy and as prosperous as we are, but we have no wish to interfere with the internal concerns of other nations, or to give advice without being asked for it; least of all as a Protestant Power would *we* think of interfering one way or the other with the Government of your Holiness.'

The Pope said, 'I do not doubt the good intentions of England, but unfortunately you do not understand this country, and your example is dangerous to the Italian minds, your speeches in Parliament excite them, and you fancy because constitutional liberties and institutions suit you, that they must suit all the world. Now the Italians are a dissatisfied, interfering, turbulent and intriguing race; they can never learn to govern themselves, it is impossible; only see how they follow Sardinia in all she tells them to do, simply because they love intrigue and revolution, whilst in reality they do not know what they want; a hot-headed people like the Italians require a firm and just government to guide and take care of them, and Italy might have continued tranquil and contented, had not the ambition of Sardinia led her to revolutionise the whole country. The Grand Duke of Tuscany, for instance, is an excellent and just man, and nevertheless, at the instigation of Piedmont, he was turned out of the country, and for no earthly purpose. I suppose you have read Monsieur About's book about Rome? well, all he says is untrue, pure calumny, and it would be easy for me to have it all refuted; but he is really not worthy of such an honour. His book, I see, has been translated into English, and I have no doubt it will be much read and believed in England. Such books and our refugees mislead your countrymen, and I often wonder at the language your statesmen hold about us in the Houses of Parliament. I always read their speeches. Lord Palmerston,

Lord John Russell, and Mr Gladstone do not know us; but when I think how kindly and hospitably Lord Granville was received at Rome last winter, and then read the extraordinary speech he made last February about us, I think the gout he suffered from here must have gone to his head when he reached England, and I wonder how Her Majesty the Queen could send for him to form a Government! Then again, Mr Gladstone, who allowed himself to be deceived about the Neapolitan prisoners—he does not know us and Italy—and Mr Cobden,—I knew him in 1847—he is always in favour of peace, and he must be very fond of animals, for when he came here from Spain he wanted me to write to that country and put a stop to bull-fights —a very good man, but I do not know his views about Italy. And Lord Stratford de Redcliffe, do you think he will be employed again? he seemed so anxious to get a place. Mr Disraeli was my friend; I regret him. But tell me, *caro mio Russell*, if you are a prophet, how all this war and fuss is to end?'

I replied, 'Your Holiness has better claims to being a prophet than I have, and I sincerely hope all this may end well for Italy; but as regards the present and the past, I must again say that I deeply regret to see your Holiness misconceive the honest views and sincere sympathies of the statesmen you have named, for the welfare of Italy; they would like to see Italy independent, prosperous, progressing and contented, and able to take care of herself without foreign troops. Your Holiness has done me the honour to speak freely and openly with me; permit me to do the same, and ask your Holiness what England must think when she sees the temporal power of your Holiness imposed upon three millions of peoples by the constant presence of French and Austrian bayonets, and when, after ten years of occupation, the Austrians withdraw suddenly, there is at once an insurrection throughout the country; and if the French were to leave Rome it is generally acknowledged that a revolution would compel your Holiness to seek refuge in some foreign country. At the same time, when the troops of your Holiness are employed as at Perugia, the Government is too weak to control them; they pillage and murder, and, instead of investigating their conduct, the excesses committed by them are publicly rewarded.'

The Pope smiled, paused, took a pinch of snuff, and then said good-humouredly: 'Although I am not a prophet, I know one thing; this war will be followed by an European Congress, and a Congress about Italian Affairs is even worse for us than war. There will be changes in Italy, but mark my words, whatever these changes are, the Pope will ever be the Pope, whether he dwells in the Vatican or lives concealed in the Catacombs.

'Lastly, I will give you some advice. Prepare and take care of yourselves in England, for I am quite certain the French Emperor intends sooner or later to attack you.'

The Pope then beckoned to me to approach, and making the sign of the Cross, he gave me his blessing in Latin, then with both his hands, he took one of mine, pressed it, and said with great warmth, 'Be our friend in the hour of need.' I have the honour to be, etc., etc.,

ODO RUSSELL

Viscount Palmerston to Queen Victoria

94 Piccadilly, 23rd August 1859

Viscount Palmerston presents his humble duty to your Majesty, and begs to state that Lord John Russell has shown him your Majesty's communication, in which your Majesty objects to a proposed despatch to Lord Cowley, on the ground that it would be a departure from the principle of non-intervention which has been publicly proclaimed as the rule for Great Britain in the late events between France and Austria. But Viscount Palmerston would beg humbly to submit to your Majesty that the intervention which all parties agreed that this country ought to abstain from, was active interference by force of arms in the war then going on, but that neither of the great political parties meant or asserted that this country should not interfere by its advice and opinions in regard to the matters to which the war related. Viscount Palmerston can assert that neither he nor any of those who were acting with him out of office ever contemplated giving such a meaning to the doctrine of non-intervention; and that such a meaning never was attached to it by the Conservative Leaders while they were in office, is proved from one end of their Blue Book to the other. The whole course of the Derby Government, in regard to the matters on which the war turned, was one uninterrupted series of interventions by advice, by opinions, and by censure now addressed to one party and now to another. Whatever may be thought of the judgment which was shown by them, or of the bias by which they were guided, the principle on which they acted was undoubtedly right and proper.

England is one of the greatest powers of the world, no event or series of events bearing on the balance of power, or on probabilities of peace or war can be matters of indifference to her, and her right to have and to express opinions on matters thus bearing on her interests is unquestionable; and she is equally entitled to give upon such matters any advice which she may think useful, or to suggest any arrangements which she may deem conducive to the general good.

It is no doubt true that the Conservative Party, since they have ceased to be responsible for the conduct of affairs, have held a different doctrine, and in their anxiety lest the influence of England should be exerted for the benefit of Italy, and to the disadvantage of Austria, have contended that any participation by Great Britain in the negotiations for the settlement of Italy would be a departure from the principle of non-intervention; but their own practice while in office refutes their newly adopted doctrine in opposition; and if that doctrine were to be admitted, Great Britain would, by her own act, reduce herself to the rank of a third-class European State.

Queen Victoria to the Lord Chancellor (Lord Campbell)

Windsor Castle, 26th December 1859

The Queen wishes to ask the Lord Chancellor whether no steps can be taken to prevent the present publicity of the proceedings before the new Divorce Court. These cases, which must necessarily increase when the new law becomes more and more known, fill now almost daily a large portion of the newspapers, and are of so scandalous a character that it makes it almost impossible for a paper to be trusted in the hands of a young lady or boy. None of the worst French novels from which careful parents would try to protect their children can be as bad as what is daily brought and laid upon the breakfast-table of every educated family in England, and its effect must be most pernicious to the public morals of the country.

1860

Lord John Russell to Queen Victoria

Pembroke Lodge, 11th January 1860

Lord John Russell presents his humble duty to your Majesty; he has just had the honour to receive your Majesty's letter of this date.

Lord John Russell has sent to Lord Palmerston the proposal he humbly submits to your Majesty.

He will therefore only venture to say that the doctrines of the Revolution of 1688, doctrines which were supported by Mr Fox, Mr Pitt, the Duke of Wellington, Lord Castlereagh, Mr Canning, and Lord Grey, can hardly be abandoned in these days of your Majesty's present advisers. According to those doctrines, all power held by Sovereigns may be forfeited by misconduct, and each nation is the judge of its own internal government.*

Lord John Russell can hardly be expected to abjure those opinions, or to act in opposition to them.

Queen Victoria to Lord John Russell

Windsor Castle, 11th January 1860

The Queen has received Lord John Russell's note of this day, in which she is not able to find any answer to her letter, or even an allusion to what she had written, viz. that Austria and France being asked to abstain from interference, such an arrangement would be partial and incomplete unless Sardinia was pledged also to non-interference. The Queen cannot make out what the doctrines of the

---

* In a despatch of 27th October, Lord John took the same ground in the case of Naples. After quoting with approval the view taken by Vattel of the lawfulness of the assistance given by the United Provinces to the Prince of Orange, and his conclusion that it is justifiable to assist patriots revolting against an oppressor for 'good reasons', he stated that the question was whether the people of Naples and of the Roman States took up arms against their Government for good reasons; and of this matter, he added, the people themselves were the best judges.

Revolution of 1688 can have to do with this, or how it would necessitate Lord John to abjure them.

Queen Victoria to Viscount Palmerston

Windsor Castle, 10th February 1860

The Queen sends a letter to Lord Palmerston which she has received yesterday evening from Lord John Russell.* She is induced to do so from a feeling that it is to Lord Palmerston, as head of the Government, that she has to look, when she may have reason to take exception to the tone of communications she may receive from members of his Cabinet. Lord Palmerston will not fail to perceive that the enclosed is not the kind of communication which the Foreign Secretary ought to make, when asked by his Sovereign to explain the views of the Cabinet upon a question so important and momentous as the annexation of Savoy to France, and the steps which they propose to take with regard to it. She need not remind Lord Palmerston that in her letter communicated to the Cabinet she had given no opinion whatever upon Italian liberation from a foreign yoke, nor need she protest against a covert insinuation, such as is contained in Lord John's letter, that she is no well-wisher of mankind and indifferent to its freedom and happiness. But she must refer to the constitutional position of her Ministers towards herself. They are responsible for the advice they gave her, but they are bound fully, respectfully, and openly to place before her the grounds and reasons upon which their advice may be founded, to enable her to judge whether she can give her assent to that advice or not. The Government must come to a standstill if the Minister meets a demand for explanation with an answer like the following: 'I was asked by the Cabinet to give an answer, but as I do not agree with you, I think it useless to explain my views.'

The Queen must demand that respect which is due from a Minister to his Sovereign. As the Queen must consider the enclosed letter as

---

* The letter ran: 'Lord John Russell unfortunately does not partake your Majesty's opinions in regard to Italy, and he is unwilling to obtrude on your Majesty unnecessary statements of his views.... Whatever may be the consequences, the liberation of the Italian people from a foreign yoke is, in the eyes of Lord Palmerston and Lord John Russell, an increase of freedom and happiness at which as well-wishers to mankind they cannot but rejoice.'

deficient in it, she thinks Lord John Russell might probably wish to reconsider it, and asks Lord Palmerston to return it to him with that view.

That Lord Palmerston may be acquainted with the course the correspondence has taken, the Queen encloses the two preceding letters.

Viscount Palmerston to Queen Victoria

94 Piccadilly, 10th February 1860

Viscount Palmerston presents his humble duty to your Majesty, and begs to state that Mr Gladstone made this afternoon his financial statement. His speech lasted three hours, from five to eight, and was admirable, detailed, clear, comprehensive and eloquent; and he did not appear to be fatigued by the effort. The statement was well received by the House, and though parts of the arrangement may, and no doubt will, be disputed and attacked as the various measures of which the arrangement is composed, pass through the House, there seems to be a fair probability that the Government will not sustain any serious defeat upon any part of the arrangement. The scheme is too extensive and complicated to admit of an abstract of it being given to your Majesty in this Report; but no doubt a condensed summary of it will be given in the newspapers of to-morrow.

Earl Cowley to Lord John Russell
(Submitted to the Queen)

Paris, 7th March 1860

My DEAR LORD JOHN,—I send a messenger this evening, in order that you may not hear from any one else of the passage of arms which took place between the Emperor and myself yesterday evening. You will find the account of it in the enclosed despatch. The more I reflect on it, the less I think that I could pass over the Emperor's conduct and language without notice. His tone and manner were really offensive, and if I had let them pass unheeded might have been repeated on another occasion. I must say that nothing could have been more friendly than His Majesty's bearing after I had spoken to him. He was profuse in his excuses, and the Empress told me later in the evening that he was *désolé*—'qu'il s'était laissé entraîner par un mouvement d'humeur,' etc. I, of course, said that I should think no more about it.

One good thing has been gained by it, that the Emperor has declared that he does not mean to act in defiance of the opinion of the Great Powers. . . .

I wish that I had not this disagreeable history to trouble you with, but do not attach greater importance to it than it merits. I look upon it as at an end. COWLEY

[Enclosure] *Earl Cowley to Lord John Russell*
(Submitted to the Queen)

Paris, 7th March 1860

MY LORD,—It is with extreme regret that I call your Lordship's attention to the following occurrence.

There was a concert last night at the Tuileries, to which the Chiefs of the Diplomatic Body were invited. On these occasions seats are assigned to the Ambassadors according to their accidental rank, and I was placed between the Nuntio and the Russian Ambassador. It is customary for the Emperor, during the interval between the two parts of the concert, to say a few words to each of the Ambassadors individually, and it is obvious that what His Majesty says to one may easily be overheard by that one's immediate neighbours.

Yesterday evening the Emperor, after saying a few words of no importance to the Nuntio, addressed himself to me in a manner and tone very unusual with him, animadverting upon the hostile sentiments evinced towards him in the English Parliament and Press. Wishing to avoid a discussion, I merely observed that I regretted that matters should be in such a state, but that His Majesty must be aware that there was quite a great irritation on this side the water. The Emperor enquired sharply whether this was to be wondered at, considering the terms and imputations applied to himself, and to the French nation, in England? They were only defending themselves against unfair attacks, His Majesty said. It was really too bad, he continued; he had done all in his power to maintain a good understanding with England, but the conduct of England rendered it impossible. What had England to do with Savoy? And why was she not to be satisfied with the declaration that His Majesty had made to me, that he had no intention to annex Savoy to France without having previously obtained the consent of the Great Powers.

'Pardon me, Sire,' I said, 'for interrupting your Majesty, but it is just what you did not say. Had you permitted me to convey that assurance to Her Majesty's Government, I will answer for it that all those interpellations in Parliament would long since have ceased, and that Her Majesty's Government and the country would at all events have awaited the decision at which the Great Powers might have arrived.'

'But I told you,' continued the Emperor, 'that I would consult the Great Powers.'

'Yes, Sire,' I replied, 'but your Majesty did not add that you would abide by their decision.'

This conversation had taken place, not only within the hearing of the Russian Ambassador, but the Emperor's remarks were addressed almost as much to my colleague as to myself. Turning then entirely towards General Kisseleff, the Emperor continued: 'The conduct of England is inexplicable. I have done all in my power to keep on the best terms with her; but I am at my wits' end (*je n'en puis plus*). 'What,' His Majesty exclaimed again, 'has England to do with Savoy? What would have been the consequence if, when she took possession of the Island of Perim for the safety of her Eastern dominions, I had raised the same objections that she has now raised to the annexation of Savoy, which I want as much for the safety of France?'

His Majesty continued to speak for a few seconds in the same strain, and I felt my position to be most awkward. With the remembrance of His Majesty's intemperate words to M. de Hübner on New Year's Day, 1859, in my mind, I did not like to leave unnoticed observations of the tendency I have mentioned. At the same time I had to bear in mind that I was not present on an official occasion, but that I was the Emperor's guest, and that it would not be right to continue a discussion in the presence of others. These thoughts passed rapidly through my mind, and I determined to be guided by a night's reflection in taking any further step in this matter. What that reflection might have produced I cannot say, but circumstances led to more immediate explanations.

As the Emperor moved on, the circle in which we were standing was not strictly kept, and after a few minutes I found myself standing a little in front, in the open space round which the circle was formed. The Emperor again accosted me, and was beginning in the same strain, when I ventured to interrupt His Majesty and to tell him that I considered myself justified in calling his attention to the unusual course he had adopted, in indulging, in presence of the Russian Ambassador, in his animadversions on the conduct of England. That His Majesty, if he had, or thought he had, any cause for remonstrance or blame with regard to England, should address himself to me, was not only natural, but would be a course which I should always beg him to take, because free discussion was the best remedy for pent-up feeling. I should answer as best I could, and endeavour to convince His Majesty when I thought him wrong. Or if His Majesty considered it right to complain of the conduct of England to the Russian Ambassador, I had no desire to interfere, provided it was not done in my presence; but what I could not approve, or consider compatible with my own dignity, or that of the Government which I represented, was that complaints respecting England should be addressed to me in the hearing of the Russian Ambassador, and to the Russian Ambassador in my hearing.

Leaving then this official tone, I added that, considering the long and intimate relations which His Majesty had been graciously pleased to permit should exist between himself and me, and knowing, as he did, the personal attachment which I bore him, and the anxiety which I had ever manifested to smooth difficulties and prevent misunderstandings between the two Governments, in doing which I had perhaps exposed myself to the suspicion of being more French than I ought to be, I had not expected to have been addressed, as I had been, in the presence of the Russian Ambassador, or to have heard words addressed to that Ambassador complaining of the sentiments of the English nation.

The Emperor frequently interrupted me, expressing his great regret at what had occurred. He could assure me, His Majesty said, that he had spoken without any bad intention—that he had just read what had occurred in Parliament the night before, and that he had been greatly hurt at the strictures passed upon his conduct; I must recollect further that he had not spoken of the Government, but of those who attacked him. Again, His Majesty begged me to think no more of the matter, repeating the assurance that he had spoken without intention.

In the course of this second conversation the Emperor again asked, but in a very different tone, why England had taken up the question of Savoy which so little regarded her. Had it been Prussia or one of the Continental Powers, His Majesty could have understood it, but not a word of remonstrance had proceeded from any one of them. I replied that I did not think the Emperor could rely on that silence as indicating approbation, but at all events, I said, the position of Her Majesty's Government was very different from that of the other powers. How was it possible, I asked, for Her Majesty's Government to remain silent in presence of the interpellations respecting Savoy which were, night after night, put to them? And if His Majesty enquired why these interpellations were put, I would answer him that, if my judgment was correct, it was not so much on account of the actual plan of annexing Savoy, as on account of the circumstances connected with the whole transaction. They were, in fact, interpellations of mistrust. And how, I asked, could it be otherwise? What could the English people think on its transpiring that in spite of His Majesty's declarations, both before and during the war, that in going to war he meditated no special advantages for France, overtures had positively been made months before, to Sardinia, for the eventual cession of Savoy; why had not His Majesty told us fairly, in commencing this war, that if, by the results of the war, the territory of Sardinia should be greatly augmented, he might be obliged, in deference to public opinion in France, to ask for some territorial advantage? Such a declaration, although it might have rendered the British Government still more anxious to prevent the war, would have hindered all the manifestation of public opinion which is now taking place.

The Emperor seemed to feel the weight of these observations, and he ended the conversation by saying, that if this question of Savoy should go further, he had pledged himself to consult the Great Powers, and that he need hardly add that if their opinion should be unfavourable to his wishes, it would have great weight with him. 'It is not likely,' said His Majesty, 'that I should act against the advice of Europe.'

I end, my Lord, as I commenced, in regretting this occurrence. I could have wished that the Emperor had not spoken to me a second time yesterday, and that I had had a little time for reflection. I feel that I spoke to His Majesty under consideration emotion, caused by the tone and manner which he had adopted; but I am certain that not a word escaped me which was not respectful to himself. To have passed the matter over, would, in my judgment, have been a fault, but on the whole I should have preferred conveying impressions to His Majesty through M. Thouvenel. I earnestly trust, however, that Her Majesty's Government will view my conduct in a favourable light.

It is but justice to my Russian colleague to state that nothing could have been in better taste than his remarks in answer to the Emperor's observations to him. I have told General Kisseleff this morning that having had an opportunity to do so, I had expressed to the Emperor the opinion that it would have been better had His Majesty avoided irritating topics concerning England in the presence of another foreign representative. It is not my intention to open my lips on the subject to any one else.

COWLEY

Queen Victoria to Lord John Russell

Osborne, 12th March 1860

The Queen, in returning Lord Cowley's private letter and secret despatch, agrees with Lord John Russell, that he has deserved praise for his mode of answering the Emperor's Napoleonic address. . . .

Lord John Russell to Queen Victoria

House of Commons, 30th April 1860

Lord John Russell presents his humble duty to your Majesty. He is sorry he cannot agree that there would be any moral wrong in assisting to overthrow the Government of the King of the Two Sicilies. The best writers on International Law consider it a merit to overthrow a tyrannical government, and there have been few governments

QUEEN VICTORIA'S EARLY LETTERS

so tyrannical as that of Naples. Of course the King of Sardinia has no right to assist the people of the Two Sicilies unless he was asked by them to do so, as the Prince of Orange was asked by the best men in England to overthrow the tyranny of James II—an attempt which has received the applause of all our great public writers, and is the origin of our present form of government.

Queen Victoria to Lord John Russell

Buckingham Palace, 30th April 1860

The Queen has received Lord John Russell's letter, and trusts he will see, upon further reflection, that the case before us is not one in which the Revolution of 1688, and the advent of William III called to the Throne, can be appealed to as a parallel. The draft warns the Government of Sardinia *'not to seek for new acquisitions,'* as the new *'Provinces* annexed have hardly as yet been thoroughly amalgamated.' Now, no public writer nor the International Law will call it morally right, that one state should abet revolution in another, not with the disinterested object of defending a suffering people against tyranny, but in order to extinguish that State and make it 'an acquisition' of its own. If William III had made England a Province of Holland, he would not have received the applause Lord John quotes. The Queen trusts that in appreciation of this distinction, he will introduce some amendment in the sense indicated in her former letter.

Lord John Russell to Queen Victoria

House of Commons, 30th April 1860

Lord John Russell presents his humble duty to your Majesty; he confesses he cannot see anything morally wrong in giving aid to an insurrection in the kingdoms of Naples and Sicily. But he admits that to do so for the sake of making new acquisitions would be criminal, and that he is not justified in imputing this motive to the King of Sardinia. Count Cavour would probably at once disclaim it.

He therefore proposes to alter these words. The despatch went this evening by the usual messenger; but, if your Majesty approves of the alteration, it can be made to-morrow morning by telegraph to Turin.

Viscount Palmerston to Queen Victoria

94 Piccadilly, 22nd May 1860

Viscount Palmerston presents his humble duty to your Majesty, and begs to state that the Cabinet met to-day at half-past twelve to consider what (if anything) should be done in consequence of the vote of the House of Lords last night. Lord John Russell, Mr Gladstone, and Mr Milner Gibson were desirous of finding some means of visiting their displeasure upon the House of Lords, but it was shown to them that the only measures which could be adopted were far too violent for the occasion, and that the House of Commons itself is powerless in the matter. When the Lords do anything inconsistent, with the asserted privileges of the House of Commons, as, for instance, inserting a taxing Clause in a Bill sent up to them, or making an alteration in a Money Bill sent up to them, the House of Commons is necessarily invited to do something afterwards in the matter, by assenting to what has been done by the Lords; and the Commons then assert their claimed rights by throwing out the Bill thus, improperly, as the Commons say, meddled with by the Lords; but when the Lords throw out a Bill there is nothing for the Commons to do, as the Bill has vanished, and the Commons are therefore furnished with no opportunity of asserting the right which they may claim. But, moreover, the Commons have always contended that the Lords cannot originate or alter a Money Bill, but it has never been contended that the Lords may not reject a Money Bill, though there are few instances of their having done so. These arguments at length prevailed, and by four o'clock it was agreed that Viscount Palmerston should give notice that he would on Thursday move that a Committee be appointed to examine the Journals of the House of Lords to ascertain the fate of the Bill thus lost like Sir John Franklin, and that on Friday he should move the appointment of a Committee to search for precedent applicable to the case.

Viscount Palmerston to Queen Victoria

House of Commons, 2nd July 1850
(8.30 p.m.)

Viscount Palmerston has had the honour of receiving your Majesty's letter of this afternoon. Nothing of much importance as to Foreign

Affairs was done at the Cabinet to-day.... The material question for discussion was the course to be pursued about the Tax Bill Report. Lord John Russell had altered his opinion since Saturday, and had yesterday sent Viscount Palmerston a Draft of Resolution which he wished to be circulated to the members of the Cabinet before their meeting at twelve to-day....

When all the other members had left the room Mr Gladstone requested Viscount Palmerston to submit to your Majesty that he could no longer continue to carry on the business of his Department.* His opinion strongly was that action and not a Resolution was required, that one of three courses ought to be pursued: either that the Paper Duty Repeal Bill should again be sent up to the Lords; or that a Bill should be sent up for suspending the Paper Duties for a year; or that a Bill should be sent up reducing those duties gradually year by year; or fourthly that with the Repeal of the Paper Duties should be coupled the imposition of Spirit Duties. Viscount Palmerston said he really could not undertake the communication which Mr Gladstone wished to be submitted to your Majesty, and earnestly entreated Mr Gladstone to reconsider the matter; he urged in detail all the reasons which ought to dissuade such a step, and he thought that he had produced some impression on Mr Gladstone....

The King of the Belgians to Queen Victoria

Laeken, 13th July 1860

MY BELOVED VICTORIA,— ... Bertie has then set out on his interesting journey,† which though not without fatigue will be full of information and satisfaction for his young mind. I am glad to hear that Albert

---

* This is said to have been an incident of frequent occurrence during the second administration of Lord Palmerston.

† In consequence of the loyal and patriotic assistance rendered by Canada during the Crimean War, and the expressed desire of the Canadians to be visited by the Queen in person and to welcome one of her sons as Governor-General, it was decided that the Prince of Wales should make a tour there. During the course of the visit, which was made in company with the Duke of Newcastle, the Prince opened the magnificent bridge over the St Lawrence; he subsequently availed himself of President Buchanan's invitation, and was received with the greatest enthusiasm at Washington. The Prince returned to England in November.

went with him, he can have no equal to his good and distinguished father for kindness, and a wise guidance of his young life. . . .

Queen Victoria to the King of the Belgians

Balmoral, 10th September 1860

MY BELOVED UNCLE,—I have no letter from you, but trust you are quite well. Here we have had a week of very fine weather, but since Saturday it has been extremely cold. We made a most delightful incognito expedition on Tuesday last, 4th, returning on Wednesday, 5th. We drove off from here quite early at eight, for twenty-one miles up to the *Geldie*, a small river—*rode* from here on ponies across the hills to Glen Fishie, a beautiful spot, where the old Duchess of Bedford used to live in a sort of encampment of wooden huts—on to Loch Inch, a beautiful but not wild lake (another twenty miles), crossed the Spey in a ferry, and posted in very rough vehicles to Grantown, again twenty miles, coming in there at nine. We passed close by Kinara where you used to be, but, unfortunately, not by the house. *No* one knew us—anywhere or at the little inn. We went under the names of Lord and Lady Churchill, and Lady Churchill and General Grey who went with us, under the names of Miss Spencer and Dr Grey! Two maids *only* went with us (whom we had sent round with our things), and *no* servants but our two excellent Highlanders, viz. Albert's first stalker or head keeper, and *my own Highland servant* and factotum—*both* excellent, intelligent, devoted people. *Only* when we had *left* was it found out. We posted to Tomantoul, a wretched village—fourteen miles, *in four hours! !* with a pair of wretched tired horses—over a big hilly road. At Tomantoul we again took our ponies and rode by Avon Side and Glen Avon, also very fine; back to Loch Bulig—eight miles from here—whence we returned home in our carriage. It was a *most delightful* and enjoyable, as well as *beautiful*, expedition. I have been besides on many other ones for the day. . . .

Viscount Palmerston to Queen Victoria

Piccadilly, 22nd November 1860

Viscount Palmerston presents his humble duty to your Majesty, and begs to submit that, as it appears from a despatch from Lord Cowley that the commercial negotiations at Paris have been brought to a conclusion, and that Mr Cobden has left Paris, the time has come for your Majesty to consider what substantial mark of your Majesty's approval your Majesty would be pleased to confer upon Mr Cobden. Mr Cobden has now for about twelve months been laboriously employed without salary or emolument in negotiating the complicated details of commercial arrangements between England and France, which cannot fail to tend to the material advantage of both countries, but more especially to the increased development of the industry and commerce of your Majesty's subjects. It would be an ungracious proceeding to leave the services of Mr Cobden with no other acknowledgement than the praises contained in a Foreign Office despatch, and Viscount Palmerston therefore with the concurrence of Lord John Russell would beg to submit for the gracious approval of your Majesty that Mr Cobden might be offered his choice of being created a Knight Grand Cross of the Civil Order of the Bath, or of being made a Member of your Majesty's Privy Council.

(*Note, in Queen's hand.*—Was agreed to offer him either to be made a P.C., or a Baronet.)*

The King of the Belgians to Queen Victoria

Laeken, 22nd November 1860

MY BELOVED VICTORIA,—I have to thank you for a most kind letter of the 20th. I hope you will see the young and very nice Empress of Austria,† perhaps you made a little excursion to Plymouth. I had, and have still, some cold, and therefore I was apprehensive of waiting at the station on the 20th in the evening; I sent Marie and Philip to receive the Empress. Yesterday before daybreak I went myself to Antwerp. I first paid the Empress a visit, and then I took her to your beautiful ship. She was much struck with it, and it was very *kind* of you, and indeed, for an invalid, invaluable.... I saw the Empress already dressed for her departure, but I think there is something very peculiar about her, which is very pleasing. Poor soul, to

---

* Mr Cobden declined both the Honours.

† The Empress Elizabeth was on her way to Madeira, in a ship placed at her disposal by the Queen.

see her go away under, I fear, not very safe circumstances, as she coughs a great deal, quite grieves one; though it certainly increased my stupid cold, still I should have been sorry not to have assisted at her going to sea. It was a beautiful day, but this night it has begun to blow from the West-south-west, which I fear will create a sea to the Westward.

Viscount Palmerston to Queen Victoria

Piccadilly, 2nd December 1860

Viscount Palmerston presents his humble duty to your Majesty, and very sincerely congratulates your Majesty upon the arrangement of a marriage which bids so fair to secure for Her Royal Highness the Princess Alice that happiness to which her amiable and estimable qualities so justly entitle her.

With respect to bishops, Viscount Palmerston would beg to submit that the bishops are in the Church what generals of districts are in the Army: their chief duties consist in watching over the clergy of their diocese, seeing that they perform properly their parochial duties, and preserving harmony between the clergy and the laity, and softening the asperities between the Established Church and the Dissenters. For these purposes it is desirable that a bishop should have practical knowledge of parochial functions, and should not be of an overbearing and intolerant temperament. His diocesan duties are enough to occupy all his time, and the less he engages in theological disputes the better. Much mischief has been done by theological bishops, and if the Bench were filled with men like the Bishops of Oxford and Exeter there would be no religious peace in the land. Nor have men chosen merely for their learning succeeded better; Thirlwall, Bishop of St David's, and Blomfield, the late Bishop of London, were chosen on account of their learning; the former is acknowledged to be inefficient, the latter greatly mismanaged his diocese. The theological learning of the Bishop of Exeter has caused much mischief to the Established Church. Viscount Palmerston would also beg to submit that the intolerant maxims of the High Church bishops have exasperated the Dissenters who form a large portion of the nation, and have given offence to many good Churchmen. The Bishop of Exeter, the late Bishop of Carlisle, and the late Bishop of Rochester, the two latter individuals kind-hearted and good-natured men, refused to consecrate burial grounds unless a wall of separation divided the portion allotted to Churchmen from the portion allotted to Dissenters —a demand which gave offence to both communities. Viscount Palmerston would beg to submit that several of the bishops whom he has had the honour of recommending to your Majesty had distinguished themselves by their classical and academical attainments, and he may mention in this respect the names of Baring, Longley, Tait, Wigram, and Waldegrave. Viscount Palmerston can assure your Majesty that although his selection of bishops has been much found fault with by the High Church, Puseyite, and semi-Catholic Party, they have given great satisfaction to the nation at large, and Viscount Palmerston has received communications to that effect, verbal and written, from persons of all classes, and political parties in all parts of the country. The people of this country are essentially Protestant, they feel the deepest aversion to Catholicism, and they see that the High Church, Tractarian, and Puseyite doctrines lead men to the Church of Rome. The disgraceful scenes last year at St George's in the East were only an exaggerated outburst of a very general and deeply-rooted feeling. Viscount Palmerston believes that the clergy of the Established Church were never more exemplary in the performance of their duties, more respected by the Laity and, generally speaking, on better terms with the Nonconformist body than at the present time.

Queen Victoria to the King of the Belgians

Windsor Castle, 4th December 1860

MY BELOVED UNCLE,— ... I add a few lines since we have seen the Empress. She came at half-past one, and stayed till a little after three. She looked very pretty, but very sad—and in speaking of her health and her return from Algiers began to cry. She seems to be much better, however, for her journey; before she could neither eat nor sleep, nor would she take notice of anything. She never mentioned the Emperor but once when she offered his compliments, and there was not the slightest allusion to politics. It is altogether very strange. She remains another week in England, and then goes back as she came. I gave her your message, and she enquired after you. Ever your devoted Niece,   VICTORIA R.

Queen Victoria to the King of the Belgians

Windsor Castle, 11th December 1860

MY BELOVED UNCLE,— ... The Empress is still here, and enjoys her liberty of *all* things. We went to town for the Smithfield Cattle Show yesterday, and visited her at Claridge's Hotel. She very civilly wanted us to avoid the trouble, but we felt that it would not be civil if we did not, and that hereafter even the French might say that she had not been treated with due respect. She looked very pretty, and was in very good spirits, but again carefully avoided any allusion to her husband and to politics, though she talked a great deal about all she was seeing! ...

1861

Viscount Palmerston to Queen Victoria

Broadlands, 1st January 1861

VISCOUNT PALMERSTON presents his humble duty to your Majesty, and begs to be allowed to wish your Majesty and His Royal Highness the Prince Consort many prosperous returns of New Year's Day, with increasing happiness to your Majesty and the Royal Family, and progressive advantage to the Nation who have the good fortune to have your Majesty for their Sovereign; and to adopt the language of Pope, he would say,

> 'May day improve on day, and year on year,
> Without a pain, a trouble, or a fear.'

This Autumn and Winter, however, have been productive of events in three of the four quarters of the Globe, which future years are not likely to repeat. The capture of Pekin in Asia by British and French troops; the Union in Europe of nearly the whole of Italy into one Monarchy; and the approaching and virtually accomplished Dissolution in America of the great Northern Confederation, are events full of importance for the future, as well as being remarkable in time present.

Viscount Palmerston submits two letters which your Majesty may feel an interest in seeing. With regard to that from Lord John Russell stating a half-formed wish to go to the House of Lords, Viscount Palmerston does not expect that the desire will be repeated when the Session begins, although Lord John said last year that he felt attendance in the House of Commons in addition to the labour of his office, more than he could well get through. He would be a loss to Viscount Palmerston in the House of Commons, especially after the removal of Mr Sidney Herbert to the House of Lords; and speaking confidentially to your Majesty with regard to the future, Viscount Palmerston would think himself doing better service by recommending the House of Lords for Mr Gladstone, than for Lord John Russell.

Mr Herbert will take the title of Lord Herbert of Lea, the title of Herbert being that borne by his elder brother during the life of the late Lord Pembroke.

The other letter from Lord Malmesbury relates to a communication which he made to Viscount Palmerston last year from Lord Derby and Mr Disraeli at the beginning of the Session, to the effect that, if the Government were then to break up from internal dissensions, the Conservative Party would support during the then ensuing Session any administration which Viscount Palmerston might be able provisionally to make, to carry through the business of the Session.* Viscount Palmerston is not aware of any circumstances which can have led to the expectation that the present administration is likely to be broken up by internal divisions in the course of this next Session. There are no questions ahead so likely to produce discord as the Reform Bill of last year, and the differences between the two Houses about the Paper Duties, about which it was very difficult to prevent Lord John and Mr Gladstone from flying off, or the Fortification Question, upon which Mr Gladstone announced to his colleagues,

* In his memoirs, Lord Malmesbury describes an interview with Lord and Lady Palmerston on 1st June 1860, apparently the one at which this communication was made. 'It is evident,' he writes, 'he [Lord Palmerston] does not wish to lose Lord John, though he would be very glad if Gladstone resigned.'

nearly a dozen times, that he was firmly resolved to resign. Viscount Palmerston has asked Lord Malmesbury to come over to him to Broadlands at any time before the 21st or 22nd of this month, which is the probable time at which the Cabinet will have to meet in London.

Viscount Palmerston finds he has not got Lord John Russell's letter at hand, but the only thing of any interest in it was the intimation which Viscount Palmerston quoted.

Viscount Palmerston to Queen Victoria

Piccadilly, 27th January 1861

Viscount Palmerston presents his humble duty to your Majesty. . . .

Viscount Palmerston saw Lord Malmesbury on Friday before the Cabinet. They both came up in the same train though not in the same carriage, and Lord Malmesbury came to Viscount Palmerston's in Piccadilly at three o'clock.

He said that he was charged by Lord Derby and Mr Disraeli with a message similar to that which he had conveyed last year, namely, that if Mr Gladstone were to propose a democratic Budget making a great transfer of burthens from indirect to direct Taxation, and if, the Cabinet refusing its concurrence, Mr Gladstone were to retire, the Conservative Party would give the Government substantial support except in the case of the Government wishing to take an active part in the war against Austria. That this did not of course mean an abstinence from usual attacks and criticisms in debate, but that no step would in such case be taken to produce a change of Government. In fact, said Lord Malmesbury, neither the Conservative leaders nor the Party wish at present to come into office, and have no intention of taking any step to turn the present Government out. Mr Bright had indeed proposed to Mr Disraeli to join together with the Radical Party, the Conservatives, for the purpose of turning out the present Government; and especially to get rid of Viscount Palmerston and Lord John Russell. Mr Bright said he would in that case give the Conservative Government a two years' existence, and by the end of that time the country, it might be hoped, would be prepared for a good and real Reform Bill, and then a proper Government might be formed.

This proposal, which it must be owned was not very tempting, Lord Malmesbury said had been declined. He also said that Count Persigny, on returning from one of his trips to Paris, had brought a similar proposal from Mr Cobden for a co-operation of Radicals and Conservatives to overthrow the present Government; but that also had been declined. Viscount Palmerston requested Lord Malmesbury to convey his thanks to Lord Derby and Mr Disraeli for the handsome communication which they had thus made to him, and to assure them that he fully appreciated the honourable and patriotic motives by which it had been prompted....

Queen Victoria to Lord John Russell

10th February 1861

The Queen has received Lord John Russell's letter enclosing the draft of one to General Garibaldi, which she now returns. She had much doubt about its being altogether safe for the Government to get into correspondence, however unofficial, with the General, and thinks that it would be better for Lord John *not* to write to him. Lord Palmerston, who was here this afternoon on other business, has undertaken to explain the reasons in detail to Lord John—in which he fully concurs.

Lord John Russell to Queen Victoria

Chesham Place, 11th February 1861

Lord John Russell presents his humble duty to your Majesty; he earnestly entreats your Majesty to consider whether any step ought to be omitted by which the peace of Europe may be preserved.

General Garibaldi is generally esteemed by Italians; even Count Ludolf speaks of him in the highest terms of praise. General Garibaldi has lost his country, and is full of resentment at Count Cavour for selling it. He respects and admires England for her disinterested conduct.

But it is evident the French Emperor is again exciting the Hungarian party. The Garibaldian legion is told to hold itself in readiness, and the *Pays* and *Patrie* are instructed to praise the Legion. They are being assembled in Genoa and Piedmont.

There is little chance of Garibaldi's refusing to take part in this expedition, and if he does proceed to the Dalmatian or Istrian coast, his name will have an immense effect.

It does not seem reasonable to throw away any chance of saving the Austrian Empire and the peace of Europe.

Lord John Russell will wait till Monday next to learn definitively your Majesty's pleasure.

The proposed letter appears to him to give some hope of preventing great misfortunes. In this belief it is Lord John Russell's duty to endeavour to prevent the frightful war which is impending.

Kossuth is fabricating paper to the extent of from 140 to 300,000,000 of florins to furnish the sinews of insurrection. In the month of March Hungary will be in a blaze. But if Italy, Germany, and France keep away, the fire may burn out of itself.

Viscount Palmerston to Queen Victoria

11th February 1861

Viscount Palmerston presents his humble duty to your Majesty, and in returning Lord John's letter begs to submit, that as Lord John is so anxious to send it, and seems so strongly of opinion that it is an effort which might be successful in dissuading Garibaldi from attempting to create disturbances in the Austrian territory by going thither with a band of adventurers, it may be best to let the letter go, though it might perhaps be improved by pointing more directly to the nature of the expedition which it advises Garibaldi not to undertake.

There may be inconveniences which may arise from the letter, but they might be dealt with; on the other hand, if Garibaldi undertakes his expedition, it would be a matter of regret if it could be thought or said that a step which might have prevented the mischief had been omitted.

Queen Victoria to Lord John Russell

Buckingham Palace, 12th February 1861

The Queen has received Lord John Russell's reiterated request for her sanction to his writing to General Garibaldi. She still entertains the same objections to the step, as implying a recognition of the

General's position as a European Power as enabling him to allow the impression to prevail, that he is in communication with the British Government and acts under its inspiration, as possibly leading to a prolonged and embarrassing correspondence, and as implying for the future that when the disapprobation of the Government is not expressed (as in the present instance), it gives its consent to his aggressive schemes. The Queen will not prevent, however, Lord John from taking a step which he considers gives a chance of averting a great European calamity. Should Lord John therefore adhere to his opinion, she asks him to let her see the letter again, upon the precise wording of which so much depends.

Queen Victoria to the King of the Belgians

Buckingham Palace, 12th February 1861

MY DEAREST UNCLE,—Many, many thanks for your dear letter of the 8th. Here we have cold again since the day before yesterday, and last night seven degrees of frost. On Sunday we celebrated, with feelings of *deep gratitude* and love, the *twenty-first* anniversary of our blessed marriage, a day which had brought us, and I may say the *world* at *large*, such incalculable blessings! *Very* few can say with me that their husband at the end of twenty-one years is *not* only full of the friendship, kindness, and affection which a truly happy marriage brings with it, but the same tender love of the *very first days of our marriage!*

We missed dear Mamma and *three* of our children, but had *six* dear ones round us—and assembled in the evening those of our Household *still* remaining who were *with us then!* ...

Queen Victoria to the King of the Belgians

Frogmore, 16th March 1861

MY DEARLY BELOVED UNCLE,—On this, the most dreadful day of my life, does your poor broken-hearted child write one line of love and devotion. *She* is gone!* That *precious, dearly beloved tender* Mother

* The Duchess of Kent died on 16th March. She had had a surgical operation in the arm, on account of an abscess, a short time before, but till the 15th the medical reports had been encouraging. On that day the Queen went to Frogmore, and was with her mother at the time of her death.

whom I never was parted from but for a few months—without whom *I can't imagine life*—has been taken from us! It is *too* dreadful! But she is at peace—at rest—her fearful sufferings at an end! It was quite painless—though there was very *distressing*, heartrending breathing to witness. I held her dear, dear hand in mine to the very last, which I am truly thankful for! But the watching that precious life going out was fearful!

Lord John Russell to Queen Victoria

Foreign Office, 30th May 1861

Lord John Russell presents his humble duty to your Majesty; he has the honour to submit letters from the Emperor and Empress of Austria of a private nature. The Cabinet decided yesterday that the ports of your Majesty's Dominions ought to be closed to the ships of war and privateers of the Belligerents in America. A letter for that object has been sent to the Law Officers of the Crown, and will be, when put into proper form, submitted for your Majesty's approbation.

Lord John Russell to Queen Victoria

Pembroke Lodge, 6th June 1861

Lord John Russell presents his humble duty to your Majesty; the despatch relating to Rome had been sent, seeming to Lord John Russell quite unobjectionable. But your Majesty will see that it was instantly suspended, and that Count Cavour is dying. The despatch was solely intended to save the poor old Pope from insult, and Rome from tumult, but beyond this it is of no consequence, and the death of Cavour may give a new complexion to the affairs of Italy.

Nothing will be done on the despatch at present.

Viscount Palmerston to Queen Victoria

Piccadilly, 8th July 1861

Viscount Palmerston presents his humble duty to your Majesty, and begs to state that Lord Elcho this afternoon moved a Resolution that the new Foreign Office should not be built in the Palladian style. Mr Charles Buxton seconded the Motion. Mr Cowper opposed it,

stating reasons for preferring the Italian style to the Gothic. Mr Layard
was for neither, but seemed to wish that somebody would invent a
new style of architecture. Mr Tite, the architect, was strongly for
the Italian style; Lord John Manners, swayed by erroneous views
in religion and taste, was enthusiastic for Gothic; Mr Dudley Fortescue
confided in a low voice to a limited range of hearers some weak
arguments in favour of Gothic; Mr Osborne seemed to be against
everything that anybody had ever proposed, and wanted to put off
the building till some plan better suited to his own taste should have
been invented. Viscount Palmerston answered the objections made
to the Italian plan, and Lord Elcho's Motion was negatived by 188
to 75. The House then went into Committee of Supply, and the
first estimate being that for the Foreign Office, some of the Gothic
party who had not been able to deliver their speeches on Lord Elcho's
Motion, let them off on this estimate.... .

Viscount Palmerston to Queen Victoria

Downing Street, 14th August 1861

Viscount Palmerston presents his humble duty to your Majesty, and
hastens to answer the enquiry contained in your Majesty's note,
which was delivered to him at Southampton. He must, in the first
place, explain that much of what was said to him by the King of
Sweden and by Prince Oscar was not clearly understood by him.
They would both speak English—which they spoke with difficulty
and in an indistinct utterance of voice—and he did not like to break
the conversation into French, because to have done so would have
looked like a condemnation of their English, of any imperfection of
which they did not seem to be at all conscious.

The King was very guarded in all he said about France; the
Prince spoke with more freedom and with less caution. The result
of what Viscount Palmerston gathered from their conversation, and
perhaps for this purpose they may be put together, because they
probably both feel and think nearly alike, though the Prince lets
his thoughts out more than the King, may be summed up as follows.

They were much pleased and flattered by the kind and friendly
reception given them by the French Emperor, and both he and they

seem to have had present to their minds that the existing Royal Family of Sweden is descended from General Bernadotte—a General in the Army of the First Napoleon. They think the French Emperor sincerely desirous of maintaining his alliance with England, believing it to be for his interest to do so. But they consider the French Nation essentially aggressive, and they think that the Emperor is obliged to humour that national feeling, and to follow, as far as the difference of circumstances will allow, the policy of his Uncle. They consider the principle of nationalities to be the deciding principle of the day, and accordingly Venetia ought to belong to Italy, Poland ought to be severed from Russia, and Finland ought to be restored to Sweden. Holstein should be purely German with its own Duke, Schleswig should be united to Denmark, and when the proper time comes, Denmark, so constituted, ought to form one Monarchy with Sweden and Norway. But they see that there are great if not insuperable obstacles to all these arrangements, and they do not admit that the Emperor of the French talked to them about these things, or about the map of Europe revised for 1860. They lamented the dangerous state of the Austrian Empire by reason of its financial embarrassments, and its differences between Vienna and Hungary. They admitted the difficulty of reestablishing a Polish State, seeing that Russia, Prussia, and Austria are all interested in preventing it; but they thought that Russia might make herself amends to the Eastward for giving up part of her Polish possessions.

They said the Swedes would be more adverse than the Danes to a Union of Denmark with Sweden. They said the Finns are writhing under the Russian yoke, and emigrate in considerable numbers to Sweden. They think Russia paralysed for ten years to come by her war against England and France, by her internal changes, and her money embarrassments. When the Prince asked Viscount Palmerston to sit down, it was for the purpose of urging in the strongest and most earnest manner that some British ships of war, or even one single gunboat, if more could not be spared, should every year visit the Baltic, and make a cruise in that sea. He said that the British Flag was never seen there, although Great Britain has great interests, commercial and political, in that sea. That especially for Sweden it would be a great support if a British man-of-war were every year to show itself in Swedish waters. He said that our Navy know little or nothing of the Baltic, and when a war comes, as happened in the late war with Russia, our ships are obliged, as it were, to feel their way about in the dark; that the Russians send ships of war into British ports—why should not England send ships of war into Russian ports? That we survey seas at the other side of the Globe, why should we not survey a sea so near to us as the Baltic; that as far as Sweden is concerned, British ships would be most cordially received. I said that this should receive due consideration; and in answer to a question he said the best time for a Baltic cruise would be from the middle of June to the latter end of August.

They both thought the Emperor of the French extremely popular in France—but, of course, they only saw outward demonstrations. They are very anxious for the maintenance of the Anglo-French Alliance; and they think the Emperor obliged to keep a large Army and to build a strong Navy in order to please and satisfy the French Nation. Such is the summary of the impression made upon Viscount Palmerston by the answers and observations drawn out by him in his conversations with the King and the Prince; most of these things were said as above reported, some few of the above statements are perhaps inferences and conclusions drawn from indirect answers and remarks.

Queen Victoria to Viscount Palmerston

Windsor Castle, 25th October 1861

The Queen has long seen with deep regret the persevering efforts made by the *Times*, which leads the rest of our Press, in attacking, vilifying, and abusing everything German, and particularly everything Prussian. That journal had since years shown the same bias, but it is since the Macdonald affair of last year, that it has assumed that tone of virulence, which could not fail to produce the deepest indignation amongst the people of Germany, and by degrees estrange the feelings of the people of this country from Germany. Lord Palmerston, probably not reading any German newspaper, nor having any personal intercourse with that country, can hardly be aware to what extent the mischief has already gone, though he will agree with the

Queen that national hatred between these two peoples is a real political calamity for both. The Queen had often intended to write to Lord Palmerston on the subject, and to ask him whether he would not be acting in the spirit of public duty if he endeavoured, as far at least as might be in his power, to point out to the managers of the *Times* (which derives some of its power from the belief abroad that it represents more or less the feelings of the Government) how great the injury is which it inflicts upon the best interests of this country. She has, however, refrained from doing so, trusting in the chance of a change in tone, and feeling that Lord Palmerston might not like to enter into discussion with the Editors of the *Times*. . . .

The Queen believes that Lord Palmerston is the only person who could exercise any influence over Mr Delane, and even if this should not be much, it will be important that that gentleman should know the mischief his writings are doing, and that the Government sincerely deplore it.

Mr Delane to Viscount Palmerston

16 Serjeant's Inn, 28th October 1861

MY DEAR LORD,—I shall be very glad to give the Prussians a respite from that most cruel of all inflictions—good advice. Indeed, I would not have intruded anything so unwelcome during the splendid solemnities of the Coronation had not the King uttered those surprising anachronisms upon Divine Right.

Pray observe, too, in extenuation of my offence that I sent a faithful chronicler to Königsberg, who has described all the splendours in a proper and reverent spirit, and done what man can do to render such ceremonies intelligible, and the recital of them not too wearisome to those who believe in Divine Right as little as your Lordship's very faithful Servant,   JOHN T. DELANE

Viscount Palmerston to Queen Victoria

Windsor Castle, 30th October 1861

Viscount Palmerston presents his humble duty to your Majesty, and begs to state that when he received a few days ago from Lord Russell the Memorandum which your Majesty intended for him, and which

QUEEN VICTORIA'S EARLY LETTERS 1861

he returned to Lord Russell, he wrote to Mr Delane in accordance with your Majesty's wishes, and he has this morning received the accompanying answer.

Viscount Palmerston would, however, beg to submit that an erroneous notion prevails on the Continent as to English newspapers.

The newspapers on the Continent are all more or less under a certain degree of control, and the most prominent among them are the organs of political parties, or of leading public men; and it is not unnatural that Governments and Parties on the Continent should think that English newspapers are published under similar conditions.

But in this country all thriving newspapers are commercial undertakings, and are conducted on commercial principles, and none others are able long to maintain an existence. Attempts have often been made to establish newspapers to be directed by political men, and to be guided by the same considerations by which those men would govern their own conduct, but such papers have seldom succeeded. The Peelite Party tried some years ago such an experiment with the *Morning Chronicle*, but after spending a very large sum of money on the undertaking they were obliged to give it up. The *Times* is carried on as a large commercial enterprise, though, of course, with certain political tendencies and bias, but mainly with a view to profit upon the large capital employed.

The actual price at which each copy of the newspaper is sold barely pays the expense of paper, printing, and establishment; it is indeed said that the price does not repay those expenses. The profit of the newspaper arises from the price paid for advertisements, and the greater number of advertisements the greater the profit. But advertisements are sent by preference to the newspaper which has the greatest circulation; and that paper gets the widest circulation which is the most amusing, the most interesting, and the most instructive. A dull paper is soon left off. The proprietors and managers of the *Times* therefore go to great expense in sending correspondents to all parts of the world where interesting events are taking place, and they employ a great many able and clever men to write articles upon all subjects which from time to time engage public attention; and as mankind take more pleasure in reading criticism and fault-finding than praise, because it is soothing to individual vanity and conceit to fancy that the reader has become wiser than those about whom he reads, so the *Times*, in order to maintain its circulation, criticises freely everybody and everything; and especially events and persons, and Governments abroad, because such strictures are less likely to make enemies at home than violent attacks upon parties and persons in this country. Foreign Governments and Parties ought therefore to look upon English newspapers in the true point of view, and not to be too sensitive as to attacks which those papers may contain.

Queen Victoria to the King of the Belgians

Windsor Castle, 26th November 1861

MY BELOVED UNCLE,—... Albert is a little rheumatic, which is a plague—but it is very difficult not to have something or other of this kind in this season, with these rapid changes of temperature; *unberufen, unberufen,* he is much better this winter than he was the preceding years.*...

Viscount Palmerston to Queen Victoria

Downing Street, 29th November 1861

Viscount Palmerston presents his humble duty to your Majesty, and begs to state that the Cabinet at its meeting this afternoon resumed the consideration of the forcible capture of the Southern Envoys from on board the *Trent* steamer upon which the law officers had yesterday given the opinion contained in the accompanying report. The law officers and Doctor Phillimore, Counsel to the Admiralty, were in attendance. The result was that it appeared to the Cabinet that a gross outrage and violation of international law has been committed, and that your Majesty should be advised to demand reparation and redress. The Cabinet is to meet again to-morrow at two, by which time Lord Russell will have prepared an instruction to Lord Lyons

---

* The Prince had been unwell, even before the receipt of the distressing news from Portugal, and began to suffer from a somewhat continuous insomnia. On 22nd November, he drove to Sandhurst to inspect the new buildings in progress there. The day was very wet, and, though he returned in the middle of the day to Windsor, the exertion proved too severe for him; on the 24th he complained of rheumatic pains, and of prolonged sleeplessness.

for the consideration of the Cabinet, and for submission afterwards to your Majesty. The general outline and tenor which appeared to meet the opinions of the Cabinet would be, that the Washington Government should be told that what has been done is a violation of international law, and of the rights of Great Britain, and that your Majesty's Government trust that the act will be disavowed and the prisoners set free and restored to British Protection; and that Lord Lyons should be instructed that if this demand is refused he should retire from the United States.

It is stated by Mrs and Miss Slidell, who are now in London, that the Northern officer who came on board the *Trent* said that they were acting on their own responsibility without instructions from Washington; that very possibly their act might be disavowed and the prisoners set free on their arrival at Washington. But it was known that the *San Jacinto*, though come from the African station, had arrived from thence several weeks before, and had been at St Thomas, and had there received communications from New York; and it is also said that General Scott, who has recently arrived in France, has said to Americans in Paris that he has come not on an excursion of pleasure, but on diplomatic business; that the seizure of these envoys was discussed in Cabinet at Washington, he being present, and was deliberately determined upon and ordered; that the Washington Cabinet fully foresaw it might lead to war with England; and that he was commissioned to propose to France in that case to join the Northern States in war against England, and to offer France in that case the restoration of the French Province of Canada.

General Scott will probably find himself much mistaken as to the success of his overtures; for the French Government is more disposed towards the South than the North, and is probably thinking more about Cotton than about Canada. . . .

Earl Russell to Queen Victoria

Foreign Office, 29th November 1861

Lord Russell presents his humble duty to your Majesty; Mr Gladstone has undertaken to explain to your Majesty what has taken place at the Cabinet to-day.

Lord Russell proposes to frame a draft for to-morrow's Cabinet of a despatch to Lord Lyons, directing him to ask for the release of Messrs Mason and Slidell and their two companions, and an apology. In case these requirements should be refused, Lord Lyons should ask for his passports.

The Lord Chancellor and the law officers of the Crown are clear upon the law of the case.

Lord Russell will be glad to have your Majesty's opinion on the draft which will go to your Majesty about four o'clock to-morrow, without loss of time, as the packet goes to-morrow evening.*

Queen Victoria to Earl Russell

Windsor Castle, 1st December 1861

Note in the Queen's handwriting.

[This draft was the last the beloved Prince ever wrote; he was very unwell at the time, and when he brought it in to the Queen, he said: 'I could hardly hold my pen.' VICTORIA R.]

The Queen returns these important drafts, which upon the whole she approves, but she cannot help feeling that the main draft, that for communication to the American Government, is somewhat meagre. She should have liked to have seen the expression of a hope that the American captain did not act under instructions, or, if he did, that he misapprehended them—that the United States Government must be fully aware that the British Government could not allow its flag to be insulted, and the security of her mail communications to be placed to jeopardy, and Her Majesty's Government are unwilling to believe that the United States Government intended wantonly to put an insult upon this country, and to add to their many distressing

---

* The draft of the despatch to Lord Lyons reached Windsor on the evening of the 30th, and, in spite of his weak and suffering state, the Prince prepared the draft of the Queen's letter early the following morning. The letter has been printed in *facsimile* by Sir Theodore Martin, who adds that it has a special value as 'representing the last political Memorandum written by the Prince, while it was at the same time inferior to none of them, as will presently be seen, in the importance of its results. It shows, like most of his Memorandums, by the corrections in the Queen's hand, how the minds of both were continually brought to bear upon the subjects with which they dealt.'

complications by forcing a question of dispute upon us, and that we are therefore glad to believe that upon a full consideration of the circumstances, and of the undoubted breach of international law committed, they would spontaneously offer such redress as alone could satisfy this country, viz. the restoration of the unfortunate passengers and a suitable apology.

Queen Victoria to the King of the Belgians

Windsor Castle, 4th December 1861

MY DEAREST UNCLE,—I have many excuses to make for not writing yesterday, but I had a good deal to do, as my poor dear Albert's rheumatism has turned out to be a regular influenza, which has pulled and lowered him very much. Since Monday he has been confined to his room. It affects his appetite and sleep, which is very disagreeable, and you know he is always *so* depressed when anything is the matter with him. However, he is decidedly better to-day, and I hope in two or three days he will be quite himself again. It is extremely vexatious, as he was so particularly well till he caught these colds, which came upon worries of various kinds. . . . Ever your devoted Niece,

VICTORIA R.

Queen Victoria to the King of the Belgians

Windsor Castle, 6th December 1861

MY BELOVED UNCLE,—I am thankful to report decidedly better of my beloved Albert. He has had much more sleep, and has taken much more nourishment since yesterday evening. Altogether, this nasty, feverish sort of influenza and deranged stomach is *on* the mend, but it will be slow and tedious, and though there has *not* been one alarming symptom, there has been such restlessness, such sleeplessness, and such (till to-day) *total* refusal of all food, that it made one *very, very* anxious, and I can't describe the *anxiety* I have gone through! I feel to-day a good deal shaken, for for four nights I got only two or three hours' sleep. We have, however, every reason to hope the recovery, though it may be *somewhat* tedious, will not be *very* slow. You shall hear again to-morrow. Ever your devoted Niece, VICTORIA R.

Queen Victoria to the King of the Belgians

Windsor Castle, 9th December 1861

MY BELOVED UNCLE,—I enclose you Clark's report, which I think you may like to hear. Our beloved invalid goes on well—but it *must* be tedious, and I need not tell you *what* a trial it is to me. Every day, however, is bringing us nearer the end of this tiresome illness, which is much what I had at Ramsgate, only that I was much worse, and not at first well attended to. You shall hear daily.

You will, I know, feel for me! The night was excellent; the first good one he had. Ever your devoted Niece,   VICTORIA R.

The Americans *may* possibly get out of it.

The King of the Belgians to Queen Victoria

Laeken, 11th December 1861

MY BELOVED VICTORIA,—*How I do feel for you from the bottom of my heart*; that you should have this totally unexpected tribulation of having dear Albert unwell, when not long ago we rejoiced that he was bearing this time of the year so well. Now we must be very patient, as an indisposition of this description at this time of the year is generally mending slowly. The great object must be to arrange all the little details exactly as the patient may wish them; that everything of that description may move very smoothly is highly beneficial. Patients are very different in their likings; to the great horror of angelic Louise, the moment I am ill I become almost invisible, disliking to see anybody. Other people are fond of company, and wish to be surrounded. The medical advisers are, thank God! excellent, and Clark knows Albert so well. Albert will wish you not to interrupt your usual airings; you want air, and to be deprived of it would do you harm. The temperature here at least has been extremely mild— this ought to be favourable. I trust that every day will now show some small improvement, and it will be very kind of you to let me frequently know how dear Albert is going on. Believe me ever, my beloved Victoria, your devoted Uncle,   LEOPOLD R.

Queen Victoria to the King of the Belgians

Windsor Castle, 11th December 1861

DEAREST UNCLE,—I can report another good night, and *no* loss of strength, and continued satisfactory symptoms. But more we dare *not* expect for some days; *not* losing ground is a *gain, now,* of *every* day.

It is very sad and trying for me, but I am well, and I think really *very* courageous; for it is the first time that *I* ever witnessed anything of this kind though *I* suffered from the same at Ramsgate, and was much worse. The trial in every way is so very trying, for I have lost my guide, my support, my all, *for a time*—as we can't ask or tell him anything. Many thanks for your kind letter received yesterday. We have been and are reading Von Ense's book to Albert; but it is *not* worth much. He likes very much being read to as it soothes him. W. Scott is also read to him. You shall hear again to-morrow, dearest Uncle, and, please God! each day will be more cheering. Ever your devoted Niece,   VICTORIA R.

Queen Victoria to the King of the Belgians

Windsor Castle, 12th December 1861

MY BELOVED UNCLE,—I can again report favourably of our *most* precious invalid. He maintains his ground well—had another very good night—takes plenty of nourishment, and shows surprising strength. I am constantly in and out of his room, but since the *first four dreadful* nights, *last* week, *before* they had declared it to be *gastric fever*— I do not sit up with him at night as I could be of no use; and there is nothing to cause alarm. I go out twice a day for about an hour. It is a very trying time, for a fever with its despondency, weakness, and occasional and *invariable* wandering, is most painful to witness —but we have *never* had *one unfavourable* symptom; to-morrow, reckoning from the 22nd, when dear Albert first fell ill—after going on a wet day to look at some buildings—having likewise been unusually depressed with worries of different kinds—is the *end* of the *third week*; we *may* hope for improvement *after* that, but the Doctors say they should *not* be *at all disappointed if* this did *not* take place till the *end* of the *fourth week.* I cannot sufficiently praise the skill, attention, and devotion of Dr Jenner, who is the *first fever* Doctor in Europe, one may say—and good old Clark is here every day; good Brown is also *most* useful. . . . We have got Dr Watson (who succeeded Dr Chambers) and Sir H. Holland has also been here. But I have kept clear of these two. Albert sleeps a good deal in the day. He is moved every day into the next room on a sofa which is made up as a bed. He has only *kept* his bed entirely since Monday. Many, many thanks for your dear, kind letter of the 11th. I knew how *you* would *feel* for and think of me. I am very wonderfully supported, and excepting on three occasions, have borne up very well. I am sure Clark will tell you so. Ever your most devoted Niece,　　　VICTORIA R.

Queen Victoria to the King of the Belgians

Osborne, 20th December 1861

MY *Own* DEAREST, KINDEST *Father,*—For as such have I *ever* loved you! The poor fatherless baby of eight months is now the utterly broken-hearted and crushed widow of forty-two! My *life* as a *happy* one is *ended!* the world is gone for *me!* If I *must live* on (and I will do nothing to make me worse than I am), it is henceforth for our poor fatherless children—for my unhappy country, which has lost *all* in losing him—and in *only* doing what I know and *feel* he would wish, for he *is* near me—his spirit will guide and inspire me! But oh! to be cut off in the prime of life—to see our pure, happy, quiet, domestic life, which *alone* enabled me to bear my *much* disliked position, CUT OFF at forty-two—when I *had* hoped with such instinctive certainty that God never *would* part us, and would let us grow old together (though *he* always talked of the shortness of life)—is *too awful,* too cruel! And yet it *must* be for *his* good, his happiness! His purity was too great, his aspiration *too high* for this poor, *miserable* world! His great soul is *now only* enjoying *that* for which it *was* worthy; And I will *not* envy him—only pray that *mine* may be perfected by it and fit to be with him eternally, for which blessed moment I earnestly long. Dearest, dearest Uncle, *how* kind of you to come! It will be an unspeakable *comfort,* and you *can do* much to tell people to do what they ought to do. As for my *own good, personal* servants—poor Phipps in particular—nothing can be more devoted, heartbroken as they are, and anxious only to live as *he* wished! Good Alice has been and is wonderful.

The 26th will suit me perfectly. Ever your devoted, wretched Child,

VICTORIA R.

Queen Victoria to the King of the Belgians

Osborne, 24th December 1861

MY BELOVED UNCLE,—Though, please God! I am to see you so soon, I must write these few lines to prepare you for the trying, sad existence you will find it with your poor forlorn, desolate child—who drags on a weary, pleasureless existence! I am also anxious to repeat *one* thing, and *that one* is *my firm* resolve, my *irrevocable decision*, viz. that *his* wishes—*his* plans—about everything, *his* views about *every* thing are to be *my law!* And *no human power* will make me swerve from *what he* decided and wished—and I look to *you* to *support* and *help* me in this. I apply this particularly as regards our children— Bertie, etc.—for whose future he had traced everything *so* carefully. I am *also determined* that *no one* person, may *he* be ever so good, ever so devoted among my servants—is to lead or guide or dictate *to me*. I know *how he* would disapprove it. And I live *on* with him, for him; in fact *I* am only *outwardly* separated from him, and *only* for a *time*.

No one can tell you more of my feelings, and can put you more in possession of many touching facts than our excellent Dr Jenner, who has been and is my great comfort, and whom I would *entreat* you to *see and hear* before you see *any one else*. Pray do this, for *I fear much* others trying to see you first and say things and wish for things which I *should not* consent to.

Though miserably weak and utterly shattered, my spirit rises when I think *any* wish or plan of his is to be touched or changed, or I am to be *made to do* anything. I know you will help me in my utter darkness. It is but for a short time, and *then* I go—*never, never* to part! Oh! that blessed, blessed thought! He seems so *near* to *me,* so *quite*

my own now, my precious darling! God bless and preserve you.
Ever your wretched but devoted Child,   VICTORIA R.
What a Xmas! I won't think of it.

Viscount Palmerston to Queen Victoria

Piccadilly, 30th December 1861

Viscount Palmerston presents his humble duty to your Majesty, and
has read with deep emotion your Majesty's letter of the 26th, every
word of which went straight to the heart. Viscount Palmerston would,
however, humbly express a hope that the intensity of your Majesty's
grief may not lead your Majesty to neglect your health, the preservation of which is so important for the welfare of your Majesty's children,
and for that of your Majesty's devotedly attached and affectionate
subjects; and which is so essentially necessary to enable your Majesty
to perform those duties which it will be the object of your Majesty's
life to fulfil. . . .

Queen Victoria to Earl Canning

Osborne, 10th January 1862

Lord Canning little thought when he wrote his kind and touching
letter on the 22nd November, that it would only reach the Queen
when *she* was *smitten* and *bowed* down to the earth by an event similar
to the one which he describes—and, strange to say, by a disease greatly
analogous to the one which took from him *all* that he loved best. In
the case of her adored, precious, perfect, and great husband, her dear
lord and master, to whom this Nation owed more than it ever can
truly know, however, the fever went on most favourably till the day
previous to the awful calamity, and then it was congestion of the
lungs and want of strength of circulation (the beloved Prince had
always a weak and feeble pulse), which at the critical moment, indeed
only two hours before God took him, caused this awful result. To
lose one's partner in life is, as Lord Canning knows, like losing *half*
of one's *body* and *soul*, torn forcibly away—and dear Lady Canning
was such a dear, worthy, devoted wife! But to the Queen—to a poor
helpless woman—it is not that only— it is the stay, support and com-

fort which is lost! To the Queen it is like *death* in life! Great and small—*nothing* was done without his loving advice and help—and she feels *alone* in the wide world, with many helpless children (except the Princess Royal) to look to her—and the whole nation to look to her—*now* when she can barely struggle with her wretched existence! Her misery—her utter despair—she *cannot* describe! Her *only* support —the *only* ray of comfort she gets for *a moment*, is in the *firm conviction* and certainty of his nearness, his undying love, and of their eternal reunion! Only she prays always, and pines for the latter with an anxiety she cannot describe. Like dear Lady Canning, the Queen's darling is to rest in a garden—at Frogmore, in a Mausoleum the Queen is going to build for him and herself.

Though ill, the Queen was able to tell her precious angel of Lord Canning's bereavement, and he was deeply grieved, recurring to it several times, and saying, 'What a loss! She was such a distinguished person!'

May God comfort and support Lord Canning, and may he think in his sorrow of his widowed and broken-hearted Sovereign—bowed to the earth, with the greatest of human sufferings and misfortunes! She lived but *for* her husband!

The sympathy of the many thousands of her subjects, but above all their sorrow and their admiration for him, are soothing to her bleeding, pierced heart!

The Queen's precious husband, though wandering occasionally, was conscious till nearly the last, and knew her and kissed her an hour before his pure spirit fled to its worthy and fit eternal Home!

Index

Abercorn, Marchioness of, 66

Abercromby, Sir Ralph, 209

Aberdeen, Earl of:
Foreign Secretary, 32
Queen's views on foreign appointments, 68
list of presents from the Imam of Muscat, 77
Queen's opinion of, 99
Corn Laws, 110, 112
takes leave of Queen on Government resignation, 124, 125, 126
Palmerston's defence of, 171
forms Government, 194
press attacks on Prince Albert, 195–6
visit of Duke of Cambridge to France, 199
his unfortunate speech in House of Lords, 201
pension for Nelson's adopted daughter, 203
Crimea War action, 204
Roebuck's censure motion, 206
resignation, 208

About, Edmond, French writer, 254

Accession of Queen Victoria, 20–1

Ackland, Sir Thomas, 121

Adelaide, Princess of Hohenlohe, early letter to Queen, 12

—, Queen (wife of William IV), 7
death of William IV, 22
letter on Queen Victoria's coronation, 29
death, 160

Adrianople, Treaty of, see Treaty of Adrianople

Albemarle, sixth Earl of, Master of the Horse, 21

Albert, Archduke, 157

—, Edward, see Wales, Prince of

—, Prince, see Consort, Prince

Alice, Princess, engagement, 271

Allt-na-Giuthasach, Queen's visit to, 182, 191

Alma, victory of, 204

America, see United States

Anglesey, Marquess of, 125

Anson, George:
Private Secretary to Prince Albert, 39
interviews with Lord Melbourne and Baron Stockmar, 42–3
Prince Albert's desire to enliven the Court, 45–6
refuses honour, 61
memorandum on Lord Melbourne correspondence, 74
purchase of Osborne, 106
advance of money to Lord Melbourne, 132

—, Sir George, 39

Anti-Corn Law League, see Corn Laws

Antonelli, Cardinal, 237, 239

Army, duelling, 91
Lord Melbourne's opinion of discipline in, 48–9
personal connection with Sovereign, 146
effective state of, 202
sent to quell Indian Mutiny, 225

Arnold, Dr, 177

Art, encouragement of, 69–70

As you like it, 89

Ashley, Lord, 166

Attwood, Thomas, Birmingham Political Union, 17

Aukland, Lord, 87, 124

Australia, wine from, 107–8

Austria, Italian dominions, 145
attacked by Sardinian Government, 147
ascendancy over Lombardy, 150
possibility of alliance with Russia, 162
war with Russia, 198
differences with Italy, 236

Austria, *continued*
differences with France, 243
war with France, 251
Garibaldi's expedition to, 277
—, Emperor of, 145
—, Empress Elizabeth of, 270-3
Ayrton, Mr, 224

Bagot, Sir Charles, Governor-General of
Canada, 68
Bala Rao, Indian Mutiny, 250
Balaklava, 204
Balmoral Castle, Queen's visit to, 182
Baltic, Navy expedition to, 199-200
Baring, E., 122
—, Thomas, 189, 224
Barrow, Sir John, 82
Beauvale, Lady, 152
Bedford, Duke of, 145, 149, 169, 222
—, Duchess of, 52, 169
Begum, the, 250
Belgians, King of, *see* Leopold
—, Queen of, *see* Louisa
Bengal Mutiny, 222-3
Bentinck, Lord George, 120, 157
Bernadotte, General, 281
Bessborough, Earl of, 126
Bethell, Sir Joseph, 227
Beverley, Lord, 110
Birmingham, political condition, 92
Bishops, appointment of, 271
Bloomfield, Lord, 169
Bonaparte, *see* Napoleon
Borthwick, Peter, 105
Bouverie, Colonel, 181
Bracebridge, Mr and Mrs, 205
Breadalbane, Marquess of, 81
Brescia, 175
Bresson, Count, aids escape of King and
Queen of France, 136
Bright, John, 160, 200, 249
Bristol, Dean of, 178
Brougham, Lord, 48, 58
Buccleuch, Duchess of, Mistress of the
Robes, 66, 111
—, Duke of, 110, 114, 116
Buchanan, President, 268
Buckingham, Duke of, 104
Buckingham Palace, state of, 104

Buckland, Dr, Irish Commissioner, 109
Bullock, Thomas, book on education,
156
Bunsen, Chevalier, 145
Buol, Count, Austrian Prime Minister,
236
Burghersh, Francis, Lord, A.D.C. to
Lord Raglan, 204
Bury, Lord, Straits Settlements, 231
Bute, Lord, 64
Buxton, Charles, 279
Byng, George, 14
Byron, Lady, 66

Cagliari, seizure of, 230
Cambridge, Duke of, 168, 199
—, Duchess of, 178
—, Prince George of, 87
Campbell, Lord, 257
—, Mr, M.P. for Weymouth, 224
Canada, visit of Prince of Wales, 268
Canning, Viscount (afterwards Earl):
Viceroy of India, 235-6
on situation in India, 250
Queen's letter of sympathy on death
of his wife, 293-4
—, Viscountess, 66, 171,
death, 293
Canterbury, Archbishop of, (William
Howley):
announcement of William IV's death,
20
Queen's opinion on evils of the Church,
181
day of prayer for Indian mutiny victims,
225-6
Cardigan, Earl of, censure on, 48, 76
Cardwell, Mr (afterwards Viscount),
189
Cartwright, Sir T., 78
Cavour, Count, Sardinian Premier, 241,
266, 279
Cawnpore, mutiny, 226
Chambers, Dr William Frederick, con-
sulting physician, 291
Charles XV, *see* Sweden and Norway,
Charles XV, King of,
Charles Albert, King of Sardinia, 145,
147, 150, 238, 266

Chartists, strength of, 140
  Kennington Common meeting, 141
Chelsea Pensioners, Bill for Enrolling and
  Arming, 91
China, English difficulties with, 228, 235
Christchurch, Dean of, 216
Church of England, 18
  opinion on Meynooth Bill, 106
Civil Service, competitive examinations,
  197
Clanricarde, Marquess of, 34, 227, 234
Claremont, residence of King Leopold,
  100, 144
Clarence, Duchess of, see Adelaide, Queen
Clarendon, Lord, 122, 124, 162, 163
  fears outbreak in Dublin, 142
  suggested as Secretary of State for
    Foreign Affairs, 149
  writes of Queen's visit to Ireland, 159–
    160
  Lord Palmerston's complaints against,
    172
  Queen's displeasure over his conduct
    on Duke of Cambridge's visit to
    France, 199
  Russian loan, 202
  suggests peace with Russia, 217
Clarendon's *History of the Rebellion,* 9
Clark, Dr (afterwards Sir James), Physi-
  cian to the Queen, 21, 289
Cobden, Richard:
  Corn Laws, 84, 115
  question of his holding Government
    office, 123
  Poor Law Commission, 131
  debate speech, 157
  unpopularity, 221–2
  refuses Government office, 248
  concludes commercial agreement
    between England and France, 270
  refuses honours, 270
Coburg, 144
Coburg, House of, see Saxe-Coburg
Coldstream Guards, at Crimea, 208
Conroy, Sir J., comptroller to Duchess of
  Kent, 3, 4
Consort, Prince (see also Victoria, Queen):
  early visits to England, 12, 34
  Queen's first impressions of, 13

Consort, Prince, *continued*
  his studies, 26
  engagement to Queen Victoria, 35
  his army rank, 37
  declaration of intended marriage, 37
  reasons against his peerage, 38
  his Gentlemen approved, 39
  his character, 41
  Lord Melbourne's complaints on his
    lack of confidence in politics, 42
  marriage to Queen Victoria, 42
  boredom with Court life, 46
  his use to the Queen, 61
  his relationship with the Tories, 63
  Fine Arts Commission, 70
  Commander of Grenadier Guards and
    Rifle Brigade, 76
  on duelling, 91
  political condition of Birmingham, 92
  visit to Birmingham, 93–4
  question of his title, 105
  Corn Laws, 110–11
  resignation of Sir Robert Peel, 116–18
  Lord John Russell's failure to form
    Government, 112–13
  installation of Lord John Russell's
    cabinet, 123–5
  strength of Chartists, 140–1
  Whig party, 161
  foreign affairs, 170–2
  opinion of Poet Laureate candidates,
    173
  Haynau affair, 176
  Papal aggression, 177–8
  1851 Exhibition, 181
  Lord John Russell's resignation, 189–90
  death of Duke of Wellington, 191–2
  Lord Derby's resignation, 194
  congratulates Gladstone on speech, 195
  Lord Palmerston's resignation and
    composition of Government, 226–9
  on Lord Palmerston's unpopularity, 234
  illness after visit to Sandhurst, 285
  his last draft, 287
  slight improvement, 288
  death, 291
Conyngham, Marquess, Lord Chamberlain, 20
Cork, Queen's visit to, 158

Corn Laws, Anti-Corn Law League, 84
  paragraph in the *Times*, 109
  proposed abolition by Sir Robert Peel,
    110, 114, 117
  settlement, 121
Coronation of Queen Victoria, 29
Cottenham, Earl of, 122
Cowley, Lord, 147, 202, 256
  Queen's high opinion of, 214
  stormy interview with Napoleon, 260–5
Cowper, Lady (later married to Viscount
    Palmerston), 39
—, Hon. William, 279
Crimean War, 204
Croker, Rt Hon. J. W., 130
Crystal Palace, 181–2
Cumberland, Duke of, 18, 21

Daily News, 242
Dalhousie, Earl of, 116, 122, 165, 209,
    216, 223
Dalkeith, Queen's visit to, 80
Davys, Rev. George, instructor to the
    Queen, 46
De Grey, Earl, Lord Lieutenant of Ire-
    land, 65
De La Warr, Elizabeth, Countess, 66
—, Lord, 67
Delhi, 222, 224, 226
Delane, John T., editor of the *Times*, 172,
    283
Denison, J. E., 178
Denman, Lord, 85
Denmark, Swedish views on union with,
    281
Derby, Earl of, *see* Stanley, Lord
Despatches, method of dealing with,
    28
Disbrowe, Sir Edward, British Minister
    at the Hague, 77
Disraeli, Benjamin:
  attack on Sir Robert Peel, 120
  House of Commons debate, 157
  writes on House of Commons pro-
    ceedings, 191
  Budget speech, 192
  feels loss of office, 195
  motion on India, 228
  Cagliari seizure, 230

Disraeli, Benjamin, *continued*
  Parliamentary reports to Queen Vic-
    toria, 230–2
  asked to join Radical party, 275
Dissenters, 122, 271
Divorce Court, Queen's objection to
  publication of proceedings in news-
  papers, 257
Drayton Manor, Queen's visit to, 91
Drummond, Edward, assassination, 83
—, Henry, M.P., 231
Dublin, Queen's visit, 158–9
Dufferin, Marquess of, story of Mrs
  Norton and the *Times*, 109
Duffield, Walter, 107
Dunkeldy, Queen's visit to, 81
Durham, Bishop of, *see* Maltby, Dr
  Edward, Bishop of Durham
—, Lord, 4

East India Company, giving of medals,
  152
Eastern Question, 202, 228
Edgecumbe, Lady Mount, 190
Edinburgh, Queen's visit to, 80, 82
Education, Queen Victoria's opinion on,
  156
Edwardes, Major, 152
Elcho, Lord, 280
Eliot, Lady Fanny (later married to Lord
  John Russell), 57, 142
—, Lord, 65
Elizabeth, Empress of Austria, *see* Austria,
  Elizabeth, Empress of
—, Landgravine *see* Landgravine, Princess
  Elizabeth
Ellenborough, Lord, 102, 116
Elphinstone, Sir J., M.P., 231–2
England, relationship with Europe, 147,
  148
  policy over Greece, 167
  foreign policy, 170–1
  relationship with France, 186–7
  war with Russia, 200
  alliance with France, 210
  peace with Russia, 216
  Indian Mutiny, 222
  difficulties with India and China, 228,
  235

England, *continued*
neutrality, 242
termination of Indian Mutiny, 248
policy over French domination in Europe, 251-2
aids insurrection in Naples and Sicily, 266
French annexation of Savoy, 259, 262, 263
preservation of peace in Europe, 276
Ense, Varnhagen von, memoirs of, 290
Ernest, King of Hanover, *see* Cumberland, Duke of
—, Prince of Saxe-Coburg, *see* Saxe-Coburg, Ernest, Prince of
Erroll, Lord, 87
Exeter, Bishop of, Gorham case, 177
—, Marquess of, 111
Exhibition of 1851, 181

Fawcett, Colonel, shot in a duel, 91
Featherstonhaugh, Mr, British Consul at Havre, arranges escape of King and Queen of France, 135-8
Feodore, Princess, 21
Fine Arts Commission, 69-70
Follett, Sir William, 85
Foreign Office, new, 279-80
Foreign Secretary, duties of, 173
Fortescue, Dudley, 280
Fould, Achille, French Minister, 241
Fox, Charles James, 75
France, anger at visit of Emperor of Russia to England, 95
policy over Tahiti, 100
Revolution, 133-9
state of, 143
policy over Austria, 147
Louis Napoleon elected President, 154
losses in Crimea War, 217
policy over Italy, 239-41
differences with Austria, 243
war with Austria, 251
annexation of Savoy, 259
commercial agreement with England, 270
—, Emperor of, *see* Napoleon
—, King of, *see* Louis Philippe

Frederick, King of Saxony, *see* Saxony, Frederick Augustus II, King of
Free Trade, 191
Freemasons, 89
Frogmore, 278, 294

Gaelic language, in schools, 156
Gaeta, 154
Garibaldi, General, 276-8
Genoa, Duke of, 199
George III, 2, 64
George IV, 3
Germany, 143, confederation, 145, *Times* attacks on, 282
Gibson, Milner, 227
Gladstone, Rt Hon. William E.:
appointed Colonial Secretary, 115-16
memorandum on victory over the Sikhs at Sobraon, 120
votes against Lord John Russell, 189
Prince Consort's congratulations on speech, 195
Civil Service examinations, 197
financial statement, 260
offers resignation, 268, 275
Glenlyon, Lord (afterwards Duke of Athole), 81
Gloucester, Duchess of (Princess Mary), 21, 178
Goethe, 76
Gordon, Sir Willoughby, 172
Gorham, Mr, and the Bishop of Exeter, 177
Goulburn, H., 32
Graham, Sir James, Home Secretary, 32, 70, 78, 80
state of the prisons, 107
votes to abolish Corn Laws, 110
defeat of Government, 124, 126
resignation of Lord John Russell, 189
Granville, Earl of, 34, 181, 189
appointed Foreign Secretary, 187-8
resignation of Lord Derby, 244
asked to form Government, 244-5
Greece, and England, 145
Lord Palmerston's attitude to, 150
affairs of, 151
draft to, 161, 169
Don Pacifico's claims, 167

Greece, Otho, King of, *see* Otho, King of Greece
Grenadier Guards, wounded at Crimea, 208
Grenville, Lord, accepts peerage, 61
Greville, Charles, 25, 172, 235
Grey, Sir George, 124, 141, 163, 178
 commissions for Army officers, 146
 Queen's visit to Ireland, 159
—, Lord, 115, 123, 124, 152, 163
Guards, embarkation for the Crimea, 198
Guizot, M., 136, 139, 143, 172, 175

Haddington, Earl of, First Lord of the Admiralty, 81, 116
Hadfield, Mr, 224
Hamilton, William, attempted assassination of Queen Victoria, 158
Hardinge, Sir Henry (afterwards Viscount), Governor General of India:
 motion on Spanish affairs, 15
 on the state of India, 102
 army promotion, 192
Hardwicke, Lord, 102, 111
Havre, flight of King Louis Philippe, 135–136
Hawtry, Dr, Headmaster of Eton, 71
Haynau, General, attack on, 174–6, 185
Herbert, Sidney (afterwards Lord Herbert of Lea), 110, 122, 189, 274
 Mrs Norton and the *Times*, 109
 sends out Florence Nightingale to Crimea, 205
Highlanders, 92nd, 81
Hill, Viscount, 48, 49
Hindoos, public offices opened to, 103
Hobhouse, Sir John, 124
Hohenlohe, Princess of, *see* Adelaide, Princess of Hohenlohe
—, Langenbourg, Ernest, Prince of, 22
Holland, Dr (afterwards Sir Henry), Court Physician, 291
—, Lady, 75
Honfleur, escape from, 136
Horsman, Mr, M.P., 231
Hospitals for sick and wounded soldiers, 209–10
Household appointments, 32, 53, 54, 65–6, 190

Howley, William, *see* Canterbury, Archbishop of
Hübner, Baron, Austrian Ambassador in Paris, 262
Hume, Joseph, 14
Humiliation, national day of prayer and, 225
Hungary, 174, 276

India, state of, 102
 Hindoos, public offices opened to, 103
 Mohammedan schools, 103
 defeat of Sikhs at Sobraon, 120
 Mutiny, 222–3
 Bill, 232
 Proclamation, 233
 motion on, 228
 termination of Mutiny, 250
Inkerman, battle of, 205
Inverness, Duchess of, 88
Ireland, Tithes, 15
 troubles in, 90
 report of Potato Commission, 109–10
 alarming state of, 142–3
 Queen's visit, 127, 158–9
Italy, and England, 145, 149
 Lord Palmerston's view on, 150
 General Haynau's proceedings in, 174
 French policy in, 236, 251
 differences with Austria, 236
 confederation, 251
 England's views on confederation, 259

Jenkinson, Lady Catherine, 14
Jenner, Dr (afterwards Sir William), Physician Extraordinary to the Queen, 291
Jersey, Earl of, Master of the Horse, 65
John, Archduke, 143, 147
Jones, Mr, Vice Consul at Havre, 136
Jowett, Reverend B., Fellow of Balliol College, Professor of Greek, 216

Kennington Common, Chartist meeting, 141
Kensington Palace, proposal to build National Gallery on site of, 180

Kent, Duchess of (Queen Victoria's Mother):
relationship with Queen Victoria, 3
character, 3
death, 279
—, Duke of (Queen Victoria's Father), death, 47
King, Mr Locke, 180
Kingslake, Mr, 209
Kinnoul, Lord, 80
Kinsky Regiment, 157
Kisseleff, General, Russian Ambassador, 262
Knowles, Sheridan, 173
Koh-i-noor Diamond, 165–6
Koller, Baron, Austrian Ambassador, 174–6, 185
Kossuth, Louis, 184–6, 277

Lamartine, M., 144
Landgravine, Princess Elizabeth, 40
Lansdowne, Marquess of, 122, 124, 156, 162
Law, administration of, 85
Lawrence, Sir Henry, death, 224
Layard, Mr, 280
Lehzen, Baroness, Queen's Governess, 14, 22
Leigh, Pemberton, elevated to Peerage, 179
Leopold, Prince (afterwards King of the Belgians):
Queen's first letter to, 7
advice on character to Queen, 8
views on hypocrisy, 11
hopes for Queen's marriage, 12
advice to Queen on Court Officials, 14
opinion of Baron Stockmar, 16, 23
views on religion, 18
advises Queen on death of King of England, 25
advice to Queen on her accession, 18–19
education of Queen, 23
opinion of the Prussians, 26
on Prince Albert's education, 29
Queen's engagement to Prince Albert, 35
opinion of Prince Albert's character, 36, 41, 108

Leopold, Prince, continued
Prince Albert's title, 37
birth of Princess Royal, 44
Queen's happiness with Prince Albert, 148
Lord Melbourne's death, 152
victory of Novara, 157
Queen's visit to Ireland, 108–9
death of Sir Robert Peel, 169
learns of Lord Palmerston's resignation and Lord Granville's appointment, 187–8
death of Duke of Wellington, 192
possibility of war with Russia, 199
Queen describes Crimean War, 204
Lord Palmerston as Prime Minister, 208
peace with Russia, 216
Queen's views on Indian mutiny, 225
Prince Consort and Prince of Wales visit to Canada, 268
Queen's visit to Scotland, 269
visit of Empress of Austria, 270–1
Queen's 21st wedding anniversary, 278
death of Duchess of Kent, 278
Prince Consort's illness, 285, 288
his sympathies on Prince Consort's illness, 289
death of Prince Consort, 291
Letters, official opening of, 143
—, Sunday delivery, 166–7
Lhuys, M. Drouyn de, 171, 202
Liberal Party, 122, 227, 245
Liddell, Mr, 224
Lieven, Princess de, 25, 172
Lincoln, Earl of, 122
Lindley, Dr, Irish Commissioner, 110
Liverpool, Earl of, 24, 65
Lombardy, 146, 150, 251
London, Bishop of, Papal aggression, 179
Louis Napoleon, see Napoleon
Louis Philippe, King of France:
visit to England, 100–2
flight from France, 133–9
death, 173
Louise, Queen of the Belgians, 4, 100–2
Lucknow, siege, 226
fall, 232
Lushington, Dr Stephen, 179
Lyndhurst, Lord, 32, 189, 201

Lyons, Richard Bickerton Pemell (afterwards Earl Lyons), 236, 237, 285, 287

Macdonald, Miss, 158
MacNaghten, Daniel, assassin, 83, 84, 85
Malmesbury, Earl of, 236, 240–1, 274
Maltby, Dr Edward, Bishop of Durham, 178
Manchester, riot, 78–9
Mangles, Mr, 224
Manners, Lord John, 280
Manning, Marie, execution, 175
Mansfield, Lord, 81
Marionette Theatre, 190
Martin, Sir Theodore, 287
Mary, Princess, see Gloucester, Duchess of
Mason, Mr, 287
Mathew, Father, 126
Mayne, Richard, Commissioner of Police, 141
Maynooth Bill, 106
Medals, Peninsular, 128, East India Company, 152, see also Victoria Cross
Melbourne, Viscount, 15, 20, 24
  forms new Government, 30
  resignation from 1839 Government, 30
  Queen's engagement to Prince Albert, 35
  censures Lord Cardigan, 48
  on army discipline, 49
  Government crisis, 50
  sugar duties, 55
  dissolves Parliament, 56
  urges appointment of Sir Robert Peel as Prime Minister, 62
  relationship of Prince Albert and Tory party, 63
  Baron Stockmar's apprehension on Queen's correspondence with, 68–9
  on discontent in England, 80
  South Wales turnpike riots, 90
  consulted by Queen on purchase of Osborne, 106
  Queen advances money, 132
  death, 152
Metternich, Prince, 142, 143, 174, 175
Michael, Grand Duke, 205
Ministers of State, duties of, 28
Militia, see Army

Militia Bill, 191
Minto, Earl of, 124, 149, 162
Mohammedan Schools, 103
Monro, Lieutenant, duel, 91
Montpensier, Duc de, 102
Morning Chronicle, 125, 284
Morning Post, 185, 242
Morpeth, Lord, 126, 141
Munster, Earl of, Governor of Windsor Castle, death, 75
Muscat, Iman, list of presents for the Queen, 77

Nana Sahib, 250
Naples, British Government apology, 155
  seizure of Cagliari, 230
  tyrannical local Government, 266
Napoleon, Louis:
  elected President of France, 154
  coup d'état, 186
  possibility of war with Russia, 198
  visit to England, 210–14
  comparison with King Louis Philippe, 212
  policy on Italy, 236
  Earl Cowley's interview, 260–5
  annexation of Savoy, 259, 262, 263
National Gallery, 180
Navy, duelling, 91
  Baltic expedition, 200
  strength of, 202
Neild, James Camden, leaves fortune to the Queen, 191
Nelson, Lord, proposed pension for adopted daughter, 203
Nepaul, 250
Neumann, Baron, Austrian Minister, 174
Newcastle, Duke of, 202, 205, 208, 268
Nicholas, Emperor of Russia, see Russia, Nicholas, Emperor of
Nicholas, Grand Duke, 205
Nightingale, Florence, 205, 217
Norfolk, Duchess of, 177
Normanby, Marchioness of, 52
—, Marquess of, 14, 147, 151, 186
Northumberland, Duchess of, first Lady-in-Waiting to the Queen, 144
Norton, Mrs, 71, 109
Norway, see Sweden and Norway

Novarra, battle of, 157
Nuneham, Queen's visit to, 58

O'Connell, Daniel, agitator, 27
O'Connor, Feargus, Kennington Common Chartist meeting, 141
Orange, Prince of, as suitor to the Queen, 12
  assistance given by United Provinces, 258
Orleans, Duchess of, 135, 186
Osborne, Queen's purchase of, 105
—, Ralph Bernal, 231, 280
Oscar, Prince, of Sweden, visit to England, 280–2
Otho, King of Greece, 151
Oudh, 250
Oxford, Bishop of, see Wilberforce, Dr

Pacifico, Don, claims against Greece, 167
Palmer, Mr, 178
Palmerston, Viscount:
  speech on Spanish affairs, 15
  on Continental Government administration, 26
  marriage to Lady Cowper, 39
  speech on Sir Robert Peel's resignation, 120
  consulted by Lord Russell on new Government, 122
  attack on Portuguese Government, 128
  Duke of Wellington's statue, 130
  escape of King and Queen of France, 135, 139
  disagreement with Queen over foreign policy, 145
  Queen's lack of confidence in, 149
  death of Lord Melbourne, 152
  draft to Greece, 161
  his lack of respect to the Queen, 165
  defends foreign policy in the House of Commons, 167–8
  further disagreements on foreign affairs, 170–2
  Haynau attack, 174–6
  Kossuth affair, 184
  his approval of Louis Napoleon's coup d'état, 186–7
  resignation as Foreign Secretary, 187

Palmerston, Viscount, continued
  insinuates that his resignation was due to Prince Albert, 196
  Roebuck's motion censuring Crimean War, 206–7
  forms new Government, 207
  view on Professor of Greek at Oxford, 216
  peace with Russia, 217
  Queen offers Order of the Garter, 218
  disunity in the Tory Party, 221
  Indian mutiny, 222–4
  resignation, 226
  his unpopularity, 234
  asked to support Lord Granville's government, 245
  forms new Government, 247
  French attitude to Italy, 252
  England's attitude to Italy, 256–7, 259–260
  abolition of paper duties bill thrown out by House of Lords, 267
  on Cobden's concluding commercial agreement between France and England, 270
  appointments of Bishops, 271
  review of political situation, 273–5
  building of the new Foreign Office, 279
  visit of the King of Sweden, 280–2
  on Times attack on Prussians and cost of newspapers, 282–5
  Trent steamship, seizure of envoys, 285
  his sympathy to Queen on death of Prince Albert, 293
Panmure, Lord, see Dalhousie, Earl of
Paper Duties Bill, abolition of, 268
Paris, treaty of, see Treaty of Paris
Parliament, new Houses of, 69
Pate, Robert, assault on Queen, 168
Paul, Captain, 136
Peel, Lady (wife of Sir Robert), 98
—, Sir Robert:
  seconds address of Condolence and Congratulation on Queen's accession, 22
  asked to form new Ministry, 31
  difficulties over appointment of Queen's ladies, 23, 51, 52
  Household appointments, 53

Peel, Sir Robert, *continued*
  relationship of Prince Albert with Tory Party, 63
  first audience with Queen Victoria, 64-5
  forms new Government, 65
  Prince Albert accepts position as Commander of Grenadier Guards, 76
  Queen's opinion of Sir Edward Disbrowe, 77
  attempted assassination, 84
  Queen's appreciation of, 105
  proposed abolition of Corn Laws, 110
  offers resignation over Corn Laws, 110
  his loyalty to the Queen, 113
  appoints Gladstone Colonial Secretary, 115
  his speech on opening of Parliament, 118
  objections to Prince Albert's memorandum of their conversation, 119
  attacked by Disraeli and Lord Bentinck, 120
  resignation, 121
  last appearance in the House of Commons, 167
  death, 168
Peelites, 284
Peers, right of audience, 70
Pensioners, Chelsea, *see* Chelsea Pensioners
People's Charter riots, 79
Perekop, Isthmus of, 204
Pery, Sir Erskine, 223
Persigny, Count de, French Ambassador in London, 240-1
Phillimore, Dr, Counsel to the Admiralty, 285
Phipis, Colonel, 190
Piccolomini, Max, 76
Piedmont, cession of Lombardy, 251
  assembly of Garibaldian legion, 276
Piedmontese, 157
Pitt, William, 61
Pius IX, Pope
  letter to Queen, 153-4
  Queen's reply, 154-5
  Papal aggression, 177-8
  his opinion of English policy, 253-6
Playfair, Dr, Irish Commissioner, 110

Poerio, 238
Poet Laureate, suggestions for office, 173
Poor Law Commission, Richard Cobden's appointment, 131
Pope, *see* Pius IX
Portugal, attack by Lord Palmerston, 128 and England, 145
Post Office, Sunday opening, 166-7
Potato Commission, 109-10
Pozzo, Di Borgo, Count, Russian Ambassador, 29
Praetorius, Dr, 71
Princess Royal, *see* Victoria, Princess Royal
Protectionists, 117, 157, 189
Prussia, Italian difficulties, 145
  Prince Consort's love for, 148
  war with Russia, 198
  Times attacks on, 282
—, King of (Frederick William IV), on French revolution, 133-5
  opinion of Lord Palmerston, 134
—, Prince Frederick William, proposed marriage to Princess Royal, 215
Punch, 178, 196
Pusey, Dr, 178
Puseyites, 99, 272

Radetsky, Marshal, Austrian General, 150, 157
Radical Party, 4, 40, 227, 275, 276
Radnor, third Earl of, 70
Raglan, Lord, 204, 205
Railways, Queen's first journey, 91
Reeve, Henry, 172
Reform Bill, 228, 231, 275
Regency Bill, 61
Riots, Manchester, 78-9
  South Wales turnpike, 90
  Birmingham, 92
  Chartist, 140-1
Ripon, first Earl of, 116
Rivers, Lord, 111
Roebuck, Mr, motion on conduct of Crimean War, 206
Rollin, Ledru, 144
Roman Catholics, Maynooth Bill, 106
  Papal aggression, 177-8

Rome, Lord John Russell's despatch, 279
  possibility of Prince of Wales visit, 237
Rosslyn, Lady, 66
Rowan, Colonel C., Chief Commissioner
  of Police, 140
Royal, Princess, see Victoria, Princess
  Royal
Russell, Lady (wife of Lord John), see
  Eliot, Lady Fanny
—, Lord John (afterwards Earl), 15, 62
  moves address of Condolence and Con-
    gratulation on Queen's accession, 22
  result of 1837 election, 25
  marriage, 57
  on Corn Laws, 110
  failure to form Government, 112
  resignation of Sir Robert Peel, 120
  undertakes to form new Government,
    122
  Queen's possible visit to Ireland, 127
  Duke of Wellington's statue, 130
  strength of the Chartists, 140
  his opinion of King Louis Philippe, 142
  Queen's opinion of foreign policy, 147
  Queen's lack of confidence in Lord
    Palmerston, 149–50
  Naples rising and British Government
    apology, 155
  draft to Greece, 161
  Lord Palmerston's behaviour, 165
  his House of Commons speech on
    censure debate, 167
  explanation to Queen on Lord Palmer-
    ston and foreign affairs, 170–2
  Haynau affair, 176
  Papal aggression, 178
  defeat of Government, 180
  Queen's praise of Prince Albert, 182
  Kossuth affair, 184
  Louis Napoleon's coup d'état, 186–7
  Lord Palmerston's resignation, 187
  resignation, 189
  tries to regain premiership, 200–1
  resigns over Roebuck's Crimean War
    censure motion, 206
  desire to go to House of Lords, 222
  Indian Mutiny, 224
  asked by Queen to support Lord
    Granville's Government, 245

Russell, Lord John, continued
  Queen writes on French policy, 252
  disagrees with Queen over Italian
    policy, 258–60
  Earl Cowley's interview with French
    Emperor, 260
  overthrow of the Government of the
    King of the Two Sicilies, 266
  his letters to Garibaldi, 276–8
  despatch to America, 279
  despatch to Rome, 279
—, Odo, Secretary of Legation to
    Florence, 237, 253–6
Russell's Modern Europe, 9
  Life, 184
Russia, possibility of alliance with Austria,
    162
  possibility of war with England, 198
  declaration of war with England, 200
  peace with England, 216
—, Nicholas, Emperor of:
  visit to England, 94, 96, 97
  death, 209
Rutland, Duke of, 66

St Germans, Earl of, Postmaster-General,
    116
Sardinia, incorporation of Lombardy, 146
  disagreement with Austria, 147
  armistice, 150
  asked to pledge non-interference, 258
—, King of, see Charles Albert, King of
    Sardinia
Savoy, annexation to France, 259, 262, 263
Saxe-Coburg, Ernest, Prince of (Prince
    Consort's brother), 12
  visit to England, 34
Saxony, Frederick Augustus II, King of,
    visit to England, 95, 96, 98
Schenk, 39
Schiller, 76
Schleswig, 145
Scotland, Queen's visit to, 80–2, 182, 191,
    268–9
Scots Fusiliers embark for Crimea, 198
  wounded at Crimea, 208
Scott, General, 286
—, Sir Walter, 290

Scutari, hospital at, 205
Sebastopol, 203, 214–15
Settembrini, 238
Seymour, Lord (afterwards Duke of Somerset), 38, 56
—, Sir Hamilton, 144
Sicily, rising in, 155, 266
provision of guns, 185
Sikhs, defeat at Sobraon, 120
Singapore, convict population of, 232
Slavery, abolition of, 51
Slidell, Mr, 286
Smith, Mr Robert Vernon (afterwards Lord Lyveden), 233
—, Sir Harry, 152
Sobraon, defeat of Sikhs, 120
Solferino, battle of, 251
Sooja, Shah, 166
Soult, Marshal, 75
South Wales, see Wales, South
Southern, Mr, Secretary of Legation at Lisbon, 128
Spain, 15, 145, 165
—, Queen of, 183
Stanley, Lord (afterwards Earl of Derby), 32, 101
wine from Australia, 107
against abolition of Corn Laws, 110
resignation, 114, 116
vote of censure on Government, 189–90
death of Duke of Wellington, 192
on Disraeli's budget speech, 193
resignation, 193–4
opinion of Lord Palmerston, 207
forms Government, 229
India Proclamation, 233
suggestion of peace to Emperor of France, 239
advises Queen on Speech from the throne, 242–4
resignation, 244
Stockmar, Baron, 26, 29, 148
illness of, 8
King Leopold's opinion of, 16
his opinion of Queen's correspondence with Lord Melbourne, 68–9
his apprehension over Queen's correspondence with Lord Melbourne, 71
on a minister's duty, 164

Straits Settlements, 231
Strutt, Mr, 201
Stuart, Lord Dudley, 185
Sugar Duties, 49, 55
Sully, Maximilien, Duc de, memoirs of, 9, 10
Sussex, Duke of, 18, 21
Sweden and Norway, Charles XV, King of, visit to England, 280–2
views on Europe, 281
—, Prince Oscar of, see Oscar, Prince of Sweden

Tahiti, dispute with France, 100
Tallenay, M. de, 143
Talleyrand, Prince, death of, 29
Tawell, Salt Hill murderer, 175
Taylor, Henry, 173
—, Sir Herbert, 16
Tennyson Alfred, 108, 173
Thiers, M., *History of the Consulate and Empire*, 214
Thouvenel, M. de, French Foreign Minister, 265
Times, paragraph on Corn Laws, 109
story of Mrs Norton, 109
Anti-Corn Law, 110
reports attempted assassination of Queen, 158
attacks on Prussia, 282
Tindal, Chief Justice, 85
Tite, Mr (afterwards Sir William), architect, 280
Tithes Bill, 15
Tomantoul, Queen's visit to, 269
Tory Party, 180
Queen's opinion of, 14, 40
oppose title for Prince Albert, 38
Sugar Duties, 56–7
treatment of Prince Consort, 63
disunity, 221
Tractarian Movement, 178
Treaty of Adrianople, 201
Treaty of Paris, 221
Trent, steamship, seizure of Envoys, 285
Turgot, M., 186
Tuscany, Duke of, 254

United States of America, 94, 121, 237, 274
  Prince of Wales' visit, 269
  Lord John Russell's despatch, 279
  right to search neutral ships, 286
Uxbridge, Earl of, 37

Venice, 147, 150, 151, 251
Victoria, Queen, ancestry of, 2
  family of, 3
  1821 childhood of, 4
    education of, 4, 5, 9
    reading, 9
    confirmation of, 10
  1837 accession to the throne, 3, 20, 21
  1838 coronation, 29
  1839 refusal to allow Sir Robert Peel appoint Ladies of Household, 33
    feelings for Prince Albert, 33
    resignation of Lord Melbourne, 30
    interviews Duke of Wellington and Sir Robert Peel, 31
    engagement to Prince Albert, 35
    appointment of Prince Albert's Gentlemen, 38
  1840 engraves seal for Prince Albert, 41
    marriage, 42
    birth of Princess Royal, 43
  1841 her scholarship, 46
    death of her father, Duke of Kent, 47
    Household appointments, 53–4
    help given to her by Prince Albert, 61
    urged by Lord Melbourne to ask Sir Robert Peel to form Government, 62
    Prince Albert's relationship with the Tory Party, 63
    her personal feelings for Sir Robert Peel, 64
    her first audience with Sir Robert Peel, 64
    on appointment of Physicians and Chaplains, 67
    her advice asked on building of new Houses of Parliament, 69
    her opinion of Sir Robert Peel, 70
    birth of Prince of Wales, 73

Victoria, Queen, *continued*
  1842 advised by Lord Melbourne on pensions, 75
    her opinion of Sir Edward Disbrowe, 77
    list of presents from Iman of Muscat, 77
    visit to Edinburgh, 80
    steam yacht, 81
  1843 her views on the McNaghten trial, 85
    Prince Consort to hold levées for the Queen, 86
    toast of Prince Consort, 87
    South Wales turnpike riots, 90
  1844 her opinion of the Emperor of Russia, 95
    visit to Emperor of Russia, 96–8
    visit of King of Saxony, 98
    visit of King of France, 100–2
  1845 state of Buckingham Palace, 104
    question of Prince Albert's title, 105
    purchase of Osborne, 105
    her opinion of Sir Robert Peel, 115
  1846 opening of Parliament, 118
    victory over the Sikhs at Sobraon, 120
    resignation of Sir Robert Peel, 120
    Lord John Russell undertakes to form Government, 122, 124
    pensions proposal, 126
    possibility of visit to Ireland, 126
    her views on Portugal, 128
  1847 Duke of Wellington's statue, 129
    her opinion on Cobden joining the Government, 131
    advance of money to Lord Melbourne, 132
  1848 abdication and flight of King of France, 135–9
    her opinion of Germany and France, 140
    Chartist strength, 141
    alarming state of Ireland, 142–3
    on etiquette of Court Ball, 144
    disagreement with Lord Palmerston over foreign policy, 145

Victoria, Queen, *continued*
  personal connection between Sovereign and Army, 166
  on the opening of her private letters, 147
  her happiness with Prince Albert, 148
  her lack of confidence in Lord Palmerston, 148–50
  Spanish marriage question, 149
  death of Lord Melbourne, 152
  letter from Pope Pius IX, 152–3
1849 correspondence with Pope Pius IX, 154–5
  Naples crisis, 155
  her opinion of the teaching of Gaelic and Welsh, 156
  attack on her life by William Hamilton, 158
  visit to Ireland, 158–9
  death of Queen Adelaide, 160
1850 on the draft to Greece, 161
  Prince Albert's character and speech, 164
  Koh-i-noor diamond, 165–6
  attacked by Robert Pate, 168
  death of Sir Robert Peel, 168
  her fears that Lord Palmerston plans war, 170
  duties of the Foreign Secretary, 173
  death of the King of France, 173
  Haynau attack, 174–6
1851 opening of Crystal Palace, 181
  visit to Balmoral, 182
  Lord Palmerston and Louis Kossuth, 184
  Louis Napoleon's *coup d'état,* 186
  resignation of Lord Palmerston and appointment of Lord Granville, 187–8
1852 opening of Parliament, 188
  her opinion of women as rulers, 189
  resignation of Lord John Russell, 189
  Lord Derby forms Government, 189–90

Victoria, Queen, *continued*
  Household appointments by Lord Derby, 190
  left a fortune by John Camden Neild, 191
  death of Duke of Wellington, 191–2
  on the recent deaths of her friends, 192
  Lord Derby's resignation, 193–4
  Lord Aberdeen forms Cabinet, 194–5
1854 press attacks on Prince Albert, 195–6
  possibility of war with Russia, 198
  sailing of the Fleet for the Baltic, 199–200
  declaration of war with Russia, 200–1
  her opinion of Lord Aberdeen, 201
  defenceless state of England, 202
  the French and Sebastapol, 203
  Battle of the Alma, 204
  march to Balaklava, 204
  Battle of Inkerman and British losses, 205
1855 Lord John Russell's resignation over Roebuck's censure motion, 206
  Government resigns, 207
  Lord Palmerston forms Government, 207–8
  her visit to the Crimea wounded, 208
  concern over hospitals, 209–10
  war medals, 210
  visit of the Emperor of France, 210–14
  fall of Sebastapol, 214–15
  Princess Royal's proposed marriage with Crown Prince of Prussia, 215
1856 Victoria Cross, 216
  peace with Russia, 216–18
  letter and gift to Florence Nightingale, 217
  memorandum on Prince Albert's status, 218–20

Victoria, Queen, *continued*
  proposes Order of the Garter for
    Lord Palmerston, 218
1857 Indian Mutiny, 222–3
  urging of strong action over India,
    223–4
  opinion of Fast Days, 226
1858 resignation of Lord Palmerston,
    226–9
  on the seizure of the *Cagliari*, 230
  Indian Proclamation, 233
1859 Prince of Wales visit to Rome, 237
  suggestion of peace to the French
    Emperor, 239
  her speech from the throne, 242–4
  on the need for defence, 242
  defeat of Government, 244
  Lord Palmerston forms Govern-
    ment, 247–8
  disagrees with Lord John Russell
    on French policy over Italy, 251
  French make peace, 252
  Pope's opinion of English policy,
    253–6
  differs with Lord Palmerston on
    England's Italian policy, 256–7
  her objection to the publication of
    divorce cases in newspapers,
    257
1860 Italian foreign policy, 258–60
  Gladstone's Budget statement, 260
  Earl Cowley's interview with the
    French Emperor, 260–5
  Abolition of Paper Duties Bill
    rejected by House of Lords,
    267
  visit of Prince of Wales to Canada,
    268–9
  commercial agreement between
    England and France, 270
  engagement of Princess Alice, 271
1861 visit of Empress Elizabeth of
    Austria, 272–3
  Lord John Russell's correspon-
    dence with Garibaldi, 276–8
  celebrates 21st wedding anniver-
    sary, 278
  death of her mother, Duchess of
    Kent, 278–9

Victoria, Queen, *continued*
  visit of King of Sweden, 280–2
  Times attacks on Prussians, 282–5
  Prince Albert's illness, 285
  America's right to search neutral
    ships, 287
  Prince Albert's slight improve-
    ment, 288
  death of Prince Albert, 291
Victoria, Princess Royal, 73, 74, 104
  birth, 43
  proposed marriage, 215
Victoria Cross, 216

Wales, Albert Edward, Prince of (after-
    wards King Edward VII):
  birth, 73
  visit to Rome, 237
  visit to Canada and Washington, 268–9
  —, South, rioting against turnpike system,
    90
Walewski, Count, 186, 227, 241
Walpole, Sir Robert, 232
Warre, Major-General, Sir William, 78
Washington, Prince of Wales' visit to,
    268
Wellesley, Lord Charles, 102
Wellington, Duke of:
  interview of Queen, 31
  illness, 47
  his health, 65
  his views on the interment of Duchess
    of Inverness, 88–9
  supports Sir Robert Peel over Corn
    Laws, 110, 114
  his influence over House of Lords, 116
  Peninsular War medals, 128
  his statue, 129
  control of Chartists, 140
  Depot plan, 188
  death, 191–2
Welsh language, in schools, 156
Wemyss, Colonel, 181
Wessenberg, Baron, 150
Weyer, Sylvain van der, 45
Whig Party, 3, 27, 40, 58, 60, 122, 143
    185–6, 194
Whiteside, Mr, 224

Wilberforce, Dr Samuel, Bishop of Oxford, memorandum on resignation of Sir Robert Peel, 121–2

tracts, 117–18

William IV of England (formerly Duke of Clarence):

tries to prevent Queen Victoria's marriage with Prince Albert, 5

relationship with Duchess of Kent, 12

William IV of England, *continued*
King of Belgium's opinion of, 13

illness, 17

death, 20

Wilson, Professor, 173

Wiseman, Cardinal, appointed Archbishop of Westminster, 178

Woburn Abbey, Queen's visit to, 60

Wood, Charles, 123–4

Wyse, Mr, British Envoy at Athens, 161